BOUNDARIES OF ORDER

Private Property As a Social System

BOUNDARIES OF ORDER

Private Property As a Social System

Butler Shaffer

MISES INSTITUTE

Published by the Ludwig von Mises Institute
518West Magnolia Avenue
Auburn, Alabama 36830
www.mises.org

ISBN: 978-1-933550-16-9

To the
Remnant

Civilization is a stream with banks. The stream is sometimes filled with blood from people killing, stealing, shouting and doing the things historians usually record, while on the banks, unnoticed, people build homes, make love, raise children, sing songs, write poetry and even whittle statues. The story of civilization is the story of what happened on the banks. Historians are pessimists because they ignore the banks for the river.

— Will Durant

Contents

Preface

I have long been interested in discovering whether social conditions can exist that maximize both individual liberty and societal order. Conventional wisdom insists this is not possible; that order and liberty are inconsistent values that must be balanced one against the other. We are told we must sacrifice some liberty in order to maintain order in society; that to believe otherwise is to engage in flights of idealistic fancy or utopian visions.

As people find their lives increasingly dominated by formal systems that suppress individual liberty, it becomes evident that the order being served has far less to do with their personal needs than with fostering the interests of the institutions in charge of the machinery of societal control. Men and women intuit a failure of expectations: that neither social harmony nor personal liberty have arisen from their submission to formalized systems of authority. As inter-group conflicts, wars, genocides, economic dislocations, and expansive policing and surveillance of people's lives continue to dehumanize societies, the possibility of discovering or creating alternative social systems has begun to energize the minds of many. Is it possible for millions to live together in ways in which social harmony and individual autonomy are neither "balanced" nor sacrificed one to the other, but become the integrated expression of what it means to be human? Can such an inquiry proceed not from religious or ideological conviction or other abstract thinking, but from an understanding of the conditions that are essential to the self-directed nature of living systems? Are there principles that would make such life-enhancing conditions possible?

I have sought such principles from a variety of sources: from so-called "moral" and "natural law" philosophies to historical insights and economic reasoning, to name a few. The problem I have with such approaches is that they are too often grounded in certain *a priori* normative assumptions from which conclusions were derived. It was not that I necessarily quarreled with the premises—I found a number of them very much to my liking—but I sensed there was a more fundamental explanation that lay hidden behind such philosophical abstractions. I felt a need to discover principles that transcended my pre-existing biases and preferences. On the other hand, my quest was clearly driven by subjective sentiments that arose from within me. A vivid moment occurred when I was in law school, and my wife and I were walking along Lake Michigan discussing my concern. I asked the question: why should I have to justify my desire for liberty on *any* grounds other than the fact that I do not choose to be coerced? Why need I appeal to any principle beyond that of my own will?

Of course, my desire for an unhindered expression of my will could bring me into conflict with others, thus causing my liberty to become a source of social disorder. The dilemma I faced might be a confirmation of the traditional view that the state must be relied upon to balance these conflicting needs. I remained convinced that these values were not contrary to one another, and that they could be reconciled by some principle I had not yet discovered. My training as a lawyer led me to suspect that the answer might have something to do with the concept of property.

As I continued my inquiries, I became acquainted with the writings of the philosopher Robert LeFevre,[1] who ran a school

---

[1]See, e.g., *The Nature of Man and His Government* (Caldwell, Idaho.: The Caxton Printers, Ltd., 1959); *This Bread is Mine* (Milwaukee, Wis.: American Liberty

in Colorado known as The Freedom School (and later named Rampart College). I studied and later taught at this school, where I discovered the missing pieces to my puzzle. LeFevre's philosophy was centered on the principle of the private ownership of property; that freedom is possible only when private ownership claims are respected; and that the existence of political systems depends upon the violation of property principles. LeFevre analyzed the property concept in terms of its constituent factors: *boundary*, *claim*, and *control*, elements I elaborate on in chapters 3, 4, and 5.

During this same time period, I discovered the writings of Konrad Lorenz[2] and Robert Ardrey[3] who first introduced me to serious studies of the territorial nature of other life forms. That animals without any formal legal systems or abstract philosophical doctrines would nonetheless function, within their respective species, on the basis of the inviolability of territorial boundaries, confirmed to me that there is something that ties together the self-directed nature of life and the orderliness that is essential to the well-being of a society. I became convinced that individual liberty and social order are obverse sides of the same coin; two ways of talking about the same thing: how we relate to one another in a physical world.

We are individuals with a variety of tastes and values who, at the same time, are social beings who have both psychic and economic needs for cooperation with one another. This requires us to have realms of personal authority within which we can act without interference from others. But, alas, our self-interest-motivated pursuits are not always restrained by a respect for the inviolability of the interests of our neighbors. We occasionally resort to personal acts of violence in order to promote

Press, 1960); *The Philosophy of Ownership* (Larkspur, Colo.: Rampart College, 1966); *The Fundamentals of Liberty* (Santa Ana, Calif.: Rampart Institute Publishing, 1988).

[2]Konrad Lorenz, *On Aggression* (New York: Harcourt, Brace & World, Inc., 1966).

[3]Robert Ardrey, *The Territorial Imperative* (New York: Atheneum Publishers, 1966).

our interests. Far more dangerous, however, has been our willingness to create institutionalized systems of violence (i.e., the state) to accomplish our purposes, a practice grounded in disrespect for property boundaries. For reasons to be addressed herein, wars against property are destructive of both liberty and social order.

It is from this perspective that this book is written. Our world is in a state of turbulence from which we can either correct the thinking that has created our problems, or face the collapse of our civilization. The fate of what it means to be a human being lies in how we respond to this crucial moment.

In completing this work, I was assisted by a number of persons whom I wish to acknowledge. Foremost has been my wife and editor-in-chief, Jane Shaffer, who insisted that I write the book and whose reading and editing comments were invaluable. She also provided some of the drawings in the book. I also wish to thank two good friends, Spencer MacCallum and David Gordon, for having closely read my manuscript and made critical suggestions that proved most helpful. My daughter, Bretigne Calvert, provided valuable assistance in the graphics that appear herein. I also need to thank Lew Rockwell, Jeffrey Tucker, Kathy White, Chad Parish, and Judy Thommesen at the Mises Institute for their help in putting the book together. Finally, I need to thank my employer, Southwestern University School of Law, in providing me with a sabbatical that gave me the time to write the substance of this book. I must also acknowledge our student newspaper, *The Commentator*, for granting permission to reprint the photograph that appears on page 38.

Chapter One
Introduction

Property is the most fundamental and complex of social facts, and the most important of human interests; it is, therefore, the hardest to understand, the most delicate to meddle with, and the easiest to dogmatize about.

—William Graham Sumner

What do the concepts of the following chart have in common, and what relevance do they have to this book?

Abortion
Airport/subway security checks/searches
Animal rights
Anarchy
Banking
Begging/panhandling
Book-burning
Building codes/permits
Business organizations
Censorship
Child custody (in divorces, adoptions)
Child-raising practices
Cloning

Conscription
>   military, jury duty

Conservation

Contracting
>   who can contract, terms of agreements

Copyrights

Crimes
>   victimizing:
>   >   murder, rape, arson, theft, burglary, manslaughter,
>   >   embezzlement/larceny, fraud, assault/battery/mayhem,
>   >   kidnapping, forgery
>
>   victimless:
>   >   drug use, prostitution, gambling, pornography,
>   >   smuggling

Cryonics

Curfews

Customs inspections/restrictions

Discriminatory practices
>   employment, conducting business, housing, pricing of
>   goods/services

Eminent domain

Employment policies

Endangered species regulation

Environmentalism

Estate planning

Ethnic cleansing

Euthanasia

Flag-burning

Food quality and standards

Freedom of:
>   assembly, press, religion, speech, association

Gay/lesbian marriage

Genocide

Global "warming," "cooling," or "change"

Gun ownership

Helmet requirements for bikers

Hoarding

Homelessness/vagrancy

Immigration

Involuntary commitments/treatments

Landlord/tenant relationship

Land use planning and regulation

Legal age

Licensing of professions:

> trades/businesses/driving

Littering

Medical treatment and practices

Minimum wage laws

National ID cards/passports

Nuclear power plants/waste disposal

Organ selling/donations

Political elections

Political systems:

> communist, socialist, fascist, welfare state

Pollution

Prescription drugs

Prices of goods and services

Privacy

Product standards

Property ownership

Rioting

Safety features on cars/homes/etc.

School systems:

> curricula, admissions standards, prayer in schools, compulsory attendance, student behavior, student clothing, student searches

Searches and seizures

Seat-belt requirements

Slavery

Smoking

Social Security/Medicare

Stem-cell research

Streets and highways:

> speed limits, who entitled to use

Strikes/boycotts
Suicide
Surveillance/wiretaps
Taxation
Torts:
>   assault/battery, trespass, negligence, intentional infliction of
>   emotional distress, strict liability, libel/slander

Torture
Traffic congestion/control
Travel
Vaccination of children
Voting
Vitamins and supplements
War
Zoning

On the one hand, this list reads like a summary of subject matter that helps to define the political, legal, and social issues of society. Public debates and media reports as to the propriety of individual or collective behavior find expression in this listing. If one were to ask people to identify the problems that most beset modern society, the leading responses would doubtless be found in this enumeration. But that fact, standing alone, affords no greater meaning to this list than would an indexing of newspaper stories.

There is a shared latent attribute to these concepts that gives them profound social significance: the meaning of each is unavoidably tied to the role of property in defining individual and social behavior. Whether we are discussing "pollution," or the "war on drugs," "abortion," or "discrimination" in housing or employment, or any of the other listed matters, we are involved in issues that have, at their core, the nature, use, ownership, and limitations on property. The disputes we have with one another largely come down to disagreements over how, when, or by whom, property is to be owned or controlled. Your neighbor's barking dog; a business competitor's use of your trademark; a city prohibiting the building of an addition to your home, or condemning your land through the power of eminent domain; your children fighting over the use of a toy; motorists squabbling over a parking space; or a family fight that arises from the reading of a will: these are just a few of the commonly experienced social problems that derive from conflicts over property.

For reasons that will be explored herein—reasons centering largely on political considerations—inquiries into these varied areas of human behavior are rarely addressed in terms of property ownership. Nevertheless, these and other human activities relate to the question of what property is, how it should be controlled and by whom, and what is entailed in "ownership." The distinction between "victimizing" and "victimless" crime, for instance, illustrates my point: the former always involves the violation of a property interest, the latter never does.

The conflicts, disorder, and destructiveness that are so expressive of modern society arise from our confusion over the nature of property as a system of social order. So insensitive have we become to the role of property as the most important civilizing influence in our world, that we have even learned to regard the infliction of our wills upon the lives and property of others as expressions of "socially responsible" conduct. So aggressive are our ambitions in the world that we do not want to be reminded that they are bought at the cost of our profound respect for the interests—and, hence, the lives—of our neighbors. We eagerly trespass one another's property interests out of an arrogance that threatens to destroy human society, if not humanity itself.

As Sumner's observation suggests, there is probably no chasm in human affairs as wide as that which separates our *desires* for property from our conceptual *understanding* of it. Property—and how it is owned and controlled—is the most basic and definitive feature of any social system. It provides the *only* means by which one is able to act in the world. Our behavior must take place within some space, with action directed upon some "thing" or intangible interest that can be controlled in furtherance of some purpose of the actor. Property is considered to be *privately*-owned when an individual is able to direct the use of a property interest to his or her ends, without having such control preempted by others. In a political context, property is owned *collectively* when such control and purpose is coercively taken from the individual and directed by an external authority. Unless otherwise indicated, I shall refer to "collective" ownership in its compulsory, political sense, distinguishing those voluntary systems (e.g., religious or philosophic communes, cooperatives) in which owners freely transfer their property interests to an association. Whatever system of ownership is in place, *someone* will exercise decisional authority over property.

In an institutionalized world dominated by abstract thought, most of us are inclined to regard "property" as a political invention, born of biases of ideology, political power, or "class-consciousness." As such, we imagine it to be a concept that can be redesigned, twisted, or modified to suit prevailing tastes, without any significant adverse consequences. Like fashions in clothing, entertainment, or lifestyles, we imagine the property principle—as distinct from the choices people make with their property—to be malleable. We treat the concept as little more than a game to be played, not being aware that, like Russian roulette, the outcome can prove deadly. Whether property is to be owned *individually* or *collectively* seems, to most of humanity, a matter to be resolved by the outcome of public opinion polls or political referenda. Men, women, and children are now paying a terrible price for the nearly universal ignorance of the nature of property and its ownership.

Property is central to our lives because of the second law of thermodynamics, which advises us that every *closed* system moves, inexorably, from a state of order to disorder, a concept known as increasing entropy. But living systems are *open*, not *closed*, and can decrease entropy, at least in the short run, by ingesting energy[1] from external sources (e.g., food). Every living thing—if it is to overcome entropy—requires the enjoyment

---

[1] I shall refer to such ingested energy, herein, as "negative entropy" or "negentropy."

of those conditions under which external sources of energy are available with sufficient regularity to sustain the individual. These external sources comprise much of what we know as "property," which every organism must be at liberty to enjoy if it is to survive. Just as there is no collective way for a species to reproduce itself, reversal of entropy can be experienced only by individual organisms. This doesn't guarantee, of course, that each being will be successful in such endeavors. The wildebeest who is busy consuming grasses may have its efforts at overcoming entropy interrupted by a lioness who is trying to do the same thing at the wildebeest's expense. Here, we begin to see a phenomenon to which we shall return later: the seemingly contradictory nature of reality. Life must consume energy if life is to continue, but such life-sustaining energy is found only in other living things. The entire life process thus becomes what has been termed a "mutual eating system," leading us to confront the harsh paradox that life can be sustained only if, in the process, life is destroyed! Might this existential fact provide an explanation—perhaps, in the minds of some, even a justification—for our mutually destructive political systems?

The answer to this question may be found elsewhere in nature. It is commonplace among species, although not universal, that the consumption of other living things be confined to members of other species; cannibalism tends to be discouraged. It is this tendency that gives rise to the need for a property principle to identify energy sources that members of a given species will respect *vis-à-vis* one another. Within a species, "life" becomes inseparable from the property question, a fact reflected in practices that deter intra-species trespasses—a topic to be examined later. Not only does our physical existence depend upon each of us occupying space to the exclusion of everyone and everything else, but requires our being able to consume energy from other living sources. The entropic nature of life, in other words, demands that we control and consume resources if we are to survive. Among members of the same species, it also requires a system for respecting one another's claims to resources. No species would long survive if its members habitually looked upon one another as energy sources to be consumed.

Despite the urgings of a materialistic culture, however, we are aware that life has more than just a biological, survival meaning: survival as *what*? Identifying and maintaining the conditions that keep us alive is *necessary*, but not *sufficient* for the meaningful life. There are men and women in penitentiaries and mental hospitals who are fed, clothed, given medical care, and provided with places to sleep, and yet few of us would regard these as fulfilling environments. Likewise, many people, kept bodily alive by life-support systems, long to have their lives end. Others, in anticipation that such a fate might await them, write "living wills" expressing their desires that machines not be employed to maintain them in a vegetative condition. The Terry Schiavo case[2] was compelling for its questioning of our sense of the meaning of "life" in a technologically-wondrous culture. Entropy, in other words, expresses itself in more than purely physical ways.

The property question has an additional, yet related, meaning beyond its relevance to individual liberty and the need to overcome entropy. Its further significance is to be found at the nucleus of a fundamental transformation now occurring in the nature and design of political and social systems. For various reasons to be explored herein, our world is rapidly becoming *decentralized*, with *vertically* structured institutions being challenged by *horizontally* interconnected networks characterized by greater spontaneity and increased personal autonomy. Society is taking on the dynamics of a giant centrifuge, spinning increased decision-making authority and control into the hands of individuals. As so much of human behavior is expressed within a material context, the implications such deconcentration will

---

[2]Terry Schiavo, a young woman, suffered cardiac arrest and was reduced to a vegetative state. For many months, she was the center of legal struggles over the question of whether she should be kept on an artificial life support system. Her feeding tubes were subsequently withdrawn, and she died on March 31, 2005.

have for how property is to be owned and controlled should be apparent.

The central question in any social system, therefore, comes down to the property inquiry: how are decisions to be made in the world, and who will make them? What kinds of organizations should we employ so that we can enjoy the advantages that come from a division of labor without sacrificing the individual liberties of others when pursuing our personal interests? What is the nature of social order, and what kinds of systems best promote a peaceful and orderly society? Are individual liberty and social order *conflicting* values that must be "balanced" by political systems, or are such qualities expressions of a *symmetry* whose patterns remain obscured through clashing belief systems?

These are just a few of the questions being asked at a time when the world is undergoing major changes in political and social organization. Social systems are as subject to the forces of entropy as living organisms. Their failure to remain resilient and adaptive to the processes of change that define life itself, can bring about their collapse. Indeed, such is the condition now confronting our institutionally-dominant world. Traditional, vertically-structured social systems are eroding, being replaced by lateral webs of independent but interlinking individuals and associations. The pyramid, with its top-down, command-and-control system of centralized authority, has been the dominant organizational model in Western society since at least the time of Plato. The assumption underlying this model is that social order can be achieved only if major decision-making is centralized within established institutions, most notably the state. This view provides the foundation for "collectivism," defined by one source as "a doctrine or system that makes the group or the state responsible for the social and economic welfare of its members."[3] Through the exercise of vertical, unilaterally-directed authority, institutional officials are presumed to be

---

[3]*Webster's Third New International Dictionary of the English Language, Unabridged* (Springfield, Mass.: G. & C. Merriam Company, 1971), p. 445.

capable of channeling the turbulent forces of human society to productive and harmonious ends. The pyramidal model functions in a chain-of-command fashion, where decisions "trickle down" from institutional leaders to the rank-and-file members at different levels in the hierarchy. Because the authority of pyramidal systems is inseparable from their control over the lives and property of people, the threat of decentralist tendencies for institutional power cannot be overstated.

Collectivism, in its varied forms, is dying. For a number of reasons, this top-down, pyramidal model now finds itself in retreat. One cause has been an increased awareness of the inability of large institutions to continue producing the values upon which a society depends for its well-being. Because of their size and proneness to bureaucratic sluggishness, institutions are less adaptable to the constancies of change inherent in all living systems. I have defined "institution" elsewhere as "any permanent social organization with purposes of its own, having formalized and structured machinery for pursuing those purposes, and making and enforcing rules of conduct in order to control those within it."[4]

Not all organizations qualify as institutions. As social beings, it is natural for us to freely associate with one another for our mutual benefit. The institutional forms that have contributed so much to the disorder in the world are those that have elevated their organizational purposes above the interests of individuals or informal groups. In so doing, they have become institutions, the most prominent of which is the *state*, with its coercive bureaucratic agencies, followed by large business corporations that align themselves more with state power than with the unstructured marketplace. Other institutions include most organized religions, schools and universities, and labor unions. In each case, an institution arises when an organization

---

[4]See my book, *Calculated Chaos: Institutional Threats to Peace and Human Survival* (San Francisco: Alchemy Books, 1985), p. 9. Reprinted Coral Springs, Fla.: Llumina Press, 2004), p. 9.

composed of autonomous, cooperating individuals becomes transformed into an end in itself.

It is common to organize with one another for social, business, religious, recreational, or other purposes. From bowling leagues to book clubs to various hobby groups, we form associations with one another that function as tools through which we accomplish shared interests. Such organizations are extensions of our individual purposes, subject to our control. A business partnership, for instance, is a vehicle allowing us to engage in a productive division of labor for profitable ends. But as the organization becomes increasingly successful, there is a tendency to preserve its effectiveness through the creation of hierarchical structures and formal rules of conduct. When the preservation of the organization becomes more important than the informal and spontaneous practices that created it, an institution has been born.

Life is a continuing process of making adjustments and creative responses in a world too complex to be predictable. Because institutions are systems that have become their own reason for being, their interests often consist in efforts to stabilize the environment in which they operate. This need to moderate or even prevent change engenders conflict with individuals seeking to promote their interests through means incompatible with those of institutions. It is at this point that institutions, particularly the state, create enforceable rules and machinery that pit the forces of restraint and permanency against autonomous and innovative processes. These practices necessarily interfere with the efforts of individuals to resist entropic forces. As such restraints metastasize throughout society, they call into question the very survival of civilization itself. As we shall see, such tensions always manifest themselves as conflicts over how property is to be owned and controlled.

Historically, the state has dominated in this struggle between the forces of stability and change. Because of the comparative advantages they enjoy by virtue of their concentrated economic interests, institutions generally prevail over individuals and smaller organizations. With the passage of time, decisions that might previously have been regarded to be within the exclusive authority of private owners to make have been preempted by various legislative, judicial, executive, and administrative branches of government. The consequence of this is that property control has become increasingly collectivized in both the United States and other Western nations, generating a great deal of social conflict.

The tensions between systems of privately-owned property and collectivism are exacerbated by the fact that the nation-state, the centerpiece of vertically-structured systems, now finds its authority in decline. There has been a drastic failure of expectations that the state could generate social and economic order. Twentieth century state-conducted wars and genocides killed some two hundred million people, while state systems of economic planning produced mass starvation, impoverishment, and death; shortages of goods and services; unemployment; inflation; and depressions. The promise that the state would protect individual liberty has been negated by expanded police states, concentration camps and gulags, death squads and death camps, systematic torture, censorship, surveillance of the lives of people, and widespread forms of police brutality. The expectation that the state would protect private property has wilted in the face of the burden of taxation, government regulation of economic transactions and land usage, asset forfeiture, and the powers of eminent domain.

There is a growing awareness that "the system" simply doesn't work as many people, especially during the time of the constitutional movement of the eighteenth century, expected it would. That movement in a sense legitimized the state. But today, the death rattle of the nation-state reverberates throughout the world. The "Iron Curtain" behemoth that served as the West's bogeyman following World War II began to erode in the late 1940s, with Yugoslavia leading the way. Later on, the surviving Soviet Union broke up into fifteen independent nations. Yugoslavia no longer exists, its erstwhile territory subdivided into six separate nations. Kosovo recently declared its independence from Serbia. Czechoslovakia—having broken away from the grips of the Soviet Union—has since decentralized into the Czech Republic and Slovakia.

Secession movements abound throughout the world, with Northern Ireland, Quebec, Tibet, Scotland, and Palestine the more prominent examples. Basque separatism in Spain, and numerous state and local secession efforts in the United States are but a few instances of large numbers of people seeking to withdraw from dominant nation-state systems. In America, parts of various cities have either seceded or sought secession in order to become independent of the principal city. Though not rising to the level of secession, a number of states and cities have been defying federal restrictions on such matters as the medical use of marijuana and the importation of cheaper prescription drugs from Canada.

At the same time, while nationalism continues to be a major political force in the world, many people are increasingly identifying themselves with and organizing their lives around various abstractions that transcend nation-state boundaries. Religion, ethnicity, culture, lifestyles, race—even membership in urban gangs—are some of the categories by which people identify themselves other than by nationality. The Internet is helping to dissolve political boundaries in favor of economic, philosophical, entertainment, political, lifestyle, and other criteria by which individuals create cyber-communities with like-minded persons throughout the world. "Societies" are beginning to be thought of less and less in purely *geographical* terms, and are increasingly being defined in terms of shared subdivisions of interests that do not necessarily correlate with place. Effective decision-making is becoming more personal, with authority moving outward, away from erstwhile centers of power.

The decentralizing processes by which individuals are increasingly gaining control over their own lives run deep. Decentralization of management in business organizations that helps to generate more profits to companies by placing increased decision-making in the hands of employees has been going on for over fifty years. Manufacturing is increasingly

done in smaller, more resilient firms, with massive, specialized factories becoming part of a growing "rust belt" in many
industrialized cities.[5] Many business entrepreneurs are experiencing the benefits, in terms of both business success and lifestyle satisfaction, of the "small is beautiful" perspective. They
have foregone the allures of corporate bigness, with its trappings of collective responsibilities to outside investors, and
retained ownership and control of their smaller enterprises
allowing them to operate in pursuit of a wider range of values
than monetary profits alone. These people are discovering the
practical advantages of living within the decentralized world
of privately-owned property.[6]

Centrally-managed corporate farms, with their mass-pro-
duced, mass-marketed, standardized fare, are experiencing
increased competition not only from "farmers' markets," but
from what is known as "Community Supported Agriculture."
In the latter case, individual farmers and buyers enter into contracts for the sale and purchase of weekly-supplied farm products (e.g., vegetables, fruit, eggs, milk, flowers, etc.). This practice—which was estimated to have grown to over 1,500 farms
by 2005—provides not only enhanced qualities of food, but a
more personal relationship between farmers and consumers
than is found in supermarket systems of distribution. In some
cases, buyers even agree to do a limited amount of farm work
during the growing season as partial compensation for what
they receive.[7] Yet another example of the decentralized supply
of life's basic necessities is found in user-owned and controlled
electric generators as supplements or alternatives to the inconstant performance of national power grids.

---

[5]See, e.g., Robert A. Sutermeister, *People and Productivity* (New York:
McGraw-Hill, 1963); Tom Peters, *Thriving on Chaos: Handbook for a Management
Revolution* (New York: Harper & Row, Publishers, 1988. Originally published
New York: Alfred A. Knopf, 1987).

[6]See, e.g., Bo Burlingham, *Small Giants: Companies That Choose to Be Great
Instead of Big* (New York: The Penguin Group, 2005).

[7]See, e.g., www.localharvest.org/csa.

Even more significantly, the traditional business model that stressed stability and linear patterns of growth of a hierarchically-structured firm, is giving way to every institution's worst nightmare: the constancy of inconstancy. The success and profitability of an enterprise is now dependent upon its being able to make responses to fluctuations whose combined influences are too complex to allow for the illusion of predictable outcomes. Management thinking that once emphasized the preservation of the status quo, is giving way to a rational spontaneity—the ability to work within informal, parallel networks that shadow, and often challenge, the formal structured authority of the firm. Advancing technologies are helping to decentralize the business environment, with computers, fax-machines, and cell-phones making it possible for more and more people to work from their homes, and for teleconferencing to connect people from different cities or countries for meetings.

Decentralization and flexibility are apparent in a variety of other areas as well. Alternative schools and health care practices continue to draw support away from institutionalized educational, medical, and pharmaceutical interests. Lawyers are increasingly turning to alternative, decentralized methods of resolving disputes, including arbitration and what is emerging as "holistic" or "collaborative" law practice. At the same time, there has been increased interest in the use of "jury nullification," by which members of a jury ignore the instructions they receive from a judge and adopt their own legal standards for guilt or innocence. Research in "nanotechnology," with molecular-scale robots performing microscopic level tasks, is stimulating interest in technological problem solving at the smallest possible level. A number of cities and regions in Europe have taken to abolishing traffic signs, leaving traffic decisions to be made by the interplay of motorists. One advocate of such change has said that "[t]he many rules strip us of the most important thing: the ability to be considerate. We're losing our capacity for socially responsible behavior." This new policy has led to a dramatic *reduction* in traffic accidents.[8]

The banking industry—perhaps the most institutionalized sector in private business—has engaged in limited experimentation with "micro-lending," a system designed to provide small loans to impoverished people who have no material collateral. The collateral upon which lenders rely is found in the promises of a handful of the borrower's fellow villagers to repay the loan. While the Grameen Bank of Bangladesh—along with its founder—won the 2006 Nobel Peace Prize for such efforts, there remains some question as to whether these systems can sustain themselves without either private or governmental subsidies. Nevertheless, the fact that such decentralist practices are being put to the test—a century and a half after first being proposed by Lysander Spooner[9]—provides encouragement that further experimentation may produce a more refined system that will be self-supporting in the marketplace. In recent decades, investment practices have evolved to provide individuals with more independent decision-making than had existed in more traditional brokerage-house practices. For instance, the emergence of mutual funds was followed by on-line discount brokerages, and later by exchange-traded funds. These and other changes have led to decentralization in the investment process.

The Internet, cell-phones, fax machines, iPods and iPhones, Tivo, websites, and blogs are the better-known technologies that increase, exponentially, our capacities for accessing and decentralizing the flow of information and decision-making proficiency among people. It has been estimated that there are over *one billion* personal computers and some twenty-two million blogsites in existence throughout the world. The established news media is firmly challenged by technologies that allow anyone not only to become a news source, but to be able to identify and even force corrections of erroneously reported news

---

[8] www.spiegel.de/international/spiegel/0,1518,448747,00.html

[9] Lysander Spooner, *Poverty: Its Illegal Causes and Legal Cure, Part First* (Boston: Bela March, 1846).

stories and photographs. Individuals with their own video and cell-phone cameras provide pictorial coverage of catastrophes and other events that centralized news sources do not. The lies, deceptions, and corruption that arise within various institutions, particularly the state, are being disclosed not so much by government officials or the so-called "mainstream media," as by independent journalists, Internet reporters, and Internet websites. Some major newspapers—confronting a diminished base of subscribers and the advertisers who depend upon that base—have turned to Internet reporting of news. Websites and so-called "niche publications" provide localized news stories or topics of personal interest to readers. In turn, the readers become active, two-way participants in both reporting and generating stories, a process that has led to increased readership and advertising.[10] There are also websites, such as Snopes.com and Hoaxbusters, that analyze and expose urban myths and hoaxes. Increasingly, the content of news is being subjected to supervision by consumers.

Authors need no longer rely on large publishing houses, as "publishing on demand" has become a viable alternative. The site, MySpace.com, is creating opportunities for musicians to circumvent established record companies and put their work online. The inexpensive availability of video cameras has decentralized the visual reporting of events, particularly over the Internet, and also spawned the widespread growth of documentary film-making as well as the phenomenon known as YouTube. Low-priced cameras and digital printers have opened the photography profession to more people. Satellite radio and cable television now vigorously compete with government-created broadcasting monopolists. Stock- and commodity-market investors control their own purchases through computers, rather than having to rely on brokerage houses. One expression of a politically unrestrained marketplace, eBay, provides a means for people to buy and sell virtually anything through

---

[10]See, e.g., Jeff Howe, "Breaking the News," in *Wired* (August, 2007): 86–90.

Internet transactions with total strangers, trading over great geographic distances.

Furthermore, PayPal is available as an alternative method for the payment of goods and services in a horizontally connected world. At the same time, some sixteen privately operating regional currencies have appeared in Germany as an alternative to the state-created euro, with sixty percent of the earnings derived from one such currency going to local charities.[11] The Internet encyclopedia Wikipedia is a continually updated system that allows visitors to edit subject-matter content, a system that has been emulated by digg.com for the reporting of news stories. Craigslist is an online service through which millions of people buy and sell items, seek employment or housing, develop social relationships, or pursue other interests. Members, themselves, provide discipline to this website by a system of flagging. On a more frivolous level, "flash mobs" make use of cellphones and the Internet to organize strangers to participate in some pointless act and then disband. One can only imagine the spontaneously creative uses to which such methods might one day be made. Perhaps no phenomenon better exemplifies the emerging decentralization of life than the success of J. K. Rowling's *Harry Potter* books. After the publisher initially put a few hundred of these books on the market—without much publicity—they became popular with children, whose playground discussions of the books snowballed into a marketplace demand that has earned the author millions of dollars.

The dispersal of human action manifests itself in still other areas. For decades, men and women have voiced a continuing decline of confidence in politics and the political process. With the emergence of websites and blogsites, however, many have begun to discover countervailing influences to the "democracy" of smoke-filled rooms, media-controlled political campaigns, and staged "debates" between establishment-certified

---

[11]Gerhard Rösl, "Regional Currencies in Germany—Local Competition for the Euro?" www.bundesbank.de/download/volkswirtschaft/dkp/2006/200643dkp–en.pdf; http://wiki-europa.info/index/php?title=Regional–currency.

candidates. Political parties find themselves having to contend with questions that concern ordinary people, rather than just the leaders of various political action collectives who presume to speak for others than themselves.

But with the decentralization of human action, politics has become a less relevant means for many people to accomplish ends that they value. Part of the explanation for this decline in the importance of politics is found in the fact that political systems have historically defined themselves *geographically,* while the world is becoming more *holistic* and beyond the limitations of geographic territory. Men and women are discovering in informal and voluntary forms of association, more effective means of bringing about social changes than those that rely on sluggish, corrupt, and coercive political machinations. While members of the political establishment chastise, as "apathetic," those who withdraw from state-centered undertakings, the reality is that increasing numbers of men and women are redirecting their energies, with an enhanced enthusiasm, to pursuits over which they have greater personal control. This redistribution of authority is both liberating and empowering, a continuing process that is generating interest—in exponential terms - in less formal systems of social behavior.

One of the more interesting phenomena is the practice, in some communities and other groups, of reaching common objectives through *consensus* (i.e., where everyone must agree with a proposal before it is undertaken). Caspar, California, an unincorporated town of some two thousand people occupying twelve square miles of territory, is one such community in which decisions are made through a process of "deliberating until we can find a way that satisfies all."[12] As with most Amish

---

[12]The Caspar residents have found this process to be not "as difficult as we thought, and that heeding and incorporating the views of the minority often saves us from grievous errors while leading us away from 'slam dunks' and quick fixes to well thought-out, longer lasting, better solutions." http://casparinstitute.org/lib/artConsensus.htm.

communities,[13] Caspar confirms the benefits that can derive from smaller, face-to-face associations. This consensus-seeking process also exists in much of Somalia, where consensus decisions are insisted upon not only as a way of achieving harmony within a community, but to make certain critical opinions are heard so as to have more information available for reaching a more sound decision. In the words of one observer:

> Decision making in the Assembly involves no casting of votes. Rather, the Assembly members keep on talking until a consensus is reached. That is why the meeting can last a long time, sometimes several months. The reason why the Assembly operates by consensus is easy to understand: *it prevents the Assembly from taking decisions that would infringe on anyone's freedom and property rights.*[14]

The dismantling of hierarchical structures has cosmological significance as well. Is there a life force—a will to exist—within the universe? If so, does it emanate from a supreme intelligence and flow, in a top-down manner, to subordinate beings? Or, does it arise autonomously, as an interconnected interplay of matter/energy? Was the universe *created*, as a product of intelligent design, or did it evolve without intention? Are our lives subject to the power of a divine authority, or is each of us the director of our behavior and destiny? Are the laws under which we live "a gift from God;"[15] a "Divine Law" derived from biblical revelation,[16] or are they, as Oliver Wendell Holmes said of the

---

[13]See, e.g., John A. Hostetler, *Amish Society*, 3rd ed. (Baltimore: The Johns Hopkins University Press, 1980); Steven M. Holt, *A History of the Amish* (Intercourse, Pa.: Good Books, 1992).

[14]Michael Van Notten, *The Law of the Somalis: A Stable Foundation for Economic Development in the Horn of Africa* (Trenton, N.J.: Red Sea Press, 2005), p. 83; emphasis added.

[15]John of Salisbury, *The Statesman's Book* (1159), in William Ebenstein, *Great Political Thinkers*, 2nd ed. (New York: Rineheart & Company, 1956), pp. 195–96.

[16]Thomas Aquinas, *The Summa Theologica* (1265–1274).

Common Law, the product of *experience*?[17] The answers to such questions are at the center of how we regard ourselves and our relationships with other people and social entities in our lives. *How* we respond to such inquiries will depend upon the content of the metaphysical models from which our thinking derives.

On a grimmer note, the processes of decentralization manifest themselves in destructive activity as well. We have learned, in recent decades, that nation-states no longer enjoy monopolies in their conduct of war: guerilla tactics, suicide attacks, and localized insurgencies have turned war, itself, into a decentralized undertaking. Powerful state military forces, armed with bombers, missiles, tanks, naval vessels, and tens of thousands of soldiers with sophisticated weapons and computerized tools, are proving to be no match for informal, decentralized, horizontally-networked groups that covertly attack and defeat them. These militia and guerrilla groups operate autonomously, each being free to quickly adapt to immediate circumstances without having to resort to direction from a centralized leadership. Militarily superior state forces with hundreds of billions of dollars of support, including the use of massive aerial bombing—the most literal example of pyramidal power—have been resisted and defeated by localized insurgency groups: the French in Indo-China and Algeria; the Soviet Union in Afghanistan; the United States in Vietnam and Iraq; and Israel in Lebanon. What makes so-called "terrorist" groups so difficult to identify and deal with is their informal, dispersed, nonhierarchical form of organization. Recall how nineteen men, armed only with box-cutter knives, were able to attack the World Trade Center buildings and precipitate the insanity of the United States' war against the Iraqi people.

Law enforcement and anti-terrorist officials in various parts of the world have noted the emerging phenomenon of informally-organized mini-groups—sometimes consisting of only two or three persons—made up of people who become angry and

---

[17]Oliver Wendell Holmes, *The Common Law* (Boston: Little, Brown and Company, 1881), p. 1.

react violently. Such groups—which have been labeled "BOGs," meaning "bunch of guys"—spontaneously appear and disappear. Their lack of formal leadership or hierarchical organization makes it difficult to identify such persons.[18] At the same time, urban gangs have effectively displaced governmental police in controlling parts of many inner cities as well as prisons.

All of this is to give a cursory flavor to the forces that are bringing about a redistribution of decisional authority in the world, a trend that established institutional interests resist. Placed in the context of this book, these changes bear a direct relation to the changing question of how, and by whom, authority is exercised over the lives and property of people.

The implications of such decentralist trends have not been lost on the political and economic establishment. The so-called "war on terror" appears to be a desperate effort by those with a vested interest in the politically-structured status quo (e.g., the state and major state-connected corporations) to resist the movement toward what I shall later explore as horizontally-networked systems. This "war," to which its promoters have given a prognosis of permanency, could more accurately be termed a "war for the preservation of the old order." If the pyramid is collapsing into horizontal networks, it is supposed that expanded police and regulatory powers, increased surveillance and torture, RFID chips[19] and GPS systems that can track the movement of individuals, restricted due process and habeas corpus rights, and other coercive means, might reinforce its crumbling foundations and reverse the decline. Despite the demonstrated failure of systems of state economic planning, the George W. Bush administration proposed broadening and further centralizing the Federal Reserve Board's powers to regulate all marketplace financial

---

[18] *Los Angeles Times*, August 16, 2007, p. A1 and p. A10.

[19] See, e.g., Katherine Albrecht and Liz McIntyre, *Spychips: How Major Corporations and Government Plan to Track Your Every Move with RFID* (Nashville, Tenn.: Nelson Current, 2005).

practices in order to deal with the problems this agency had caused![20]

When the Bush administration renamed this "war" the "Global Struggle Against Extremism," it admitted to its purpose of perpetuating a pyramidally-structured society. While "terror" is a strategy of violence, "extremism" has no necessary relationship to coercion or destructiveness. Indeed, one dictionary defines "extreme" in terms of "exceeding the ordinary, usual, or expected," then adding "situated at the farthest possible point from a center."[21] If the preservation of centralized, institutionalized, command-and-control systems is to be regarded as a social value, the voices or systems that represent the processes of change will be considered "extremist" influences to be marginalized or destroyed. History informs us of the men and women who have been labeled "heretics," "seditionists," "terrorists," "radicals," "counter-revolutionaries," "possessed," "traitors," or "extremists," who have been punished or killed for conduct or opinions that deviated from a sacred center. Because our hierarchically dominant world is, by definition, the "center" from which to measure the deviations that define "extremism," the institutionally self-serving nature of such campaigns should be evident.

Perhaps the earliest, and most far-reaching, indicator of the emerging decentralization of society was the collapse of politically planned and directed national economies. Nowhere has the pragmatic contrast between private ownership of property and state collectivism been more sharply drawn than in these diametrically opposed approaches to the organization of economic life. A stark distinction has been established as to both the quantitative and qualitative conditions under which humans are to live in society by comparing the real-world consequences of systems grounded in individual liberty versus those premised on coercive authority. As the marketplace reestablishes itself

---

[20]Reported by the Associated Press, March 28, 2008. See www.msnbc.msn.com/id/23853415/.

[21]*Webster's Third New International Dictionary*, p. 807.

following decades of dismal utopian experiences with state socialism and centralized planning, inquiries into the nature of spontaneously derived order have energized thoughtful minds. The experiences of the twentieth century have made it clear that the material well-being of humankind is better served through voluntarily organized marketplace systems than through political direction and supervision. That the foundations of either such system lie in the question of how property is to be owned and controlled in society will be the dominant theme throughout this book.

As the destructive and dehumanizing twentieth-century history of a politically-dominated world has demonstrated, the crisis in our lives is caused *not* by events, but by the thinking that produces and interprets such events. Our understanding of the world is unavoidably tied to the *images*, the *models* that our minds have created to describe it. In the words of Richard Weaver, "ideas have consequences,"[22] and it is to our thinking that we must repair if we are to emerge from the present crisis that is destroying our world.

We have long fooled ourselves that we can relate to nature and events in some "objective" fashion, like a camera that faithfully records what it observes. Contrary to such a view, our understanding of the universe, or the society in which we live, or even ourselves, is inextricably tied to subjectively-crafted models put together by our thinking. The content of our consciousness is largely the product of an intermixing of our unique, personal experiences; what our parents, teachers, friends, and the media have taught us; books we have read; and the abstract concepts we have put together in our minds to create as consistent a paradigm as possible that explains the complex nature of our world. If our lives are to change to more beneficial ends, we must look to the models upon which we have constructed our world. We have learned to see the universe in a particular way, and each of us has the capacity to transform such thinking. The underlying

---

[22]Richard Weaver, *Ideas Have Consequences* (Chicago: University of Chicago Press, 1948).

theme of this book is that our traditional institutional model is not only no longer useful to, but actually destructive of, the purposes for which we have long embraced it. This book will suggest and explore an alternative model for the peaceful and productive conduct of society.

Perhaps a valuable lesson can be learned from the history of scientific thought. As Thomas Kuhn has observed, scientific revolutions, which he defined as paradigm shifts that cause scientists to view their world differently, begin in crisis. Earlier scientific theories become increasingly unable to explain anomalous events in the world, leading some scientists to begin a search for new theories. In words relevant to our inquiry herein, Kuhn states that "[f]ailure of existing rules is the prelude to a search for new ones."[23] The crisis begins to escalate into a state of turbulence, generating "the essential tension" associated with trying "to live in a world out of joint."[24] For example, the inconsistencies between Ptolemaic astronomical theory and pre-Copernican observations of the heavens represented such a bifurcation point. Through the interplay of the forces of "stability" and "change," scientists began to develop a more complex model that helped to accommodate the earlier theories to the anomalies. As established thinking was confronted by new explanations, the systemic chaos provided the catalyst for developing a more complex and orderly system of understanding. But, as Kuhn is quick to emphasize, the older theory is never rejected just because it no longer conforms to nature. Only when a better model is available will a paradigm shift occur.[25] Even then, the new model need not be superior in all respects to the old, but only comparatively better.

Similar dynamics are at work in our understanding of social behavior. Contrary to some of our simplistic notions about human progress, significant changes in our thinking have

---

[23]Thomas S. Kuhn, *The Structure of Scientific Revolutions*, 2nd ed. (Chicago: University of Chicago Press, 1970), p. 68; originally published, 1962.

[24]Ibid., p. 79.

[25]Ibid., pp. 77–79.

arisen not through gradual, accretive processes, but by the revolutionary overthrow of older paradigms by newer ones. The belief that governments were ordained by God collapsed, at least in Western society, as people turned, instead, to the idea of a "social will" arising out of a "social contract." Being better equipped to resolve inconsistencies evident in the traditional model, the new paradigm supplanted the old. Such changes occur rather abruptly, being followed by relatively stable periods that will later be interrupted by yet another paradigmatic coup. Such punctuated processes have been observed in other fields of study as well, such as Stephen Jay Gould's models of evolutionary change.[26] The influences of stability and change continue to work their syntheses.

For the same reasons that led members of the scientific community to respond to crises by transforming their thinking, we are now in need of a better model upon which to base our understanding of social systems. Our traditional model has proven itself too destructive of life to any longer satisfy even the most meager definitions of pragmatic purpose, much less those more profound inner needs that are subject to neither measure nor calculation. Nor is it any longer capable of rationalizing its inherent contradictions. There is a growing crisis in confidence, as reflected in the turbulence of modern society, to which humans must respond if civilization itself is to be salvaged. Such a response can no longer be of the cosmetic nature of political "reform," but must amount to a fundamental change in our assumptions about how societies come to be organized.

What many regard as the most powerful of curses begins, "May you live in interesting times." We are living in interesting times. Few have the opportunity to observe either the collapse or fundamental transformation of the civilization within which they live. Such an occasion appears to be before us. The world into which we were born will not be the same one from which most of us will depart. Whether our future will be more free,

---

[26]Stephen Jay Gould, *Ever Since Darwin* (New York: W.W. Norton & Company, 1977), pp. 118, 271.

peaceful, and productive; or whether it will be more repressive, violent, and destructive, may depend on the content of the thinking we carry with us.

A focal point of such thinking involves an exploration of the competing interests of individual liberty versus obedience to collective authority. "Liberty" is not some abstract philosophic principle, although it is often incorporated into various ideologies, but a way of describing the autonomous nature of life in its myriad forms. "Liberty" is *life* pursuing what it wants to pursue, through its self-directed energy. Because liberty and spontaneity express the essence of living systems, this book is about how—and by whom—authority is to be exercised in our lives. Are you and I to have effective decision-making control over our lives, or is this power to reside in others? Because control is the defining factor in the ownership of property, such questions raise the deeper inquiry into where our sense of ownership resides. Whether or not we choose to claim self-ownership has more than an arcane, abstract significance. It goes to the very essence of what it means to be a free man or woman. As we shall discover, individual liberty and self-ownership are synonymous terms; we are free only insofar as we insist upon the exclusive authority to direct our own energies and other resources.

Our assertion of self-ownership confronts the doctrine of eminent domain, a concept essential to the authority of all political systems. Eminent domain expresses the proposition that the state has a supervening claim to all property interests within its domain, which it may exercise at any time it chooses. Such powers are not confined to the more familiar area of real property, but include ownership claims over persons. Conscription, the regulation and taxation of one's productive activities, control over what substances a person may ingest, capital punishment; and compulsory education, are some of the major instances of the eminent domain principle, which presumes individual interests to be subservient to those of the state. It is this doctrine that is being challenged by the development of decentralized, horizontal, interconnected social practices.

If we are to move beyond the turbulent and destructive organizational models that consume rather than enhance human life, we must make conscious efforts to think in concrete terms about what forms our social behavior will take and what practices it will embrace. One inquiry has to do with the question of how property is to be owned and controlled in our world. Does life belong to the *living*, or to the *institutions* that have traditionally claimed a preemptive authority over mankind? At long last, we must explore the most fundamental of social concepts that those who would control the lives of others have insisted we ignore.

This is the kind of examination we have never been encouraged to undertake. In our highly-structured world, authority has been centralized in institutions, particularly the state, none of whom have been interested in our asking such questions. But centralized authority necessarily implies centralized control over the lives and property interests of us all. To the degree our personal decision-making has been preempted, we have lost control, hence the effective ownership, of our lives. But if our world is moving toward more decentralized, horizontal systems, the authority to direct our lives will also become decentralized. Of necessity, this will lead us to a consideration of the questions: do we, in fact, own ourselves, and do we desire to do so?

However we answer these questions will prove most unsettling to our institutionally-conditioned minds. Most of us, particularly those of us of "senior citizen" status who have endured more years of such operant conditioning, will not find comfort in such explorations. Nonetheless, in the face of the many fundamental changes already occurring in our world, even asking such questions will effect a redistribution of authority. It is to engage in mechanistic thinking to suppose that "information" or "technology" will magically transform our lives; only a fundamental change in our thinking can accomplish such ends. We must make a conscious choice to assert our claim to self-ownership. Having done so, with a full understanding of what is implicit in making such a claim, the control over our lives will shift from institutions to our individual selves.

This book, then, is more than just an inquiry into the nature of property as "things"—including real estate—as the restricted understanding of our materialistic culture tends to suggest to us. Neither is it just about the accumulation of wealth, although it embraces the liberty of men and women to pursue wealth if such ends have transcendent meaning to their lives. "Property" has a far richer human dimension to it than this, something that men and women of ascetic dispositions have often failed to understand. It involves the question of *how* and by *whom* decisions are to be made about people and "things" in the world in which we live. The deeper significance of property lies in defining our relationships to one another as well as our personal sense of being, particularly as such factors delineate our respective areas of decision-making authority. As the common origins of the words suggest, "property" is a way of describing "proper" behavior: that conduct is "proper" when performed by the individual whose "property" interests are affected thereby, and when such an actor restricts his or her decision making to what he or she owns.

This is a book, in other words, about *social metaphysics*, an exploration of the interrelated nature of peace, freedom, order, and property, and how these factors are dependent upon the nature of the social systems through which we organize ourselves with others. It is an examination of the relationship between *property* and *authority*, and of their connection to both individual liberty and order in any society. Property is the most important and yet, paradoxically, the least understood of all our social practices. In spite of the preoccupation that mankind has with getting, keeping, protecting, controlling, buying, selling, regulating, or confiscating property, we live in almost complete ignorance of its functional nature, or of its social and spiritual significance in our lives. The reason for this lack of clarity is understandable: political institutions, which have been the principal architects of our thinking, depend upon varying degrees of preemption of our authority over our lives and property interests. If we really understood how liberty, as well as our material and spiritual well-being, is dependent upon our capacity to exercise control over what is ours, we might never consent to such institutional intrusions upon our property interests.

One could go so far as to state that our understanding of property is, in social terms, still at a pre-Copernican level. Very few thinkers have undertaken a comprehensive analysis of the subject, and most of those have tended to be apologists for existing political and social arrangements, or ideologists of one persuasion or another. Even most defenders of private ownership have failed to identify any firmer foundation for their case than some eighteenth century myths about "natural law" or "moral imperatives." So weak has been the modern case for private ownership that to even raise the proposition as a sufficient basis for decision making is to risk being labeled a "reactionary" who would "take us back to the nineteenth century."

It is difficult, in exploring a subject that calls into question both the entire institutional structure and the thinking that pervades our lives, to avoid being charged with expressing one's subjective, normative preferences. I am well aware, however, of Heisenberg's warnings about the observer being an integral part of what is being observed. I will go even further and insist that all we can ever know about the world is fashioned subjectively within our minds as products of our prior experiences and formal learning. This is not to suggest that our opinions are necessarily in error, but only that, no matter how much effort or good intentions we bring to bear, we can never fully rise above the content of our thinking in describing and analyzing the world in which we live.

With this caveat in mind, the conclusions I draw herein will be as free as possible from deductions drawn from ideologies, moral imperatives, historical determinism, natural law, right reason, or any other abstract principles by which people have endeavored to explain their opinions. My efforts to avoid resting my conclusions on little more than my own subjective preferences is made difficult by the fact that our scientifically-modeled, materialistic culture insists upon a *quantitative* analysis of phenomena as a standard for "truth." As will become evident, much of the approach I take in this book rests upon an analysis of *qualitative* factors that are essential to an understanding of conditions that make social systems conducive to the satisfaction of human needs. "Peace," "liberty," and "social order" are difficult—if not impossible—subjects to be addressed in a purely quantitative manner. On what basis, for example, can one do a thorough, quantitatively-based analysis of Auschwitz, the Soviet gulags, the bombings of Hiroshima, Nagasaki, and Dresden, or the slaughter of hundreds of thousands of innocent Iraqis as a reaction to 9/11? How does one withdraw from consideration of the "costs" and "benefits" of such actions the costs to the degradation of human beings which alone allows them to be treated as *atrocities*? For reasons that go to the essence of what I regard as the humanizing nature of private property, I am both unable and unwilling to separate qualitative values from my description of the human condition.

Though I openly confess to the charge that my views herein represent nothing *more* than my subjective opinions, they also represent, as do the writings of everyone else, nothing *less*. Each of us is unable to do otherwise. I will do my best, however, to not hide my opinions behind dogmatic a priori assertions of values disguised as fact. I offer them to you not out of some momentary flight of whimsy, but as the product of decades of focused study and thinking on the subject. They represent the best of what I am capable of contributing to the question now before all of mankind: how can we aid and abet the transformation of our social systems so that they can maximize the opportunities for individuals to satisfy their material and spiritual needs in voluntary cooperation with others? I shall approach the subject as an integrated examination of our material and spiritual, as well as individual and social, requirements for living peacefully and productively in the world.

Chapter Two
The Eroding Structure

As our populations expand, as a world-wide movement from countryside to city embraces all peoples, as problems of housing, of broken homes and juvenile delinquency, of mass education and delayed independence of the young rise about us in our very human midst, as David Riesman's "the lonely crowd" comes more and more aptly to describe all humankind, have we not the right to ask: Is what we are witnessing, in essence, not the first consequence of the deterritorializing of man? And if man is a territorial animal, then as we seek to repair his dignity and responsibility as a human being, should we not first search for means of restoring his dignity and responsibility as a proprietor?

— Robert Ardrey

I must explain, at the outset, that this book is not simply an abstract discussion of the property concept. One must consider the relative importance of property principles within the broader context of particular metaphysical models that are presumed to both describe phenomena and prescribe systems and behavior that conform to a given model. If a particular paradigm has been accepted to explain the regularities in nature, efforts will be made to broaden the acceptance of that model as widely as can reasonably be accomplished. Because this book explains the nature of property from the perspective of a traditional model of social beliefs and systems, and proposes an alternative paradigm—one that already seems to be emerging—it is essential to begin with an historical analysis of what has brought us to our present situation.

For centuries, Western civilization has functioned on a model, developed by Isaac Newton, that presumed the universe to be composed of basic building blocks—atoms having become the preferred explanation—held together, and their behavior regulated, by discernible "laws" (e.g., laws of motion, gravity, light, thermodynamics, etc.). This provided a mechanistic and reductionist model that helped provide, within the realm of human society, the metaphysical base for the emergence of modern institutionalized systems of social order. Implicit in such a view is the idea that nature is structured in relatively simple patterns of calculation that can be accurately identified and measured. Because of the presumption of certainty inherent in such a model, it has long been an article of faith that, given sufficient information, it is possible for human beings to predict the consequences of events in both our physical and social worlds. Indeed, the universe came to be regarded as a giant clockwork, destined by the second law of thermodynamics to run down. If nature, including human action, was predictable, it was also controllable, a presumption upon which vertically-organized systems have depended for their existence.

While Newtonian thinking provided the intellectual base upon which the sciences built, political systems had long been grounded in similar assumptions about the governance of societies. Plato's *Republic*,[1] dating back to the fourth-century B.C., provided what one scholar has called "The first work that deserves to be called political science."[2] Plato envisioned a pyramidal governmental system in which society would be structured into a hierarchy of rulers, followed by a class of soldiers and administrators whose function would be to regulate the lowest class: the *producers*, whose existence makes society

---

[1] *The Republic of Plato*, trans. by F.M. Cornford (Oxford: Oxford University Press, 1945).

[2] William Ebenstein, *Great Political Thinkers*, 2nd ed. (New York: Rinehart & Company, 1956), p. 2.

possible. That this arrangement continues to define modern political society is a proposition I trust requires no independent citation of authority! The imagery of such thinking can be seen in the Washington Monument towering above the District of Columbia.

The mechanistic model of a predictable and controllable universe has underlain programs of state planning and control, including the regulation of economic behavior, health care, the environment, foreign policies, education, wildlife management, urban renewal, transportation systems, and monetary policies, to name but a few. From the more ambitious undertakings of the erstwhile Iron Curtain systems, to the proliferation of legislative codes, administrative rulemaking, and judicial decision-making, all of which combine to dominate Western societies, modern assumptions about the necessity for the imposition of order differ from the mindset of the ancient lawgiver, Hammurabi, only in the expanded scope of their application. The belief that order must be intentionally generated and imposed upon society by institutional authorities continues to prevail.

This centrally-directed model is premised upon what F.A. Hayek called "the fatal conceit," namely, the proposition "that man is able to shape the world according to his wishes,"[3] or what David Ehrenfeld labeled "the arrogance of humanism."[4]That such practices have usually failed to produce their anticipated results has generally led not to a questioning of the model itself, but to the conclusion that failed policies have suffered only from inadequate leadership, or a lack of sufficient information, or a failure to better articulate rules. Once such deficiencies have been remedied, it has been supposed, *new* programs can be implemented which, reflective of this mechanistic outlook, will permit government officials to "fine tune" or "jump start" the economy, or "grow" jobs, or produce a "quick fix" for

---

[3]F.A. Hayek, *The Fatal Conceit: The Errors of Socialism*, W.W. Bartley III, ed. (Chicago: University of Chicago Press, 1988), p. 27.

[4]David Ehrenfeld, *The Arrogance of Humanism* (New York: Oxford University Press, 1978).

the ailing government school system. Even as modern society manifests its collapse in the form of violent crime, economic dislocation, seemingly endless warfare, inter-group hostilities, the decay of cities, a growing disaffection with institutions, and a general sense that nothing "works right" anymore, faith in the traditional model continues to drive the pyramidal systems. Most people still cling to the belief that there is something that can be done by political institutions to change such conditions: a new piece of legislation can be enacted, a judicial ruling can be ordered, or a new agency regulation can be promulgated. When a government-run program ends in disaster, the mechanistic mantra is invariably invoked: "we will find out what went wrong and fix it so that this doesn't happen again." That the traditional model itself, which is grounded in the state's power to control the lives and property of individuals to desired ends, may be the principal contributor to such social disorder goes largely unexplored.

Faith in the traditional model began to erode with work done in the field of "quantum mechanics." The Newtonian dream of being able to describe the universe as a kind of cosmic erector set has been upset by a view of subatomic behavior in which spontaneity seems to offer a more plausible explanation for events than does mechanics. Traditional beliefs that phenomena could be explained as simple deterministic, cause and effect patterns, like David Hume's vector analysis of the behavior of billiard balls, have given way to an awareness of more dynamic and mysterious interactions among particles than had before been imagined. One can still play a very adept game of pool using Newtonian principles, but his system is no longer sufficient to explain complex dynamics.

Just as distressing to adherents of the Newtonian paradigm was the realization that, at the subatomic level, change occurred not through gradual processes of evolution, such as a molecule of water progressively getting warmer as it was subjected to heat, but through "quantum leaps." While the collective temperature of the water could be said to gradually increase, for any specific molecule such a change came about instantaneously, as a jump from an unheated to a heated state. What this means is that prediction—hence, the ability to control—is impossible at the subatomic level, and must give way to estimates of *probabilities,* based on the law of large numbers. Even our atomic "building-block" assurances about the existence of matter have, at the subatomic level, been shattered. The on-again, off-again character of particles led Einstein to characterize "matter" as "frozen energy,"[5] much as Emerson had described the world as "thickened light,"[6] or some physicists to speak of particles in terms of "tendencies to exist."[7] To have a science that no longer admits being able to control specific complex events, a presumed power that has been further diminished by the study of complexity and chaos, has been quite devastating, not only to many scientists themselves, but to members of the institutional order, whose authority has depended upon the appearance of such ability.

Quantum mechanics has been a major contributor to the breakdown of traditional centrally-directed models of order. With an understanding of events focused on the margins of subatomic behavior, the universe begins to look less and less like an assemblage of parts subservient to some whole, and more like patterns of reciprocal interconnectedness. This emerging model may find an analogy in the pointillistic art style of Georges Seurat,

---

[5]See Harald Fritzsch, *An Equation That Changed the World: Newton, Einstein, and the Theory of Relativity* (Chicago: University of Chicago Press, 1964), p. 180; Timothy Ferris, *Coming of Age In the Milky Way* (New York: HarperCollins, 2003), p. 194.

[6]Ralph Waldo Emerson, "The Scholar," a lecture presented to Washington and Jefferson Societies at the University of Virginia, June 28, 1876.

[7]Fritjof Capra, *The Tao of Physics* (Boston: New Science Library, 1983), p. 133.

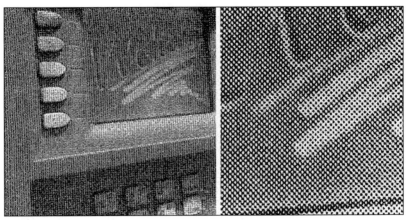

Newspaper picture, with section enlarged

or of photographs in a newspaper. In each, the picture is seen only as the composite of individual dots of paint on a canvas, or ink on a page of newsprint.

Though our eyes are accustomed to seeing the pictures as single, complete entities, a closer examination reveals their individualized composure. The reality of the pictures is found only in the interconnectedness of the dots (or "quanta"). Without the individualized dots, there is no picture. Like the fast moving series of still photographs that produce what we call "motion pictures," these dots create the illusions we think of as "reality." As Einstein has helped us to understand, our visions of the world are dependent upon the perspective—including our paradigms—from which we view events.

The most devastating blow to the long-established model of order is coming from the emerging science of "chaos," which is revealing the integrated complexity of the universe and the processes by which such complexity spontaneously generates order. We have long been familiar with the phenomenon of apparently regular behavior suddenly becoming erratic. A water faucet will drip at a fairly regular rate, increasing its flow proportionately to any additional supply of water. For a time, the relationship between input and output is *linear* in nature (i.e., any change in the pattern of flow is proportionately related to input changes). For example, if "x" produces "y," "x + 1" will produce "y + 1."

There comes a point, however, where a further increase in input will produce disproportionate effects, generating erratic patterns. At this bifurcation point, a linear and basically predictable system is thrown into non-linearity and randomness. "X + 4" now produces not "y + 4," but "z," with "z" representing turbulence. Like the proverbial straw that broke the camel's back, the consequence of adding one more unit is to create a nonlinear effect. These occurrences of nonlinearity are also seen in such examples as air turbulence, the flow of rivers, arrhythmic heartbeats, and the smoke from a cigarette whose rising regularity suddenly breaks up into erratic patterns.

Until recently, scientists and others have been content to dismiss such turbulence as random disorder. Because of the second law of thermodynamics, such irregularity has heretofore been accepted as only a confirmation of the entropic nature of the universe. But in the study of chaos, we are beginning to discover that, even within apparent disorder, patterns of orderliness and regularity can be found. Using computers as their principal tools, chaos scientists have identified behavior patterns in nature that recur, but do not precisely repeat themselves in any predictable manner. In the continual branching patterns of a river system, or a tree, or a cauliflower, we find examples of a recurring self-similarity that scientists have named "fractals." Fractals are a means by which systems most efficiently organize themselves by continually repeating successful patterns at different levels of scaling. Even nonlinear and seemingly random events, in other words, reveal a deep, hidden order, organized around so-called "attractors," which are the functional principles around which turbulence and perceived chaos regularize themselves. Earthquake fault lines, arrhythmic heart patterns, or brain wave patterns during a seizure, are just a few examples. Irregularity, in other words, has been found to have a certain regularity to it.

In spite of the regularity that has been discovered, it must be emphasized that chaotic systems are, by definition, nonlinear in nature (i.e., output changes are out of proportion to changes in input). Furthermore, a system can be rendered chaotic by even the most seemingly insignificant factor, whose effects are then fed back into the system, thus greatly multiplying its initial influences. This process by which a factor is able to produce a multiple of itself is known as "iteration," and can operate either to stabilize a system or to generate change.[8] In the regularities that keep iterating themselves deep within the behavior that we have heretofore regarded as disordered chaos, we are discovering a more dynamical and complex conception of order.

An awareness that order can arise spontaneously and without conscious design has begun to alter our views concerning the forms and functions of social organizations. As Hayek has observed, "we are able to bring about an ordering of the unknown *only by causing it to order itself,* . . . not by deliberately trying to arrange elements in the order that we wish them to assume."[9] We are also developing a better understanding of how a healthy, creative order involves a continuing interplay between the forces of *stability* and *change.*

Because of such complex, nonlinear influences, our ability to predict outcomes associated with such behavior becomes impossible over any extended period of time. It is the unpredictable nature of complex systems that is most troublesome to practitioners of the traditional model of order. Predictability depends upon an awareness of all the factors that bear upon an event in question—what chaos scientists call a "sensitive dependence on initial conditions."[10] To overlook any factor, no matter how minimal its apparent significance, will eventually produce exaggerated errors in what we try to foretell. These and other factors contribute toward making complex systems increasingly unpredictable with the passage of time. In what has come to be known as the "butterfly effect," chaos theorists offer the metaphor that the flapping of the wings of a butterfly over the Andes

---

[8]John Briggs and F. David Peat, *Turbulent Mirror* (New York: Harper & Row, 1989), pp. 66–68.

[9]Hayek, *The Fatal Conceit*, p. 83; emphasis in original.

[10]James Gleick, *Chaos: Making a New Science* (New York: Viking Penguin Inc., 1987), p. 44.

will influence the weather in Tibet. As regular and permanent as our solar system appears, even planetary orbits—which are subject to numerous disturbing influences—remain unpredictable over a long period of time.

Our inability to identify and accurately measure the multitude of factors influencing complex systems not only makes extended forecasting impossible, but it makes historic explanations equally subject to error. There has probably been no topic of human history more thoroughly examined and debated than the cause of what Edward Gibbon called "the decline and fall of the Roman Empire." There is not even agreement among historians as to whether Rome "fell" or was only "transformed" from what it had once been. One scholar has identified as many as 210 explanations for this watershed occurrence.[11]

There are numerous factors at work that make it impossible to ever have sufficient information to allow for the prediction of outcomes in complex systems. The first is the logistical difficulty of marshalling and accurately assessing all relevant information. Complex systems are subject to a number of variables, whose existence, fluctuations, and interactions may be both unknown and immeasurable. Furthermore, the interplay of positive and negative feedback loops can influence complex systems in unexpected ways. Additionally, our senses have a capacity for processing only a tiny fraction of the reality to which they are exposed. We are biologically incapable of even perceiving all of the factors acting upon events in our lives, including the dynamics by which such factors interrelate. Furthermore, our capacities for synthesizing all of the information that we do perceive is limited by our tendencies to experience information overload, which can cause us to periodically anesthetize or even shut down our minds.[12] Contrary to our hubristic assumptions about our capacities for understanding, there

---

[11]See Alexander Demandt, "210 Theories." http://crookedtimber.org/2003/08/25/decline-and-fall.

[12]See, e.g., Marshall McLuhan, *Understanding Media: The Extensions of Man* (New York: The New American Library, 1964).

are simply far too many matters affecting our lives that will forever be beyond our epistemological grasp.

Our lack of ability to foretell the future becomes even more pronounced with the increased complexity of the systems and/or the extension of time frames being considered. This is why government economic planning has been such an unmitigated disaster for millions of people. Hayek has thus identified the shortcomings of central planning: "the totality of resources that one could employ in such a plan *is simply not knowable to anybody*, and therefore can hardly be centrally controlled."[13] Centralized decision-making increases, exponentially, the interconnected factors at work upon situations for which one is trying to anticipate outcomes. On the other hand, a given individual acting on matters of his immediate concern has far fewer factors to consider in making a decision, thus reducing the range of uncertainty. While his ability to predict outcomes remains subject to the limitations posed by complexity, should his prognosis prove erroneous, the impact of his mistake will be much more confined.

As Hayek has expressed it, the spontaneous ordering of social systems requires us to "allow each individual element to find its own place within the larger order." This process

> requires that dispersed information be utilized by many different individuals, unknown to one another, in a way that allows the different knowledge of millions to form an exosomatic or material pattern. Every individual becomes a link in many chains of transmission through which he receives signals enabling him to adapt his plans to circumstances he does not know.[14]

We shall discover, further on, how a system of privately-owned property is not only essential to such self-organizing processes but, by decentralizing decision-making, serves to *localize*, rather than *universalize*, the consequences of erroneous judgments.

---

[13]Hayek, *The Fatal Conceit*, p. 85; emphasis in original.

[14]Ibid., pp. 83–84.

Closely related to these matters is the fact that all of our knowledge of the world is both *subjective* and *abstract* in nature. Our understanding has been produced by our mind organizing itself around various abstract concepts, and then cataloging and interpreting our experiences by reference to such concepts. If, as I believe, we do live in an objective universe, we can never experience its reality except as subjectively held opinions. We *translate* our world by reference to the mental constructs we have created for ourselves, which makes our understanding *different* from the world itself. We seem fated to dealing with the world by reference to such abstractions as "trees," "rivers," "justice," "furniture," "mankind," and "thunderstorms," concepts that inhere in our minds, not in what they describe. Alfred Korzybski reminded us of the metaphorical nature of our thinking when he declared that "the map is not the territory."[15] The words and other symbols that we employ never precisely equate with what they are used to describe and must, therefore, be *interpreted* when being applied in our world.

Through more precise use of language, we can narrow the range of uncertainty, but some amount of "fuzziness" remains because words are never the equivalent of what they seek to describe.[16] To assist us in our efforts, we turn to dictionaries, which are collections of words (abstractions) we use to interpret other words. Even a photograph has a great deal of information loss. It provides a two-dimensional representation of an observable three-dimensional event, thus lacking the perspectives of depth, time, and energy. Because our concepts are based upon limited prior experiences, and, therefore, less than complete knowledge, there is an unavoidable information loss between

---

[15]In Ken Wilber, *The Spectrum of Consciousness* (Wheaton, Ill.: The Theosophical House, 1977), p. 41.

[16]As any competent attorney knows, ambiguous language breeds conflict. Thus, language in a loan agreement that requires a borrower to pay a "fair and reasonable" rate of interest, is an invitation to a later dispute. But more specificity does not end the problem. Agreeing upon a 7 percent rate of interest does not tell us how such interest is to be calculated. The amount borrowed? The unpaid balance? Whether the interest is to be compounded? Etc.

the concept and the event itself; between the word and what the word is supposed to represent. As such, our opinions must always be regarded as incomplete and tentative in nature. We must develop an awareness not only of the importance of using sufficient clarity in our words so as to allow us to function with one another, but of the inherent uncertainties in language that foster conflict.

Our mind presents us with an additional problem: it functions on a dualistic model of perceiving and organizing the world into mutually-exclusive categories. We organize our experiences, through both formal and informal methods of learning, around "either-or" concepts. Something is either "A" or "non-A," "animal" or "vegetable," "hot" or "cold," a process that unavoidably leads us to see the world as a series of *divisions*. That the rest of the universe functions in an indivisible manner, without any apparent awareness of the partitions into which our minds have organized it, is a further limitation on our capacities for understanding.

Thus, when we deal with some event in the world, we are bound to interpret its causal explanations and meaning in light of what our prior experiences tell us are relevant to consider. Such interpretations will always be done by minds that are both limited as to content and separated from other phenomena. What we already know, in other words, restricts the range of our inquiries about the unknown, a fact that creates an inevitable gap between our beliefs and the universe in which we live.

The study of quantum physics has afforded us another insight into the limitations of our capacities for obtaining sufficient information upon which to make predictions. Werner Heisenberg's "uncertainty principle" informs us that we cannot simultaneously measure both the location and the momentum of a physical object; that the act of focusing our attention on something influences what we end up seeing. The behavior of subatomic particles is affected by the fact that they are being observed, just as the insertion of a thermometer into a container of a hot liquid will alter the temperature of the liquid. One finds this phenomenon in television coverage of

political demonstrations, wherein the appearance and enthusiasm of demonstrators rises when the cameras are turned on,
and diminishes when the television reporters leave. Nor can
we overlook the influence of observer bias—whether intended
or unintended—in choosing what phenomena upon which to
focus attention. Because a scientific experiment is always an
interplay between *fact* and the *theory* upon which the experiment is conducted, what the scientist ends up observing is the
external world's response to human thought.

In the command-and-control thinking spawned by our
adherence to the pyramidal model, there remains a latent tendency to believe that the accumulation of more information can
overcome uncertainties and the unpredictable nature of a complex world. But such thinking is illusory, for the reasons stated.
Our task is not to manage complexity, which implies trying to
control it for intended results, but to *respond* to its presence. An
example of this latter approach is found in the warnings given
to participants in whitewater river-rafting: should you fall over-
board and be drawn beneath the raft, do not fight the turbulence
but give in to it, and you will return to the surface on the other
side. Those who fight the turbulence often end up drowning.

There is an arrogance, bordering on a presumed omniscience,
connected with an insistence upon vertically-structured systems
for the control of the complex and spontaneous events that comprise nature, including human society. The appetites for such
systems are fed by desires for certainty in an inherently uncertain world, and for security from the inevitable vicissitudes of
spontaneous change. The fallacy that centrally-managed power
structures can put such fears to rest is being confronted by a
growing awareness that decision-making authority is best left
in the hands of individuals who, responding to the singular and
marginal nature of the events before them, are best able to minimize the potentially adverse consequences of uncertainty.

What clearer example of our inability to foresee the course
of complex events could be found than the failure of so-called
government "intelligence" to predict four of the more dramatic
occurrences of recent decades: the fall of the Shah of Iran, the

tearing down of the Berlin Wall, the collapse of the Soviet Union, and the attacks on the World Trade Center on 9/11? Despite untold tens of billions of dollars spent on gathering the most detailed information about the Middle East, the "Iron Curtain" countries, and international "terrorism," government officials were unable to anticipate these momentous events.

The record of economic planning by the state is even more abysmal. The "oil crisis" created by the Nixon administration's imposition of price controls was troublesome to most Americans having to endure the resulting shortages. Cars lined up at gasoline pumps were reminiscent of Russians standing in lines to purchase everyday household needs. The deadly consequences of such planning, however, were no better revealed than in the governmental policies in the past half-century in China. As a result of Mao Tse Tung's "Great Leap Forward" program, begun in 1958, millions of people were forced to leave their farms in order to work in factories, resulting in what two scholars have estimated as a 61 percent decrease in grain production[17] which, in turn, led to the starvation deaths of anywhere from 20 to 43 million people. In following years, the Chinese government instituted its "One Child Only" program—legally restricting the number of children a couple could have—some of the effects of which have included increased numbers of abortions, infanticide, and the practice of small children being left to die.

Ignorance of the inconstancies of complicated systems has also produced catastrophic consequences in various government conservation and environmental protection programs. Employing computerized mathematical models—whose capacities for planning are also dependent upon an awareness of all interconnected influences—government agencies have often produced the adverse outcomes they were intended to prevent.[18] So presumptuous are the political faithful in their ability

---

[17]Wei Li and Dennis Tao Yang, "The Great Leap Forward: Anatomy of a Central Planning Disaster," in *Journal of Political Economy* 113 (2005): 840–77.

[18]See, e.g., Orrin H. Pilkey and Linda Pilkey-Jarvis, *Useless Arithmetic: Why Environmental Scientists Can't Predict the Future* (New York: Columbia University Press, 2007).

to circumvent the uncertainties inherent in complexity, that one federal court, dealing with the disposal of radioactive wastes in Nevada, insisted that the Department of Energy predict the effects thereof for a period extending from 300,000 to 1,000,000 years![19] That such an extended prognostication could not take into account such uncertainties as earthquakes, climate changes, soil erosion, the area being hit by a comet or asteroid, or any of a number of other unforeseeable factors, did not seem to diminish the court's confidence in its capacity to formulate rules to accomplish such ends. Such an effort would be as absurd as trying to foretell—on the eve of mankind's emergence on earth—the course of human history.

Why should our understanding of chaos and complexity raise doubts about the adequacy of hierarchical systems? Because the ability to plan outcomes is essential to any system of formalized control, be it the state or a business organization, chaos theory challenges the foundations upon which our traditional social practices have been built. For our world to be predictable and controllable, it must be *mechanistic* and *linear* in nature. But, the illusions of the behaviorists to the contrary notwithstanding, there is nothing *less* mechanistic and linear in nature than the human mind, whose intricacies and capacities have yet to be matched by even the most sophisticated computers. When one multiplies the uncertain and constantly fluctuating qualities and preferences of the individual by the hundreds of millions of individuals comprising modern, complex societies, and then multiplies these factors by their recurring feedback effects, the unpredictable nature of human behavior increases to exponential levels of uncertainty. When one further considers the myriad of purely physical factors that interact and interconnect with one another—themselves producing iterations of their own unforeseen effects—the inconstant and variable nature of the world becomes even more apparent.

---

[19] Ibid., pp. xi, 50.

The dismal failure of state systems of economic planning, provide the most vivid example of this phenomenon. The hubris of government planners has never been a match for spontaneous market forces that know no masters; unlike the marketplace pricing system, administered pricing practices of state socialism have been unable to determine efficiencies. The world is simply too complex for any groups of human minds to calculate its labyrinthine interconnections. The Achilles' heel of socialist systems has been their failure to resolve this calculation problem.

Two political leaders grasped the truth of this. Over four centuries ago, Emperor Charles V acknowledged the futility of trying to universalize social order, when he observed: "To think that I attempted to force the reason and conscience of thousands of men into one mould and I cannot make two clocks agree."[20] French president Charles deGaulle reached the same conclusion in observing, centuries later: "How can anyone govern a nation that has 246 different kinds of cheese?"[21] If prediction within complex systems becomes impossible, the rationale for institutional authorities to centrally control social conduct in order to achieve some desired end is swept away. Chaos theory, in other words, is calling into question the entire logic upon which our highly structured world of institutional direction and governance has been predicated.

Through the study of chaos, we may be able to transcend the dualistic patterns of our thinking, and to understand that what we polarize as "order" and "chaos" may represent a continuous, interconnected process. Consider, for instance, the following image on the top of the next page. What does it represent to you? Is it nothing more than a collection of random, disordered splotches? Or, do you see the beginnings of a Jackson Pollock painting? Perhaps it is a photo of bird droppings on a car. If you are unable to find a recognizable pattern; what about figure 2?

---

[20]John Bartlett, *Familiar Quotations*, 13th ed. (Boston: Little, Brown and Company, 1955), p. 95.

[21]www.brainyquote.com/quotes/authors/c/charlesdeg134421.html.

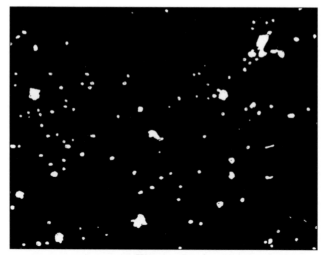

Figure 1.

Figure 2.

Do you recognize this, at once, as major sections of North America? If so, why did you not immediately perceive figure 1, which is an enlarged segment of figure 2, taken from a nighttime satellite photograph? Figure 1 provided you with no recognizable pattern with which to connect it, while figure 2 did. In other words, the "chaos" of figure 1 became the orderly presentation of figure 2 *not* because of any inherent qualities of either, but because your *mind* discerned a familiar pattern in the latter.

These photos can help demonstrate the important lessons being drawn from the study of chaos, namely, that what any of us may regard as "disorder" may only represent an "order" whose patterns we have not yet identified, or which conflict with our expectations. As with learning in general, it may be that only new patterns of order are being discovered. Did the substance of what you saw change, or only your interpretation thereof? If we think of order as a kind of information system, our failure to discover the underlying harmony or regularity may lead us to conclude that we are facing disorderly conditions. But isn't the difference between what we think of as order and disorder accounted for only by the state of our understanding rather than by the rest of nature? Has the universe suddenly changed from "chaos" to "order," or has there only been a change in our perspectives—encouraged, perhaps, by the availability of improved technologies—such that we are now able to discover these hidden patterns of order? And isn't the process of discovering order in what seems to us disorderly, only a synonym for *learning*? Harlow Shapley expressed the point in these words: "Chaos is but unperceived order; it is a word indicating the limitations of the human mind and the paucity of observational facts. The words 'chaos,' 'accidental,' 'chance,' 'unpredictable,' are conveniences behind which we hide our ignorance."[22]

Quantum mechanics and the study of chaos are transforming our assumptions about the certain and foreseeable nature of the world. While many continue to express faith in the proposition that "the more complex society becomes, the greater the need for centralized, governmental regulation," the truth lies elsewhere. Because of the unpredictability factor, it is *simple*— not *complex*—systems that can more easily be organized from the top-down. The more complex a society becomes, the less

---

[22]Harlow Shapley, *Of Stars and Men: The Human Response to an Expanding Universe* (Boston: Beacon Press, 1958), p. 63.

capable political systems are to provide for social order—if, indeed, they ever were—and the more we must rely upon spontaneous and informal processes. Politics is a means for trying to enforce a simplified model of structured regularity upon a complex, nonlinear world. Our lack of awareness of the inner complexities of the world, including human society, helps generate much of the confusion and conflict in our lives.

Contrary to the tenets of our institutionally-directed thinking, conditions of *non*equilibrium, of *instability*, are essential to the health of any system. If a system is to survive, it must continue to renew itself, a process that implies variation, diversity, and change, a movement toward a more orderly condition. "Life," itself, emerged and continues to develop through spontaneous responses to nonequilibrium conditions. If biological stability were the only consideration for living systems, life might never have had the occasion to develop beyond the bacterial stage. Life became more complex, in other words, only by partially abandoning the linear regularity of single celled forms. Only by becoming more chaotic did life become more complex and proliferate itself.[23] Life is a continuing interplay between *organizational form* and *spontaneity*, not an effort to stabilize some momentarily advantageous strategy. But it is this reciprocal process that institutions find threatening to their presumed needs for stability and permanence. Rather than seeing the long-term benefits to themselves in remaining adaptable to the forces of change, institutions tend to regard continuing transformation as a threat to their interests. In order to minimize the effects of this perceived menace, established systems—which insist upon being regarded as ends in themselves—have been attracted to mechanisms for the structuring of human conduct. But such efforts enervate the health of any vibrant system. In the words of Edmund Sinnott: "Constancy and conservatism are qualities of the lifeless, not the living."[24] The early Greek

---

[23]Briggs and Peat, *Turbulent Mirror*, pp. 70ff.

[24]Edmund Sinnott, *The Biology of the Spirit* (New York: The Viking Press, 1955), p. 61.

philosopher, Heraclitus, recognized this truth some twenty-five hundred years ago when he observed that "nothing endures but change."[25]

The fate of Western civilization may depend on whether— and how—we respond to the turbulence in which we now find ourselves. Efforts to maintain static, equilibrium conditions may prove as fatal to a society as to an organism or business firm. One historian, Carroll Quigley, has identified such practices as leading to the collapse of civilizations.[26] This is brought about when "instruments of expansion" (i.e., those systems within a civilization that have incentives for invention, saving, and investment) become institutionalized (i.e., ends in themselves, rather than the *means* for producing the negentropy upon which that civilization depends for its survival). River valleys—e.g., the Tigris-Euphrates in Mesopotamia, the Nile in Egypt, the Ganges in China, the Indus in India—became generators of the earliest civilizations. They could be characterized as "instruments of expansion" as irrigation was introduced, allowing people to more fruitfully sustain themselves through agriculture. In a complex industrialized society, these "instruments of expansion" can take a variety of forms: the economic system for the production and exchange of goods and services, technology, agriculture, the sciences, medicine, and the arts being some of the more prominent examples. Information, itself, is rapidly becoming a dominant creative instrument for what may prove to be a civilization in transition. What has proven to be such a productive instrument for Western Civilization—particularly the American version—has been the concept and practices of private ownership of property. This sytem has given real-world expression to the creative energies that lie within the self-interests of free men and women.

---

[25]John Bartlett, *Familiar Quotations*, Justin Kaplan, ed., 16th ed. (Boston: Little, Brown and Company, 1992), p. 62.

[26]Carroll Quigley, *The Evolution of Civilizations* (Indianapolis, Ind.: Liberty Press, 1979).

When such instruments become institutionalized and structured, they lose those qualities that are essential for resisting
entropy: resiliency, creativity, and the capacity for growth—
conditions that are dependent upon an environment receptive
to change. Having transformed their *raison d'etre* from that of
fulfilling specific functions, to preserving their organizational
structures, institutions tend to exhibit varying degrees of rigid-
ity and an unwillingness to adapt their behavior to the environmental and internal turbulence to which healthy systems would
ordinarily have to respond.[27] The failure of the Roman army to
convert from its long-established infantry base to cavalry, for
example, allowed Germanic barbarian horsemen to subdue
Rome.[28] Business organizations that are unable or unwilling to
deviate from established practices in response to more creative
or efficient competitors, provide further examples of institutional ossification.

Because the negentropic behavior of other organizations and
individuals are often inconsistent with the primacy of institutional interests, efforts are undertaken to restrain any incompatible conduct, and to channel behavior in institutionally serv-
ing ways. Such efforts may be *voluntary* (e.g., private cartels,
trade association codes of ethics[29]) or *involuntary* (e.g., statutes,
administrative agency regulations) in nature. In either event,
rules regarding the decision-making of owners over their property begin to proliferate. When such rules are agreed to voluntarily—i.e., as contracts—there is no more conflict with property
interests than there is with any marketplace transaction. Other
market participants, not being bound by such contractually-
based rules, remain free to make responses that frustrate these
efforts to restrain trade. Furthermore, the self-interests even of
those agreeing to such restraints will rise up to defeat the effort.

---

[27] Ibid., pp. 101ff.

[28] Ibid., p. 103.

[29] See my book, *In Restraint of Trade: The Business Campaign Against Competition*, 1918–1938 (Lewisburg, Pa.: Bucknell University Press, 1997).

This is why voluntary cartels and price-fixing agreements have been such weak mechanisms.

On the other hand, when the power of the state is invoked; when legislative and judicial processes are employed on behalf of institutional interests (e.g., by propping up ailing industries, providing subsidies, or inhibiting competitive change in various regulatory ways), such practices prevent entropy from working its way out of the system. Malinvestments become protected, inefficient firms have their lives extended beyond what market disciplines would tolerate, and creative alternatives are discouraged. All of these have a restrictive effect on how people direct their energies or other property interests. Because such regulations interfere with the negentropic behavior of others, conflicts begin to multiply, producing even more pervasive restraints in a futile effort to alleviate such frictions and restore the orderliness these measures have upset. The proliferation of inefficient firms and practices provokes a major political response. This may take the form of government loan guarantees to corporations, restrictions on the importation of lower-priced goods, sanctimonious campaigns against "cheap" foreign labor, or other protectionist measures. Such practices contribute to the institutionalization of the "instruments of expansion" that threaten the health of a civilization.

As their own purpose for being, institutions are desirous of maintaining the status quo which they represent. As such, they find enforced standardization of behavior essential for limiting the responses they would otherwise have to make to the actions of others. In economic matters, this would include, among others, such government programs as the licensing of business firms and professions in order to restrict the entry of competitors; the establishment of product, employment, and trade practice standards; the imposition of wage and price controls; import restrictions on foreign products; and zoning laws and land-use restrictions; or other inhibitions upon innovation, to name but a few.

Regardless of whose immediate interests are being served by any particular government regulation, the practice invariably increases the costs and inefficiencies of marketplace activities. Not only do such regulations increase transaction costs, their mandate often increases the prices of goods and services.[30]By its very nature, imposing requirements upon marketplace participants beyond what they would otherwise have freely negotiated, increases the costs of productive human action, and limits the options that facilitate the creative and efficient use of resources.

Government regulation fosters inflexibility and increases structuring of economic activity by restricting the uses owners can make of their property. For instance, it is easier for larger firms to distribute the fixed costs of regulation over a greater volume of products than it is for smaller firms with a lesser output. The added per unit production costs resulting from compliance with such regulation will be lower for the larger firm, giving it a comparative advantage when it comes to the pricing of its products. For the same reason, someone who develops a fundamentally new or innovative product might first have to satisfy a lengthy and expensive process of government-mandated testing or licensing before being allowed to produce and sell the product. Unless this person is financially capable of absorbing such up-front costs, he or she might be inclined to sell the creation to a large firm that could more easily bear such costs. In such ways have government regulatory practices promoted both increased concentration within industries as well as disincentives for generating the creative alternatives that keep a civilization vigorous.

State-mandated conservation practices are another form of government regulation designed to protect established firms from energetic competition. While the avowed purpose of such programs has been to "preserve natural resources," they have had the actual and intended effect of maintaining higher prices for products in such industries as petroleum, lumber, and coal

---

[30]Murray L. Weidenbaum, *Government-Mandated Price Increases: A Neglected Aspect of Inflation* (Washington, D.C.: American Enterprise Institute for Public Policy Research, 1975).

by restricting increased supplies. Again, conservation programs are usually directed against the owners of resources in order to stabilize the interests of existing firms.[31]

Another factor that contributes to a weakening of the dynamics necessary to sustain a vibrant economy is found in Joseph Schumpeter's analysis of the development of business organizations. He shows the significance of how property is owned and controlled by distinguishing between "owner"— and "manager"—controlled systems. The perspectives of owners, he posits, tend to be more long-term oriented, as contrasted with the shorter-term outlooks of managers. In his view:

> [T]he modern businessman . . . is of the executive type. From the logic of his position he acquires something of the psychology of the salaried employee working in a bureaucratic organization. . . . Thus the modern corporation, although the product of the capitalist process, socializes the bourgeois mind; it relentlessly narrows the scope of capitalist motivation; not only that, *it will eventually kill its roots.*[32]

Capitalism, in the course of its development, "tends to automatize progress,"[33] he adds. An owner-entrepreneur risks his energies and financial resources in the uncertainties of the marketplace, an undertaking that proves disappointing to most who try. In the course of developing his enterprise, the successful entrepreneur will likely get funding from investors and lending institutions who are now more concerned with preserving the value of their interests than with further venturesome pursuits by the firm's creator. Accordingly—and particularly as ownership of the firm increasingly comes into the hands of pas-

---

[31]I have dealt with these and other efforts by members of the business community to employ the powers of the state to restrain competition in my earlier book, *In Restraint of Trade.*

[32]Joseph Schumpeter, *Capitalism, Socialism, and Democracy*, 3rd ed. (New York: Harper & Bros., 1950), p. 156; emphasis added.

[33]Ibid., p. 134.

sive investors—the entrepreneur's control is replaced by that of hired managers, attuned to practices designed to help preserve existing interests.

With *management* divided from *ownership*, an emphasis on cautious and conservative policies becomes separated from the risky practices that could either further enhance the profitability of the firm, or bankrupt it. Although the dynamics of chaos would emphasize the need for any vibrant system to remain resilient to changing conditions by altering its existing practices, the voices of prudence and hesitancy more often prevail. With preservation of the organization now an ascendant principle, corporate interests—whose concentrated nature provides them more political influence than that of other market participants—seek governmental restraints and other state-conferred benefits designed to reduce the risks of additional, more innovative, or more aggressive competition. In such ways does the widespread institutionalization of the "instruments of expansion" begin to erode the creative processes that sustain a civilization, and contribute to its collapse.

The metamorphosis identified by Schumpeter found reinforcement in the classic work by James Burnham, *The Managerial Revolution*.[34] A system of private capitalism—with the control of enterprises exercised by their owners—was being replaced by managerial hierarchies that would centrally direct economic decision-making. This transformation would have profound significance not only for traditional business and political institutions, but for what is implicit in the personal and social meaning of property.

As we shall discover in subsequent chapters, conflict is likely to emerge whenever *ownership* is divided from *control*. In the case of a business firm, a manager may have purposes of his own that differ from those of an owner. As an employee with shorter time-preferences, he may be more interested in having a greater portion of company earnings directed to salaries

---

[34]James Burnham, *The Managerial Revolution* (New York: The John Day Company, Inc., 1941).

than to plant expansion. Likewise, as in so-called "hostile take-overs," the hostility that often arises is between the managers and the owners. The acquiring firm may pay a sizeable amount of money to the managers, whose jobs would be jeopardized by the merger, in order to elicit their cooperation in the merger process. Such payments become part of the acquirer's cost of purchasing the enterprise, an amount that would otherwise be available to the stockholders.

In the same way, conflict occurs whenever the state, through its regulatory practices designed to enforce standardized con-duct, insinuates itself into an owner's control over his or her property. With ownership and control fragmented, it becomes increasingly difficult for an individual or a firm to make cre-ative adaptations to a constantly changing world. Such diffi-culties are greatly exacerbated when, as now, the speed of both communication and technological innovation demand swifter responses than are otherwise allowed by bureaucratically-struc-tured mandates. When decision-making authority is unified in the hands of an owner, however, symmetry—not conflict—tends to prevail. Whether the owner is then able to make appro-priate responses to a constantly inconstant world will depend upon his or her creative talents that are unhindered by formal restraints.

One other area of human activity the state has always insisted upon controlling is the definition and enforcement of standardized rules of law governing transactions and personal disputes. For instance, people will always have disputes with one another, as well as a need to resolve them. The question needs to be asked: must resort be had to governmental court systems or, as the increasing use of arbitration, mediation, col-laborative/holistic practices illustrate, might marketplace pro-cesses satisfy these needs as effectively as they provide for other goods and services? Such an inquiry calls into question the con-cept of "judicial review," which is premised on the state's court system defining legal principles and standards of conduct to be made uniform within a given jurisdiction. In marketplace trans-actions, individually-driven preferences of buyers and sellers generate a multitude of transactions of diverse terms and conditions, without presuming a need for definitive and uniformly enforced standards for food, music, household products, clothing styles, etc., or their prices. For the same reasons, we may discover the value of competition in the resolution of disputes, without a need for superintending authorities to review such decisions. If auto mechanics, building contractors, grocers, and orthodontists are capable of providing their goods and services without a presumed need to have their transactions reviewed and approved by others, might not disputes get peaceably and efficiently resolved by a variety of independent means? What we may discover is that judicial review is but one of the methods by which the institutionalization of society has come about, by centralizing and standardizing the rules that operate among people.

Chapter Three
Foundations of Order

An important scientific innovation rarely makes its way by gradually winning over and converting its opponents: it rarely happens that Saul becomes Paul. What does happen is that its opponents gradually die out and that the growing generation is familiarized with the idea from the beginning.

— Max Planck

How does the uncertain and unpredictable nature of complex systems and the diffused character of private property ownership relate to the health of a civilization? If a civilization is to remain resilient to the constancies of change, what transformations—if any—in our assumptions about organizational forms must be undertaken to accommodate the creative dynamics? In an environment of instant communication and responses spread over an entire planet, does the traditional top-down model of social order prescribed by an elite for the many have any relevance? Can a civilization expect to survive as a viable system in a world of decentralized fluctuation on the basis of the same kind of thinking with which Machiavelli advised his royal clientele? Upon what conditions is the health of a society dependent?

Consistent with Quigley's analysis, Arnold Toynbee suggests that a civilization begins to break down when there is "a loss

of creative power in the souls of creative individuals,"[1] leading to a diminished capacity of that civilization to successfully
respond to challenges. As the civilization disintegrates, there is
a qualitative transformation in which the "differentiation and
diversity" that characterized a *growing* civilization is replaced
by "a tendency toward standardization and uniformity."[2] The
final stages of disintegration are marked by increased milita-
rism and the resort to "forcible political unification in a universal state."[3]The present preoccupation with aggressive wars
by the American government, and its use of the "war on terror" to further its ambitions for world empire reflect a political system vainly struggling to shore up its crumbling foundations. By contrast, says Toynbee, "[w]hat we are looking for is
a free consent of free peoples to dwell together in unity, and to
make, uncoerced, the far-reaching adjustments without which
this ideal cannot be realized in practice."[4]

    Historians Will and Ariel Durant reached a similar conclu-
sion. In their view, the development or decay of a civilization
depends upon whether—and how—challenges to existing practices would be met. The answer to this question turns "upon
the presence or absence of initiative and of creative individuals with clarity of mind and energy of will . . . capable of effective responses to new situations."[5] As with organic systems,
"civilizations begin, flourish, decline, and disappear—or lin-
ger on as stagnant pools left by once life-giving streams."[6] Historian Jacob Burckhardt echoed these insights, declaring that
"the essence of history is change," and "the way of annihilation
is invariably prepared by inward degeneration, by decrease

---

[1]Arnold J. Toynbee, *A Study of History* (New York: Oxford University Press,
1958), p. 245.

[2]Ibid., p. 555.

[3]Ibid., pp. 244, 364, 552.

[4]Ibid., p. 552.

[5]Will and Ariel Durant, *The Lessons of History* (New York: Simon & Schuster,
1968), p. 91.

[6]Ibid., p. 90.

of life."[7] Civilized society, said William von Humboldt, is the expression of "human development in its richest diversity."[8]

Such dynamics reflect an ongoing tension between the unimpeded efforts of organisms to pursue their individual self-interests—activity that is synonymous with "liberty"—and the determination of others to confine such behavior within bounds that are compatible with established interests. Herein is to be found the cradle of institutionalism, whose essential premise is that the self-interests of some are to have priority over the interests of others, and that restrictions upon the activities of the latter may be justified by the presumed superiority of purpose of the former.

The efforts of one organism to live at the expense of another is, when confined to members of the same species, a form of cannibalism. But these institutionalizing traits encounter resistance from organisms seeking their *own* interests. There is a life force that is both self-interest driven as well as resilient enough to respond to efforts to restrain its self-seeking nature. One sees this phenomenon in such economic behavior as so-called "black markets" and smuggling (i.e., people covertly circumventing legal restrictions on the free trade in goods and services), as well as the ineffectiveness of cartels to sustain themselves without the use of coercion to enforce them.[9] The tendency is also seen in people emigrating from one nation to another in order to seek the comparative advantage of a less inhibiting environment. The role played by "frontiers" in the creative development of society is a topic to which I shall return in chapter four.

But when the institutionalizing restraints become so pervasive and of such intensity as to deprive life of too many options

---

[7] Jacob Burckhardt, *Force and Freedom: Reflections on History*, James H. Nichols, ed. (New York: Pantheon Books, 1964), p. 103.

[8] Quoted in John Stuart Mill, *On Liberty* (Indianapolis, Ind.: Hackett Publishing Company, Inc., 1978); originally published 1859.

[9] See, e.g., Mancur Olson, *The Logic of Collective Action* (Cambridge: Harvard University Press, 1965), pp. 2, 9–10, 36; Murray N. Rothbard, *Man, Economy, and State* (Princeton, N.J.: D. Van Nostrand Company, Inc., 1962), vol. 2, pp. 579–86.

for its free expression, the fate of civilization itself is called into question. An irreconcilable conflict arises between institutional interests and those of life itself, which, unless reversed, may make inevitable the collapse of life-inhibiting structures.

The study of chaos and complexity may help us to better understand the dynamical processes that can foster both the health and the decay of societies. Complex social systems—with their labyrinthine interconnections of manifold influences—play out regularities that are far beyond our capacities to foresee, but which we ignore to our embarrassment or peril. The constant adaptations of the marketplace illustrate the unpredictable order within complexity. Even the modern practice of insurgency group warfare expresses itself in identifiable patterns. As Oxford University physicist Neil Johnson has shown, "the same basic patterns" arise. "As you increase the number of casualties, the number of clashes is much fewer,"[10] confirming that even within what most would regard as the disordered nature of modern warfare, patterns of behavior will repeat themselves. As contrasted with top-down, state-run military systems, insurgency groups will pulsate in coming together for an attack, disband, and later regroup.

As with other complex systems, societies are subject to the processes of chaos. Fluctuations within subsystems may generate increased turbulence that can reach a bifurcation point, at which the system may begin to function chaotically. Should this turbulence continue unabated, the system will experience either an entropic decline (e.g., western Rome) or total collapse, or transformation into a more refined order. Both the collapse of civilizations and the emergence of creative, liberalizing periods have often been preceded and/or accompanied by extensive social upheaval and conflict. Neither course is predetermined. There is nothing inevitable in a complex world. A society may reverse its entropic course and, through spontaneous self-organization,

---

[10]Neil Johnson quoted in Jonah Lehrer, "Reading the Terrorist Mind," November 8, 2006, at scienceblogs.Com/cortex/2006/11/reading_the_terrorist_mind.php; and in "Universal Patterns Underlie War," in *Seed Magazine* (December, 2006).

evolve into a more sophisticated and complex system. These creative responses generated such life-enhancing periods as the Renaissance, the Enlightenment, and the scientific and industrial revolutions. In spontaneous, unplanned ways—in which individuals were free to act upon and within the world—complexity and chaos have been catalysts for the development of ever more complex systems of order.

The work of Ilya Prigogine and Isabelle Stengers[11] has added another counterintuitive understanding to how systems, including a society or civilization, are able to reverse entropic declines. The mechanistic interpretation of the universe as a giant clockwork fated, by the second law of thermodynamics, to collapse into entropic death, is being challenged by the model of "dissipative structures"[12] that permit living systems to use entropy to renew themselves. Such systems exchange matter and energy with their environments and, in the process, use the resulting entropy to spontaneously generate more complex systems of order. From life itself, to a whirlpool, to a galaxy, systems interact with their surroundings to maintain their forms. In this way—contrary to our expectations from the second law of thermodynamics—orderly systems can arise out of disorder. The universe, in other words, may not be running down; it may just be getting started!

If our metaphysical assumptions about the world are undergoing major transformations, we must expect significant alterations to occur in the nature of our social systems. Because we seem to have a need for our philosophic opinions and behavior to become synthesized, the organizational arrangements we create will tend to reflect a desired coherence. As our thinking moves from mechanistic and fragmentary conceptions of reality to a more organic and interconnected model, we should expect the forms and practices of social organizations to undergo major changes. Our traditional thinking about systems must be

---

[11]Ilya Prigogine and Isabelle Stengers, *Order Out of Chaos: Man's New Dialogue With Nature* (Boulder, Colo.: Shambhala, 1984).

[12]Ibid., p. 12.

revised. Contrary to what we have long presumed to be true, the study of chaos is making us aware that greater complexity in social organizations demands not that we imbue vertically-constituted institutions with greater authority, but that we begin to dismantle such structures. The pyramidal archetype under which we have been living has fostered division and social conflict *because* it centralizes authority in institutional entities to deal with complex matters for which they are inherently incapable. If this model is collapsing in favor of more informal systems, decision-making power can be expected to become decentralized into the hands of individuals and less-structured groups.

A movement from vertically-imposed to horizontally self-generated systems is facilitated by an awareness of the principle of "self-organization." One source defines this as "a process in which the internal organization of a system, normally an open system, increases in complexity without being guided or managed by an outside source."[13] This concept is at the core of the debate over whether "order" within any system is a quality to be prescribed by external forces, or is autonomously-generated from within an organism by the interplay of matter and energy working to continually renew—through "autopoeisis" (i.e., the process by which living systems self-organize through productive networks)—the internal system. Self-organization expresses the inherent—albeit often unseen—order that prevails within a system, a process that renders authoritatively-prescribed forms at best a redundant, and at worst a destructive force. The biological and physical sciences provide endless examples of both organic (e.g., the development of an organism from conception onward), and chemical (e.g., crystallization), processes of self-organization in nature. If seemingly non-conscious entities can generate such spontaneous systems, might it be possible for human beings to do so as an unintended consequence of their interconnected self-interested activities? An understanding of the dynamics of self-generated order reinforces

---

[13]See en.wikipedia.org/wiki/Self-organization.

alternative social models of decentralized authority and horizontal organization.

If "order through fluctuation"[14] is essential to the continuing revitalization of a system, then we need to revise our model of societal order as well as the organizational systems through which we interact and cooperate with one another. If "interconnectedness" is to replace "subservience;" and "fluctuation" and "variety" are to be substituted for "stability" and "uniformity;" then new organizational premises must be discovered. Our present thinking, and the systems such thinking has generated, are in a state of crisis. Our present well-organized madness has proven itself too destructive and too degrading, leading to a massive failure of expectations. For the sake of our living well— perhaps of our living at all—humanity is in need of a major paradigm shift regarding the nature of order in society.

As already indicated, our world is rapidly becoming decentralized, with computerized systems and other technologies providing much of the impetus for change. The pyramidal model—born of mechanistic and reductionist premises that no longer explain the interconnected nature of complex systems— is in need of replacement. A candidate for a paradigmatic change may be found in the interplay between "chaos" theory and complexity, on the one hand, and what I shall call a "holographic" model of order, wherein *vertical structures* are replaced by *horizontal networks*.

Western civilization is in a critical, confused state. As Kuhn informs us, "[a]ll crises begin with the blurring of a paradigm."[15] That his analysis applies not only to scientific thought, but to social thinking as well, is reflected in his observation that "[p]olitical revolutions are inaugurated by a growing sense, often restricted to a segment of the political community, that existing institutions have ceased adequately to meet the problems posed by

---

[14]Erich Jantsch, *The Self-Organizing Universe* (New York: Pergamon Press, 1980), p. 28.

[15]Kuhn, *The Structure of Scientific Revolutions*, p. 84.

an environment that they have in part created."[16] Such revolutions, he adds, "aim to change political institutions in ways that
those institutions themselves prohibit. . . ."[17] If, as seems to be
the case, modern society is experiencing a "blurring" of the prevailing authoritarian model upon which it has long been based;
and if there is a "growing sense" of the failure of the existing
system to resolve the problems it has helped to generate, the
question arises as to the form an alternative paradigm might
take.

To help envision the nature of the transformation that is
occurring, resort might be had to solid geometry. The *pyramid* of
the state-dominated society might be contrasted with that of a
sphere. The pyramid is characterized by polarized relationships
of authority and subservience, of power and weakness. As one
sees in the structure of a traditional organization chart, relationships are *vertical* in nature; decision-making flows from the top
downward to those who are to carry out the authoritative direc-
tive. Such dualities do not prevail in the holographic world of a
sphere. There is no preferred position to be found on the surface
of a sphere; no favored location from which power could either
accumulate or flow. Spheres—such as a marketplace—have neither "tops" nor "bottoms," but multilateral connections.

At the risk of over-simplification, holography is a technological process by which an object is photographed with the use of
a laser beam that is split into two separate beams, the "object"
beam and the "reference" beam. With use of mirrors and lenses,
the object beam is used to create a diffused light pattern. The
two beams interfere with one another in such a way as to create
a pattern that is then recorded on the photographic film. After
the film has been developed, a laser beam is directed through
the backside of the holographic film. The diffracted light that
emerges recreates the original three-dimensional image with
which we have become familiar.

---

[16]Ibid., p. 92.

[17]Ibid., p. 93.

One of the more interesting features of holography is implicit in the Greek origins of the word itself. From *holos* (meaning "whole") and *gramma* (meaning "message"), we get hologram, or the "whole message." If you cut the original film (the "image master") into parts, and direct the laser beam through any piece thereof, you will still be able to reproduce the *entire image*! Unlike an ordinary photograph taken by a camera—in which a portion of the negative will reproduce only that portion of the image—in a hologram the complete image is stored everywhere on the film. Any portion of the image master, in other words, is capable of reproducing the entire hologram. Like fractals, which repeat their simple patterns on more complex scales, holograms may be yet another manifestation of the order that lies hidden in our daily experiences. Perhaps fractals and holograms are only two different ways in which our minds have thus far been able to describe the patterns by which nature harmonizes particular events into general patterns.

A holographic model of thinking contrasts with the dualistic manner in which our minds deal with the world. Dualistic thinking is premised upon our world being subdivided into mutually-exclusive concepts, including the separation of the individual—as an *individual*—from the *community*. A holographic paradigm, on the other hand, is grounded in an awareness of the integrated wholeness of nature, whose elements and meanings are radiated throughout rather than concentrated. The *whole* is manifested in each *part* or, to be more precise, in the *interactions* among the parts. This model finds analogous expression in Emerson's transcendentalist philosophy, wherein each of us is not only able to connect up with a life force in nature, but are embodiments of this force. Thoreau's reference to "the infinite extent of our relations"[18] carries the same sense of interconnectedness. In Hindu and Buddhist philosophy, the metaphor known as "Indra's Net" describes a complex web of threads held together by numerous shiny pearls, whose respective surfaces reflect one

---

[18]Henry David Thoreau, *Walden; or, Life in the Woods* (Boston: Ticknor and Fields, 1854), chap. 8.

another, as apt an image for a holographic paradigm as can be imagined. A holographic view gives real-world meaning to the "butterfly effect," in that each of us is *individually* capable of acting upon the world in profound, godlike ways. In popular culture, the motion picture *It's A Wonderful Life*—in which George Bailey discovers how different the world would have been had he not been born—expresses this phenomenon.

The systems with which we organize ourselves with one another are largely fashioned from the metaphysical models we embrace. In turn, the principles upon which our societal architecture is based produce consequences that may be beneficial or harmful to our well-being. Perhaps the distinction between two forms of the same chemical element can illustrate the significance of different organizational forms. *Graphite* (pencil lead) is one of the softest materials known. Its molecules are layered in parallel patterns that make the bonds between each layer of atoms weak and capable of easy separation. This is what allows us to transfer pencil lead to a piece of paper. *Diamonds*, on the other hand, are the hardest known substance in nature. Their atoms are tightly bound together in interlocking patterns that are difficult to separate. Despite such fundamental differences, each of these substances is composed of pure carbon. It is how their respective molecules are organized that gives them either weakness or strength.

Beyond the fact that our lives are also carbon-based, what relevance does this analogy have to the social implications of property? If our relationships are based upon mutual respect for our individuality and the inviolability of our respective boundaries, there will be no contradiction between individual and social interests. The organizations we develop will be tightly interconnected by trust; the bonds that hold us together will be so firm that institutional systems will find it difficult to intrude their purposes into our lives and divide us into conflicting groups. Our present social organizations are built more upon the graphite model, wherein our connections with one another are so weak as to be severed with little effort. Instead of a mutual trust and respect that gives individually-supportive social systems internal strength, we are easily mobilized by a fear of one another that generates mutual distrust. In bonding with the institutional forces that separate us from one another, we provide institutional systems with the power to dominate life.

We have a desperate need to develop social systems that obtain their strength from the interplay of individuals cooperating to achieve mutual purposes. This requires us to rethink our assumptions about the source and nature of order in our lives: is it a quality that is vertically-imposed upon us, or one that is horizontally-generated by the confluence of tens of millions of people pursuing their diverse interests? Holographic thinking may provide us the basis for such alternative systems.

A holographic paradigm is an expression of the labyrinthine interconnectedness of complex systems. Whether we are considering economies, ecosystems, plate tectonics, epidemics, planetary polar reversals, climates, or other phenomena whose behavior is influenced by an unknowable array of intervening factors, our world is far too complicated to allow us to deal with it as fragmented parts, or to any longer permit the illusion of it being manageable to foreseeable ends. The formal structures to which we have long been accustomed, are being toppled by irresistible dynamic forces. With the vertical in decline, a holographic model—with its decentralist implications—will likely prove itself the most effective system for generating social order as an unintended consequence of each of us responding to the complexities in our lives.

By its very nature, a holographic social system diffuses all authority over human action. Centralized power is replaced by decentralized networks, with decision-making residing in autonomous but interrelated men and women who respond to one another through unstructured feedback systems and processes some have referred to as "emergence."[19] Social relationships are characterized by individuals freely choosing to

---

[19]Steven Johnson, *Emergence: The Connected Lives of Ants, Brains, Cities and Software* (New York: Scribner, 2001).

cooperate with one another for the accomplishment of mutu-ally-desired purposes. Social behavior would be represented by the interconnectedness of independent persons, not the sub-servient obedience of subjects. The Internet provides a perfect metaphor for such systems, wherein individuals communicate directly with one another, without any need for institutional "gatekeepers"[20] to superintend such intercourse.

Within a holographic organization, authority flows horizon-tally, or laterally, with members communicating and exchang-ing directly with one another, rather than through formal inter-mediaries. The function of leaders within such a system is not to direct, control, and supervise members, but to coordinate and facilitate (e.g., to make certain that raw materials are avail-able for work, to maintain clear channels for feedback, or, as the phrase used to be employed to describe the role of college administrators: to keep the snow off the sidewalks). Order is more spontaneously derived as a by-product of the behavior of all members of the organization, not the creature of institutional design or authoritative pronouncement.

Any comparison between vertically-structured and hori-zontally-networked social systems must include a focus on the question of how order originates. The vertical, "positiv-ist" model presumes order to be the product of human inten-tion and design; of consciously formulated rules created to impose standardized conduct upon members of society. Such thinking is grounded in a "fear of trusting uncontrolled social forces,"[21] focusing upon systematically directed uniformity as essential to an orderly society.

The horizontal, holographic model, on the other hand, is premised on order being the unintended consequence—a side effect—of people pursuing their respective self-interests. It

---

[20]According to a *Reuters* news report of February 11, 1998, Hillary Clin-ton made a statement in Washington, D.C., suggesting that the Internet might require an "editing or gatekeeping function."

[21]F.A. Hayek, *The Constitution of Liberty* (Chicago: University of Chicago Press, 1960), p. 400.

consists of those regularities that arise without any planning or purpose to create them. The marketplace, with the pricing system constantly adjusting—without outside direction—to the fluctuations in supplies and demands for goods and services, is the most vivid and familiar example of such spontaneously-derived order. No one—buyer or seller—enters into economic transactions for the purpose of fostering equilibrium pricing, but such are their contributions to the informal order of the marketplace. In holographic systems, individuals, not the state, are acknowledged as the conductors of their own affairs on the basis of terms they freely negotiate with one another, and with disputes resolved on the basis of such self-negotiated rules, as well as the broadly based customs, practices, and expectations of the community. In such alternative systems, the substance of social order is found in the regularities that arise, spontaneously and without any intention to do so, from the interplay of human behavior.

The contrast between these ways of conceptualizing order can be seen in how we think about that force we call gravity. Under the traditional, pyramidal model, gravity has been thought of as a kind of regulatory force imposed upon matter through external means. We even speak of gravity as one of the numerous "natural laws" by which nature has imposed its regularities upon the universe. While few people would take this as a literal proposition, or continue to insist that nature has "created" such "laws" and "imposed" them upon us pursuant to some subject/object relationship, the words that we use continue to reflect that kind of mindset. In much the same way that our reference to "sunrises" and "sunsets" can subtly reinforce a pre-Copernican perspective, our antiquated views of gravity can provide unconscious support for a broader concept of order.

If we were to think about gravity in the language of a holographic model of order—as physicists in fact do—we would understand that it is not a quality imposed upon us from beyond, but arises out of the relationship of two or more bodies. If you and I are carrying on a conversation in a room, gravity could be thought of as just one expression of how we relate to one another; as well as how we and the chairs relate to each other, to the building in which we are located, the other people in the building, as well as to the interrelatedness of all these other people and things to one another, and so on. Everything in the universe relates to everything else in just such ways. When we think of our world in terms of such incalculable interrelationships, and comprehend the uncertainty that arises from such complexity, we begin to see the humor in our simplistic beliefs about centrally-directed systems, be they societies or the rest of the universe. So considered, gravity—like all the other regularities we discover in our world—takes on a more profound and complicated meaning than is to be explained by the metaphor of an apple falling on Newton's head!

The marketplace is an example of a self-organizing, holographic system in which decision-making is widely diffused among persons whose self-serving behavior generates beneficial consequences to others. In contrast with state planned and regulated economies, a free market is directed by no one. The informal processes of the pricing system—which functions as an attractor for economic activity, operating independently of the interests of any given market participant—communicate information about the preferences of both buyers and sellers. On the basis of such information, individuals may modify their choices which, when combined with the responses of others, may alter the signals in the pricing structure to which further adjustments will be made, ad infinitum. The market, in other words, is a self-sustaining, self-adaptive system for producing and exchanging goods and services among strangers.

But the marketplace, as a spontaneous, self-organizing system, can function only in an environment in which private ownership is acknowledged as a fundamental social principle. Respect for the inviolability of private property is the defining characteristic of a free market system. Only when individual owners assess their own risks and bear all the costs and benefits of their actions; only as they commit their own resources

toward a desired end; and only when the range of their decision-making control is defined by the boundaries of what *they*
own, can the self-disciplining nature of the marketplace function. The self-interested motivation to act for the enhancement
of what one owns diminishes in intensity when we make decisions regarding the property of others. Unlike owners, politicians and bureaucrats can engage in actions that cost them
nothing, but which impose financial burdens upon affected parties. History is replete with the errors of judgment, tyrannical
behavior, political fiascoes, and adverse consequences of collective delusions, brought about by the practice of some persons
making decisions over the lives and property of others.

Externally undirected, self-organizing behavior is also
observed in the spontaneous responses complete strangers
make to a natural disaster—such as a tornado, hurricane, or
earthquake—or to a major accident. Individuals quickly come
together, assess the problems, agree upon a division of labor and
then, when they have accomplished their group task, return to
their homes. The effectiveness of such immediate reactions is
contrasted with the bureaucratically sluggish, hindering, red-
taped responses of governmental agencies that often delay
rather than facilitate recovery. Those who haven't discovered
the advantages of self-organization over institutionally-structured behavior, are invited to compare the spontaneous efforts
of tens of thousands of individuals, businesses, and churches to
come to the aid of New Orleans residents following hurricane
Katrina, and the non-responsive—and often impeding—actions
of governmental agencies during and following this disaster.[22]

Self-organizing practices are not confined to humans.
Throughout the rest of nature, different life forms exhibit the
same kind of reciprocally advantageous conduct, or symbiosis. The entire life process is grounded in this kind of symbiotic, holographic interconnectedness, which comprises an eco-
system. The well-being of carnivores is dependent upon the

---

[22]See, e.g., Llewellyn H. Rockwell, Jr., *Katrina and Socialist Central Planning*,
10/10/2005, at http://www.mises.org/story/1934.

presence of a sufficient number of herbivores whose existence, in turn, depends upon an adequate supply of plant life. We humans breathe in oxygen—emitted by plants—and expel carbon dioxide, which, in turn, is consumed by the plants. What is entropy (or waste) for us is negentropy (or energy) for our plant cousins.

Various plant and animal species use one another for their respective survival and proliferation advantages. Fruit trees produce sweet-tasting, nutritious, seed-bearing fruit that animals—humans included—will carry away to eat, with the undigested seeds passing intact through the animal, to be fertilized by the feces. As Michael Pollan has observed, potatoes, apples, marijuana, and tulips have—with human help—evolved characteristics that appeal to our preferences, in order that we might cultivate them and transport them to other locations where they can thrive.[23] Have we been "exploiting" these plants for our benefit, or have they been "exploiting" us for theirs, or is the entire concept of exploitation just another expression of divisive thinking?

Examples of cooperative and symbiotic relationships among species are found throughout nature. Flowers supply insects with food, in exchange for which the insects pollinate the flowers. Some of these plant/insect exchanges have become so sophisticated that certain flowers can only be pollinated by specific insect species, a fact that reminds us of another pattern of interrelatedness: evolutionary processes can foster both greater *diversity*—making a species more adaptable to change—as well as greater *specialization*—making a species more vulnerable to the consequences of change. Over-specialization can create tendencies for non-adaptability that can weaken or destroy a species. In the emerging study of "ecological anachronisms," we are becoming aware of how specific plants and animals have evolved mutually dependent relationships (e.g., various fruits evolving seed dispersal systems suited to particular animals

---

[23]Michael Pollan, *The Botany of Desire* (New York: Random House, 2001), pp. xiv ff.

that can maximize the plant's opportunities for propagation). While cooperation, rather than conflict, has generally proven to be a viable arrangement, the partnership was oftentimes too narrowly confined. When the targeted animals became extinct, the highly specialized reproductive strategies of the plants created a botanical crisis, often leading to drastic reductions in plant populations.[24] Perhaps the rest of nature has an important lesson for us humans. Just as other life systems may be threatened by a resistance to multiple strategies for survival, civilizations can be destroyed by institutional structuring that inhibits resiliency to changing conditions.

Other cooperative strategies among species reflect the advantages of symbiosis. Grazing animals, through their eating habits, prevent more vigorous plants from taking over and crowding out other plant species, thus assuring a greater variety of plant life. Likewise, various plants produce toxins or thorns, which help to discourage grazing animals from eating too much of any one kind of plant, thus helping to maintain a balance in plant species. Such plants seem to have worked out their own solutions to the "tragedy of the commons" problem![25] Similar animal species will hunt at different times of the day, or will have different preferences for prey, as ways of reducing interspecies competition.[26]

Contrary to the mindset that sees the various species—particularly humanity—as being in a continual war with one another, life exhibits an amazing symbiosis. Cooperation, both within and among species, has led to the proliferation of life forms on earth, a point well developed by Peter Kropotkin in his classic work *Mutual Aid*.[27] It has been estimated that there are more

---

[24]Connie Barlow, *The Ghosts of Evolution: Nonsensical Fruit, Missing Partners, and Other Ecological Anachronisms* (New York: Basic Books, 2000), p. 198.

[25]Peter H. Raven, Ray F. Evert, and Susan H. Eichhorn, *Biology of Plants*, 6th ed. (New York: W.H. Freeman and Company, 1999), pp. 366, 642.

[26]Robert Augros and George Stanciu, *The New Biology: Discovering the Wisdom in Nature* (Boston: New Science Library, 1987), p. 93.

[27]Peter Kropotkin, *Mutual Aid* (London: Heinemann, 1902).

trees growing in North America today than there were before Columbus's arrival over six centuries ago.[28] I strongly suspect that there is more corn growing in Nebraska in any current year than existed on the entire face of the planet at that time. In fact, this major world food source didn't even exist until early humans cultivated it from a mix of wild grasses. From London[29] to New Jersey, America's most densely populated state, wildlife is prospering in urban centers. Gardens, garbage cans, and domesticated pets—food sources provided by humans—have attracted birds and mammals from the countryside. New Jersey is experiencing an increase in the black bear population, while it is estimated that there are now more wild deer living in that state than were there before European settlers arrived.[30] These wild animals are probably coming to the cities for the same reasons as their human counterparts: to make a living. Domesticated animals have experienced similar results: chickens, cows, pigs, goats, dogs, cats, cattle, and sheep, have greatly increased their numbers by appealing to human tastes. Henry

---

[28]Stephen Moore and Julian Simon, *It's Getting Better All the Time* (Washington, D.C.: Cato Institute, 2000), p. 204.

[29]See "Life Is Thriving in Animal City," *The Sunday Times* (London), November 5, 2006. The article states, in part:

> There's now a school of thought that the true home of nature is the modern city, not the countryside, because of a remarkable shift of biodiversity over the past few decades. Animals and plants appear to be conquering the cities simply because the overfertlised soil of the country is becoming an ever-more inhospitable place for them.

www.timesonline.co.uk/tol/news/article625151. Ece?print=ye. Another news reports tells that there are an estimated 10,000 foxes living in London. Cassell Bryan-Low, *The Wall Street Journal*, April 26, 2006, reprinted by *Pittsburgh Post-Gazette*, April 26, 2006. www.post-gazette.com/pg/06116/685240-82.stm.

[30]*Black Bear in New Jersey: Status Report* (New Jersey Department of Environmental Protection, 2004), www.state.nj.us/dep/fgw/pdf/2004/bear_report04.pdf; David Kocieniewski, "Audubon Group Advocates Deer Hunting," *The New York Times*, March 15, 2005; Ann Broache, "Oh Deer!," in *Smithsonian* Magazine, October, 2005 (www.smithsonianmag.com/science-nature/Oh_Deer.html?c. The *Smithsonian* article states, in part: "In some parts of highly urbanized New Jersey, up to 60 deer live in a square mile, according to the state's Division of Fish and Wildlife, compared with just 5 to 10 deer per square mile before the land was settled by Europeans."

George made the point quite well: "Both the jayhawk and man eat chickens, but the more jayhawks, the fewer chickens, while the more men, the more chickens."[31]

But nature, including mankind, is not consistently organized along symbiotic lines. Parasitism—a phenomenon characterized by one organism (the "parasite") deriving its negentropic energies from another organism (the "host") without a reciprocal benefit—also exists in plant and animal life. Leeches, ticks, various bacteria and fungi, among others, survive by feeding off the energies of a host.[32] Within human society, parasitism manifests itself in the form of thievery and fraudulent transactions, both of which are based upon a disrespect for the property interests of the victim. In more than metaphorical fashion, all of human interaction can be reduced to such *symbiotic* relationships as are found in the marketplace, or *parasitic* behavior such as exists in victimizing crime and political systems. In either case, the question of whether or not the property boundaries of another are to be regarded as inviolate defines the systems.

In the language of chaos theory, Western civilization in general, and its American branch in particular, are in a state of turbulence. Fundamental changes are occurring around us, but we are not inclined to see them. It is as though we were living in the eye of a hurricane, where relative calm and regularity prevail. Our immediate surroundings appear normal, our family lives and work environments are subject to no more disruption than usual, while we tend to dismiss impending storm warnings.

But at the periphery of our world, destructive forces are tearing apart the foundations of our society. As with a real hurricane that brings down trees, buildings, power lines, billboards, and transportation facilities, societal turbulence is confronting perpendicular structures whose elevated centers of gravity make them vulnerable to collapsing forces. The social hurricane moves laterally, its centrifugal energies overpowering any

---

[31]Moore and Simon, *It's Getting Better All the Time*, p. 17.

[32]Epiphytes—plants that grow on other plants without parasitizing it or without any evident symbiosis—are distinguished here.

resistance it meets. The institutional order declares war against the turbulence, and acts desperately to reinforce the weakened footings of its antiquated structures. Persons living in hurricane regions, on the other hand, have learned the futility of fighting the storm. As the study of chaos and complexity advises us, our survival depends upon our discovering the orderly patterns within the turbulence to which we can adapt our efforts to productive, life-sustaining ends.

We may, of course, continue to accept the institutional order's explanations for the tempest as well as its proposed remedies. But neither *terrorists* nor *immigrants* have been the cause of the decline of Western civilization any more than were the invading barbarians the cause of the fall of the western Roman Empire. Each such group was but a *symptom*, among many, of the vulnerability of a civilization that had become weakened by its own contradictions and lack of responsiveness to the conditions upon which life depends. Should we continue to delude ourselves that *outside* forces are responsible for our *inner* collapse, and that more powerful mechanisms of state coercion are all that is needed to correct our course, our civilization will most likely continue toward its entropic fate.

On the other hand, the creative implications of chaos and complexity remind us that turbulence need not result in social collapse, but may provide us with opportunities to develop alternative practices that allow us to transcend our present destructiveness. In the words of Erich Jantsch, "the dismantling of social control hierarchies and strengthened autonomy of the subsystems"[33] provide the means for discovering more orderly, life-enhancing social systems. Such changes are already occurring. Into the void generated by the increasingly enervated institutional order, are arising new, informal, and relatively unstructured systems that serve the interests of those who choose to associate with them. The decentralized nature of the emerging social systems has been no better stated than in the words of the

---

[33]Erich Jantsch, *The Self-Organizing Universe* (New York: Pergamon Press, 1980).

2003 Nobel Peace Prize recipient, Shirin Ebadi. She described the organizational model used by Iranian feminist groups in these words:

> They are very strong. Their approach is unique because they have no leaders. They do not have a head or branch offices. . . . The movement is made even stronger by not having leaders. If one or two people lead it, the organization would weaken if these leaders were arrested. Because there is no leader, it is very strong and not stoppable.[34]

Decentralization leads to a more robust, resilient organization. Centralized authority provides a jugular vein which, when attacked, can greatly damage or destroy the entire system. If you topple the head of a pyramidal organization, the structure may collapse. On the other hand, as Ebadi points out, if you eliminate a key figure in a decentralized network, the system quickly adapts. The distinction between the ease with which Nazi Germany was able to force the central governments of Holland, Poland, and France to surrender, and the impossible time the Germans had in their efforts to subdue the decentralized French underground, illustrate the contrast. Such is the emerging model in which the collectivist doctrine "in union there is strength"—which has made us vulnerable to the power ambitions of others—is being replaced by an awareness that in autonomous and decentralized systems we can maximize both our liberty and the benefits from social organization.

In 1951, John Steinbeck provided an interesting contrast between vertically-structured and horizontally-networked systems. Surmising that "perhaps our species thrives best and most creatively in a state of semi-anarchy, governed by loose rules and half-practiced mores," he contrasted the likely social consequences that would occur from the "sudden removal of twenty-five key men" in the governments of Nazi Germany or the Soviet Union, with the United States.

---

[34]From an interview with Shirin Ebadi, conducted by Mandana Afshar, in *Amnesty International Magazine*, Winter 2006. www.amnestyusa.org/winter_2006/a_contrary_opinion/page.do?id=1105568.

"A too greatly integrated system or society," he warned, "is in danger of destruction since the removal of one unit may cripple the whole." In America, on the other hand, "we could lose our congress, our president and our general staff and nothing much would have happened. We would go right on. In fact we might be better for it. . . ."[35]

If, as seems to be the case, our traditional organizational forms are disintegrating, it will be incumbent upon us to reexamine our basic assumptions concerning how we relate to one another. Whether we are to live in a pyramidally-structured, centrally-directed society, or a holographically-modeled society in which authority is decentralized among individuals, will be reflected in how property is owned and controlled. The reason for this should be apparent: decision-making is always over human lives and property interests. Each such system tells us where the focal point of human action is to be found. Will decisions be made and conduct imposed by a few upon the many, or will individuals undertake such responsibilities for themselves in free association with others? For centuries, we have indulged ourselves in social and political illusions that presume the insignificance of private property ownership, and we are now paying the price for our delusions in the conflict, violence, warfare, genocide, and other dehumanizing practices that beset us all. In one form or another, we are at war with our fellow humans because we neither respect the inviolability of *their* interests nor demand that of our *own*.

As Sumner reminds us, property is the most fundamental of all our social concepts, and yet we have relatively little conscious understanding of either its nature or importance. In our materialistic and monetarily defined culture, most of us regard property as little more than "things" or other interests to be owned and used, and measure the success in our lives in terms of the quantity and value of the things that we have accumulated. We largely fail to understand the deeper

---

[35]John Steinbeck, *The Log From the Sea of Cortez*, (New York: Penguin, 1951) pp. 257–58.

social and spiritual meanings of property; that how property is owned and controlled tells us how, and by whom, decision-making authority is exercised in our lives.

A holographically-modeled system would, by definition, be incompatible with political systems that rely upon centralized force to control the lives and property of subjugated people. Social order would be thought of less as the product of central planning than of informal and spontaneous self-generation. Only a system of privately-owned property—in which authority to make decisions rests in the hands of individuals—is consistent with a diffused model of social organization.

Life functions in a material context: if they are to survive, organisms must occupy space and consume resources to the exclusion of everything and everyone else. This is not a normative proposition—a matter of ideological faith—but a statement of indisputable fact. From the simplest to the most complex life forms—be they animal or vegetable—every living thing is engaged in a continuous process of possessing and absorbing some portion of its physical environment.

At the same time, in a complex and uncertain world, for an organism to remain viable, it must be able to respond to specific conditions and events within its immediate environment with the resources available to it. Life functions at the margin. A species neither "survives" nor "dies" in some collective manner, other than as a consequence of the success or failure of individual members to sustain themselves by resisting entropy. This fact, alone, should alert us to the importance of decentralized private ownership to our survival.

In a quantum world of possibilities and "tendencies to exist," the absolutism of Newtonian physics will be found wanting. Institutional demands for uniformity and standardization must give way to autonomy and spontaneity as the organizing principle. If we are to reverse our downward course, we ought to heed Toynbee's warning: "[a]s differentiation is the mark of growth, so standardization is the mark of disintegration."[36] Erich Jantsch

---

[36]Toynbee, *A Study of History*, p. 589.

has provided this succinct statement of the premise that must underlie our efforts: "[t]he more freedom in self-organization the more order."[37]

When we are acting for our own purposes and with our own resources—instead of presuming to act on behalf of multitudes who have never acquiesced in our decision-making over them—the range of both the options available to us and the consequences of our conduct are more narrowly circumscribed. An awareness of the indeterminate and unpredictable nature of complex systems, as well as the subjective nature of our understanding and the preferences we pursue, act as a check upon our hubris. If we err in our judgments, the resulting harm is greatly confined. In either event, whether our actions benefit or harm us, others can learn from what we have done and calculate such lessons into their own conduct.

Such thinking has underlain the philosophy of pluralism, which recognized both the individual and societal benefits of the kind of diversity that has long been submerged in the stultifying concrete of uniformity, egalitarianism, factionalism, and other expressions of institutionalized thinking. The pluralistic practices that foster the individuality and the consequences, from which all of us may learn, depend upon a decentralized system of decision-making authority in society. If we are to have the resilience to make life-enhancing responses to the world— to assess risks and other costs, and to settle upon an efficacious course of action—we must enjoy the autonomy to act upon our portion of the world without interference from others, a liberty to be found only in a system of privately owned property.

In answering the question as to how and by whom property is to be owned and controlled, we shall be telling ourselves how we regard both ourselves, and others. Are we but the producers of the material values that serve both personal and organizational ends, or is there an underlying dignity to our being that precedes such physical needs? Are we individuals entitled to pursue our own ends through the control of our own resources,

---

[37]Jantsch, *The Self-Organizing Universe*, p. 40.

or are we but the means to the ends of others, to be exploited and disposed of as befits their purposes? Are we worthy of the respect of others—as well as ourselves—as self-directed individuals?

"Authority," one dictionary informs us, is the "power to require and receive submission: the right to expect obedience: superiority derived from a status that carries with it the right to command and give final decisions."[38] Authority relates to the decision-making processes in our world, and decisions are always made about *some thing* by *some person*. By its very nature then, the concept of authority relates to how and by whom decisions are to be made over the lives and property of people. Whether such authority is exercised by each individual over his or her life and other property interests, or whether it is exercised by others over such individuals, determines whether societies will enjoy liberty and be free of conflict.

The property concept is so basic to our lives that most of us have never bothered to think about its meaning or implications. How property is to be owned and controlled is the most functionally relevant social question in any culture. It begins with that most basic inquiry: *do individuals enjoy self-ownership?*, a topic to which we shall return in chapter five. Property is a purely social concept, having meaning only as it relates to our relationships with other people. If, for example, I were the last person on earth, I would have no need for a property principle upon which to govern my behavior. Let us imagine that I have a toolbox in my possession. There being no other person to challenge my authority over the toolbox, I would be free to do with it as I chose. I would have no more need for an appreciation of "property" principles than I would for a lock on the doors of whatever house in which I chose to reside. Everything in the world would be a potential resource available to me in my efforts to sustain myself. The question of "who is the owner of this tool box?" would have no meaning to me whatsoever.

---

[38] *Webster's Third New International Dictionary of the English Language, Unabridged*, p. 146.

Such was the initial condition experienced by Robinson Crusoe upon his arrival at the island.

But now introduce another human being to my world—a modern version of Friday—and the two of us must arrive at an understanding as to which of us will make decisions about what resources, as we each pursue our self-interests. A preliminary question we must ask each other—as was also implicit in the Crusoe-Friday relationship—is whether each of us will acknowledge the other as self-owning beings, or whether we shall look upon each other as but another resource to be owned and controlled for our personal ends. Whether we expressly articulate the issue this way or not, our relationship will be defined by how we resolve the property question. This matter cannot be avoided, no matter how well-intentioned each of us might be, or how well we get along with one another, or what methods we might agree upon for resolving the problem: we may even agree to share the tool box. Whatever the outcome, the problem is an unavoidable fact of our existence, as each of us endeavors to consume the energy that will keep us alive and allow us to realize our self-interested ends. What makes this a social issue is not my exercise of control over the toolbox, but the presence of a potential competitor—or even a cooperator— regarding how, and by whom decisions regarding the toolbox will be exercised. The *property* question, in other words, has nothing to do with my relationship to the toolbox, but with my relationship to my *neighbor* concerning the toolbox.

As the property concept illustrates, to think of our relationships with others in holographic terms is not to repress one's sense of individuality in favor of a new-and-improved collective dogma. Consistent with our emerging understanding of the dynamics of complexity, it is to see ourselves and others in terms of *relationships* grounded in the kind of existential equality that presumes no person to have rightful authority over another. As we learn to see our individual uniqueness and self-interested nature as the qualities we share with all others; as we begin to comprehend how a holographic model ends the divisions we have created amongst one another; we may reverse our destructive course. We may discover how to live cooperatively in society without either diminishing the importance of our sense of self, or regarding our neighbor as an exploitable resource.

Chapter Four
Boundary: What Can Be Owned?

"That dog is mine," said those poor children; "that place in the sun is mine."

—Blaise Pascal[1]

Because "property" has meaning only within a social context, how it is to be owned and controlled defines the nature of a given society. An analysis of the concept must begin by identifying the functional elements of property, and inquiring into their personal and social implications. These elements—which will be explored at length in this and the following two chapters—are those of *boundary, claim,* and *control*. While these concepts will be discussed separately, it must be emphasized that they are as interconnected to an understanding of property as the heart, lungs, and circulatory system are to the functioning of the body. Our inquiry into each of these three elements will occasionally cross over from one to the other.

A discussion of the nature of property must begin by identifying the interest—the entity—that is subject to being owned. This is the *boundary* element, the "what" that can be owned, the

---

[1]Blaise Pascal, *Pensées* VII (1670).

definition of the property itself. We are familiar with "boundaries" as they relate to the ownership of real property—e.g., iron pipes driven into the ground at each corner of the property, or fence-lines encircling a piece of land—but we are less familiar with the *conceptual* nature of boundaries, and of the important role they play in defining the range of our decision making. Boundaries are the means by which *liberty* and *peaceful order* become integrated in society. As the saying "good fences make good neighbors" reminds us, it is the failure to identify and respect boundaries that is at the heart of our social conflicts.

The boundary element circumscribes not just the physical dimensions of an item of property but, more importantly, the identification of the extent of decision-making authority over such an interest. The boundary line that separates your land from mine, for instance, has less to do with describing the character of the land itself than with defining the limits of our respective decision-making. All property—even so-called "intangible" interests—has dimensions to it, even if their configurations are not visible. This means that all property must consist of an identifiable interest that can be subjected to the control, the will of one we call an owner.

Property boundaries are what make peaceful and productive society possible. They are a way of signifying to one another the range of our respective interests; telling us what it is over which each of us may "properly" exercise authority. In much the same way that the boundaries of a tennis court delineate the area within which the game is to be played—with each player staying on his side of the court and without trespasses from the fans—property boundaries describe the field within which owners may act without interference, or the necessity of securing permission from others.

It is important to emphasize that boundaries are not limitations on the decision-making authority of an owner; they only define what it is over which one has authority. Within the bounds of his or her property, the owner is an unfettered decision-maker. Let us assume that I own a brick, and I assert the authority to do whatever I want with what is mine. Would that proposition entitle me to throw my brick through your picture window without your permission? The answer is clearly "no." I may exercise complete decision-making over what is *mine*, but not over what is *yours*. I may throw my brick through my picture window, or hit myself over the head with it, for in doing so I am exercising control only over what I own. To say that I may do as I will with what I own necessarily precludes me from doing as I will with what you own. Our respective property boundaries define—and thus limit—the range within which each of us may be unrestrained actors. As an owner, my decision making properly ends where my property boundaries end. Should I go beyond these limitations, I become a trespasser, just as you will if you forcibly prevent me from acting upon what is mine.

The following illustration may prove helpful in understanding this meaning of "boundaries." Let us imagine that I have bought a new car, financing the purchase with a loan from a bank that insists upon a chattel mortgage to secure my obligation to repay the loan. Both the bank and I have property interests in the car. The boundaries of the bank's interest preclude me from damaging or destroying the car, and may even obligate me, as a condition in our contract, to keep the car insured. Its interest does not, however, extend to being able to drive the car, or controlling where I might drive it, or who I might carry as passengers: these are property interests within my boundaries. Once I have repaid the loan, the bank's interest evaporates, and my boundaries extend to the full decision-making authority over the car. With our respective boundaries clearly defined, there is no way that our property interests can be in conflict, *unless* one of us chooses to transgress the other's interests.

This self-limiting nature of property boundaries is a crucial concept to grasp if one is to understand how privately-owned property is an essential system for harmonizing *individual liberty* and *societal peace*. "Life" requires both cooperation with and separation from other living beings, particularly members of our own species. A system of property is the social expression of this fact of nature—just as it is with other species—affording a principle for informally allocating the *spatial* and *energy consumption* needs of all life-sustaining activity. We are so accustomed to living under political systems that introduce division and conflict into our world by separating our lives and other property interests from our individual control, that we accept divisive definitions of property. Because the state trespasses upon us by presuming the authority to control our lives, we come to believe that such transgressions are an integral part of property ownership. We have become so conditioned to the practice of the state defining the legal scope of our decision making, that most of us cannot comprehend the idea of property as a self-defining system of social order. We conflate what is *legal* with what is *rightful,* and become insensitive to trespasses upon our property interests, and disrespectful of the boundaries of others. We become more concerned with what the law demands of us than with what we, or our neighbors, desire to do with what is ours.

It is essential to an understanding of the boundary concept that we be clear as to its mutually exclusive implications. Because we tend to confuse our *ownership* interests in property with the items of property themselves, we suppose that property interests can be in conflict. Let us imagine that you own a parcel of real estate, and you agree to sell me the mineral rights to this land. After the transaction has been completed, our respective spatial boundaries would look like this:

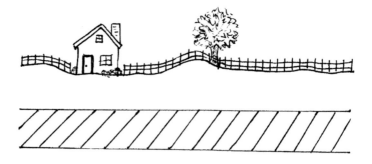

Figure 1.

The boundaries of what you own would consist of everything within the parcel (i.e., surface, subsurface, and air rights) except for the shaded portion (i.e., the mineral interests) that I now own. Because a contract is only an agreement to transfer ownership claims, the terms of our agreement redefine the boundaries of what each of us had owned previously. My mineral rights are not in conflict with, nor a restriction upon your property interests. The boundaries of what you own have been redefined, but your ownership control in what remains is as complete as it was before.

But what happens if my efforts to remove my minerals cause your house to subside: would that amount to a trespass or other interference with your property interests, and would this mean that my ownership interests (i.e., the right to control my mineral rights) are now in conflict with your interest in not having your property subside? Because contracts define the boundaries of the ownership interests being transferred, the answer to this question will depend upon what we had agreed to in our contract for the sale of the mineral rights. If I agreed to provide "subjacent support" in order to prevent subsidence, then our mutual boundaries would be defined to reflect this. My boundaries would again, be reflected by the shaded area, while yours would be enlarged, by our contract, to include the supports. Should I now attempt to remove these reinforcements, I would be trespassing upon your property interests, *not* by causing your

Figure 2.

house to subside, but by interfering with the support interest you had retained.

The reverse of this hypothetical is subject to the same analysis. If, by contract, I have the right to remove all the minerals without providing subjacent support, the boundaries of your property interests will be defined in a more limited way, while my interests would now include the right to cause subsidence that was incidental to my mining operations. Since, presumably, the purchase price for these mineral rights would be higher in the latter situation than it would be were we to agree to provide for subjacent support, we can infer that the price differential reflects our mutual understanding that I am purchasing a larger property interest (with more extensive boundaries) when I do *not* have to provide support, and a smaller interest when I *do* have to provide such support. As long as each of us abides by our agreement, there is no way in which our respective property interests—as measured by clearly defined spatial boundaries—can come into conflict. While a conflict could arise from our failure to specify such boundaries with sufficient clarity, it is the imprecision of our boundaries, not the nature of the property itself, that generates the conflict. Conflict arises when the property interests of one person are trespassed by another. In this sense, a trespass is but the imposition of costs on others. If, in the face of an agreement that clearly accords me the right to remove my minerals without providing you support, you are able to get the courts to enjoin my actions, you would derive, at my expense, a property interest for which you had not negotiated. This is just one of the many ways in which the state violates property interests.[2] Over the course of time, conditions may

---

[2]See, e.g., *Pennsylvania Coal Co. v. Mahon*, 260 U.S. 393 (1922). This case involved a coal company that owned coal-bearing land. The company had conveyed surface rights to the plaintiffs, while specifically retaining sub-surface rights to mine coal from beneath that land. The plaintiffs also waived all rights to seek damages for any subsidence that might occur. Years later, the Pennsylvania legislature enacted a statute prohibiting any mining of coal that might result in surface subsidence. The plaintiffs sought to enjoin the company from mining its coal without providing for subjacent support. The U.S. Supreme Court denied the plaintiffs' cause of action, declaring the statute—as applied

arise that neither of us had anticipated, leading us to modify the terms (the boundaries) of our contract. But in a system that respects individual autonomy and the inviolability of property interests, such an alteration—a novation—will arise, as did the initial agreement, from the parties themselves.

This hypothetical example is not simply a theoretical one. That a number of discrete property interests—each owned by a different person—may exist within one parcel of land, without conflict, is found in early California mining law. The same parcel of ground might be subject to one claim for placer mining (i.e., to extract minerals from sand or gravel by a washing process), to another claim for *quartz-ledge* mining, to yet another for *fluming* purposes (i.e., to divert water by means of an inclined channel), and to another claim for the diversion of spring or stream water on the parcel.[3] Closer to home, urban properties usually exhibit multiple levels of ownership interests (e.g., a leasehold, mineral rights, mortgage interest, easements, and a landlord's fee simple interest) within the same parcel of land, wherein different owners are able to conduct themselves without conflict. The language of the agreements creating these interests, along with public recordation that would give subsequent parties notice of such claims, would define the respective boundaries of each property interest.

Such tendencies for multiple levels of ownership in the same territory are not confined to humans, but are found in the division of boundaries among various species. It has been observed, for instance, that as many as five different species of warblers will feed on the same kind of worm in the same spruce tree, but with each species occupying different levels of the same tree. Likewise, such estuary sea life as oysters, mussels, gar pikes, and snappers—each with a different level of tolerance for the

---

in this case—a taking of the coal company's property, particularly as upholding the injunction would have given them "greater rights than they bought."

[3]See, e.g., Charles Howard Shinn, *Mining Camps: A Study in American Frontier Government* (New York: Alfred A. Knopf, 1948), p. 259; originally published, 1884, by Charles Scribner's Sons.

saltiness of sea water—will establish territorial boundaries based upon the varying degrees of salinity of the water.[4]

There is something about the functional nature of boundaries that extends far beyond their relevance to property alone. Because of the dualistic nature of our thinking, boundaries provide the means by which our minds separate and distinguish one concept or category from another. Through considerable effort or intuitive insight, we are often able to transcend the divisions created by our structured thinking, and to see the universe more holistically. Because such an awareness may help us dissolve the lines of separation that can keep us in deadly and destructive conflict with one another—a topic to which we shall return—I believe it is necessary to devote a broader inquiry into the role boundaries play in our lives, an examination that will then bring us back to their significance in matters involving property.

There is a symmetry at work in all of this, the recognition of which may help us integrate what the dualistic nature of our minds insists upon seeing as *isolated*, or even *contradictory*, phenomena. *Light* and *darkness*, and *space* and *matter* define each other's boundaries in mutually exclusive ways. The movement of my fingers, for instance, alters the configuration of the space that surrounds them, redefining the relationship of each to the other. Any item of property I desire to claim derives its identity from the boundaries that surround it. So, too, the boundaries of your interests are necessary to a definition of what is *mine* (i.e., what is yours to control delimits what is mine, and vice-versa).

Our daily lives are unavoidably tied up with boundary questions. The work that we do ("that's *my* job"), the homes in which we live, the computer websites through which we communicate with others, and our very sense of "self" are carefully delineated in terms of boundaries. Even the remarkable orderliness of freeway driving is dependent upon adherence to boundaries. Tens of thousands of motorists drive at high speeds, separated by a scant few feet of space, each endeavoring to stay in "his" or

---

[4]Augros and Stanciu, *The New Biology*, pp. 95ff.

"her" lane, aware of the immediate life-and-death consequences of a mistake in judgment that might precipitate a boundary trespass we know as an "accident." When we are aware of how our politically-generated boundary trespasses have their own destructive, anti-life implications, we might become as cautious in what we advocate as governmental policies as we are in the behavior of our fellow motorists.

Boundaries are dynamic information systems, whose qualities relate not just to defining property interests, but also to many areas of life. Learning, for example, is a process by which we cross the boundary that separates the known from the unknown. *Learning* consists of transcending, or even dismantling, the boundary lines by which we have categorized our prior experiences. An openness to the unfamiliar is essential to learning, just as the willingness to cross the boundaries separating the known and the structured from the unknown and the unstructured, is the mark of a creative person. On the other hand, we have organized our learning through neatly arranged concepts, categories, academic disciplines, belief systems, and other structures grounded in definitional boundaries. Those who have attached themselves to such formalized thinking—a trait one sees in ideologies, religions, and academia—are ever vigilant in seeking to preserve the inviolability of their boundaries. Boundaries play a very important role within academic disciplines. What university campus does not channel learning into rigidly-defined "disciplines," and discourage speculative inquiries that have no recognized boundaries? What university departments do not remain on the alert for poachers from other disciplines, a phenomenon that has been given the territorial name of "turf wars?"

Economic analysis and the study of *genetics* are each concerned with changes that occur along the margin of events. The economist is interested in knowing how one additional unit of supply of a commodity will affect its price, while the geneticist—whose motto is "cherish your mutations"—learns much about biological processes by studying an organism whose structure deviates from the norm. *Words* and other intellectual concepts are distinguished by subtle nuances whose exclusive boundaries provide meaning, or "definition." When we want to know the details of anything, be it a basic element, a chair, a particular fruit or vegetable, we speak of its "properties," and do so in terms of boundary descriptions that differentiate the subject matter from all others. It is also noteworthy that, when Korzybski wrote of the distinction between *abstractions* and the *reality* they are intended to represent, he employed the property metaphor of "territory." His observation reminds us to not confuse the boundaries separating the *world* from our *thoughts about* the world.

The universe is whole and interrelated, but in order to understand it, our mind compares and contrasts our experiences, looking for identifiable patterns. With the help of analogies and distinctions, we divide the world into discrete categories, each with its identifiable boundaries, and then deceive ourselves that such divisions represent reality. It is when we are playing around at the boundaries that separate these concepts—as when exploring contradictions—that which we begin to get intuitive glimpses of the underlying wholeness of the world. This is what makes boundaries such a magical, creative place, if only we can muster the courage to move into the realm of the unknown.

We can think of this territory beyond the known as a *frontier*, a realm within which uncertainty, autonomy, and spontaneity represent the norm, and where the turbulence of change is the continuing dynamic. It is at the boundary separating the frontier from the more established regions, the unstructured from the structured environments, that liberty and creativity often flourish. We are seeing such dynamics in the rapidly transforming world of computerized technology and the Internet. But to enter a frontier, be it of physical, intellectual, or psychological dimensions, we must be prepared to give up our attachments to whatever defined our interests in the structured world we are leaving behind.

If we desire to remain creative people, we must develop an appreciation for frontiers, and for the dynamics that take place at boundary lines where our present understanding confronts the unknown. In its earlier decades, America became as free, creative, and materially productive as it did because of its frontier nature. Its relatively unstructured social environment served as a frontier for millions of European immigrants who left the relative certainty of their institutionalized homelands for the opportunities existing in an uncertain land. Many of their Medieval ancestors, in their time, had left their subject status and gone to undeveloped lands in Europe. In these frontiers, they cleared forests and set up new settlements, an undertaking that "conferred liberty on the colonizers . . . [and] elevated them from slavery and serfdom."[5] Frontiers have long held out to men and women the promise that a portion of the world could become theirs to own and control for their purposes. In such environments, people have been free to innovate and adapt themselves to new situations without being compelled to conform to the demands of an established hierarchy of authority.

In the same way, the undeveloped West—a flexible concept that continually redefined itself as western Pennsylvania, then Ohio, then Nebraska, then Utah, then Oregon—served as a frontier for those living in the more institutionally established eastern states. When early Dutch settlers tried to impose a feudal system along the upper Hudson River, they found little interest expressed by those who had the option of easily moving elsewhere. The frontier served as a boundary separating the more established from the relatively undeveloped into which people could freely move. As such, frontiers provided environments of decentralized and limited political authority, wherein independence and alternative social systems could flourish. It was this relationship that pressured eastern states not to become too restrictive of the activities of those trying to further their interests. This arrangement provided Americans with an effective check upon the more established states' tendencies for institutional

---

[5]William Chester Jordan, *Europe In the High Middle Ages* (London: Penguin Books, 2002), p. 10.

rigidification and, in the process, allowed people to remain free and productive for many decades.[6]

Frontiers are not defined geographically as much as they represent a state of mind, a willingness to see opportunities in relative uncertainty. Imagination—the capacity to see beyond the boundaries of the known—has long been the frontier for creative minds. To believe that a physical environment by itself, without any volition on our part, has the power to transform us is to engage in mechanistic thinking. Indeed, there were many settlers in the early west, who, insisted upon what they perceived as the "protection" of the state (e.g., in the form of a military presence). Implicit in the dynamics along a frontier is the interplay between "stability" and "change;" between the established and the new, along with the existence of individuals capable of and willing to pursue alternative courses of action. The liberty to commit one's life and property interests to such opportunities is central to this process. The implications of this have been noted by Alfred North Whitehead: "the vivid people keep moving on, geographically and otherwise, for men can be provincial in time, as well as in place."[7]

One of the most significant boundaries we encounter is related to our learning and other creative activities. Having learned what we believe to be a sufficient body of knowledge, we resist efforts to think beyond the boundaries of the known (i.e., to "think outside the circle") and to explore the unknown. Scientists, inventors, and philosophers have been among the more noted examples of persons discouraged or even threatened by those who insisted upon what one writer labeled "the saber-toothed curriculum."[8] The ways in which our minds create barriers ("boundaries") that circumscribe our behavior were

---

[6]An interesting account of such influences can be found in Frederick Jackson Turner's classic work, *The Frontier in American History* (New York: Henry Holt and Company, 1920).

[7]Lucien Price, *The Dialogues of Alfred North Whitehead* (Boston: Little, Brown and Company, 1954), p. 50.

[8]J. Abner Peddiwell, *The Saber-Tooth Curriculum* (New York: McGraw-Hill, 1939).

reflected in events leading up to the running of a sub-four-minute mile. For years, it was assumed that running a mile in less than four minutes was impossible, and while many came close none was able to accomplish the task until 1954, when the Englishman Roger Bannister ran the mile in 3 minutes, 59.4 seconds. It was not long after that boundary-breaking event that many other runners accomplished the same feat.

As our social world continues its apparent transformation into horizontal networks, we are likely to find ourselves at the boundaries of a new frontier: *society* itself. As decentralization expands the realms of our personal authority, we will find ourselves exploring radically new social assumptions concerning what it is appropriate for each of us to control, and how to freely cooperate and exchange with one another. We may then discover the informal systems of order and other spontaneous processes that work, beneath the surface of events in our lives, to instill the peaceful and productive conditions that make society decent. As we continue to explore such new territory, we may discover one another in totally new relationships, as well as the social harmony that arises as an unintended consequence of the pursuit of our respective self-interests.

The dynamics of chaos and complexity that help to transform our understanding of the world—including the organizational premises of our social systems—are particularly relevant to our inquiry. One of the central features in this emerging field of study involves the boundary transition that occurs when a system moves from linear regularity to chaotic turbulence. Bifurcation points represent boundaries, separating entropic and negentropic courses of conduct. As such, something either *destructive* or *creative* can occur along boundary lines. The study of such processes reveals patterns of heretofore undiscovered order embedded within our complicated world, regularities that take on the qualities of new boundaries. Related dynamics occurring along boundaries are seen in creative acts, wherein innovation confronts the outmoded; novelty challenges the status quo.

Humor seems to be a reflection of our unconscious mind's awareness of the harmony found in seemingly contradictory relationships. Whether we are considering jokes, puns, sight gags, witticisms, irony, or satire, humor provides a pleasurable meaning because it gives us the opportunity to integrate what our conscious mind tells us is to be segregated. James Thurber described "humour" as "emotional chaos remembered in tranquility."[9] It operates along the boundary lines separating the *expected* from the *unexpected*, sometimes bouncing back and forth from one side of the line to the other, giving us glimpses of the complementary nature of the world. This is what gives puns their potency: a word or phrase used to communicate different meanings than when such expressions are used in a different context. Puns challenge the boundary lines of what we like to think of as the mutually-exclusive meanings of our abstractions.

Optical illusions also generate fuzziness along boundary lines. Is the staircase ascending or descending? Do we see a vase, or two faces looking at one another? Is it a beautiful woman, or an old lady? M.C. Escher developed a unique art style in which different objects shared common boundaries in one of the better-known expressions of symmetry. We find amusement in these patterns that alternate, but which our dualistic minds find difficulty in seeing simultaneously.

As we have seen, there is an unavoidable information loss in the use of abstractions—particularly words—as we endeavor to understand and negotiate with the world. Words must always be interpreted and, in our efforts to do so, we discover that they often have an elusive quality to them; that they can play tricks on us as we struggle to define their respective boundary lines. They have no inherent meaning, and when we turn to a dictionary for help, we discover that they can only be defined in terms of *other* words, *other* abstractions. We are familiar with the common role of *synonyms*, wherein different words may mean the

---

[9]*New York Post*, February 29, 1960. See also www.bartleby.com/63/92/5392. html; also, www.kirjasto.sci.fi/thurber.htm.

same thing (e.g., "poetry" and "verse"). Even differing words of seemingly opposite denotation may be used synonymously. In modern usage, for example, "hot" and "cool" can have the same meaning, just as—in my teenage years—the phrase "what's going on?" meant the same as "what's coming off?" But the same word—a *contronym*—will sometimes have a diametrically opposed meaning. The word "sanction," for instance, may mean either a form of *approval* or of *punishment*. "Custom" may refer to something that is *common* or, alternatively, something produced for special order. The word "oversight" can mean either to *pay attention* to something, or to *fail* to do so.

Many of our conflicts arise from a failure to acknowledge the hazy nature of all abstractions. Like Humpty Dumpty, we are inclined to the proposition that "when I use a word, it means just what I choose it to mean—neither more nor less."[10] Our world would become less strife-ridden were we to become aware that the boundaries of our concepts do not have the concrete and objective meanings we like to imagine they enjoy.

As a social system, boundaries have a dualistic quality: whether our relationships with others are peaceful or violent is reflected in the degree of respect we accord their inviolate nature. A socially troublesome aspect of boundaries is found in the practice of identifying ourselves through what Fritz Perls has called "ego-boundary" abstractions.[11] We learn to identify ourselves in terms of collective abstractions. While our more distant ancestors identified themselves with their tribe, clan, or race, most of us modernly identify ourselves with our nationality, race, religion, social class, gender, ideology, economic interests, geography, or other abstractions.[12] Through such thinking,

---

[10] Lewis Carroll, *Alice's Adventures in Wonderland* (1865).

[11] See, e.g., Frederick Perls, *Gestalt Therapy Verbatim* (New York: Bantam Press, 1971), pp. 7ff.; originally published 1969 (Moab, Utah: Real People Press). See, also, Ludwig von Bertalanffy, *Robots, Men and Minds* (New York: George Braziller, 1967), p. 33, who characterized the practice as the "ego barrier."

[12] I have developed a more thorough analysis of this in my *Calculated Chaos: Institutional Threats to Peace and Human Survival* (San Francisco: Alchemy Books, 1985); reprinted (Coral Springs, Fla.: Llumina Press, 2004).

we define "who we are" by reference to various social sub-groupings that are either institutional in nature, or are exploited for institutional purposes. Through this same thinking, we embroil ourselves in wars, genocides, racial confrontations, and even riots between competing fans over the outcome of soccer games. These are among the more violent consequences of our failure to respect the inviolability of one another's "ego-boundaries." We think of ourselves in terms of such abstractions, a holdover from the most primitive ways of regarding ourselves. We become *integrated with* those who share our boundaries, and *alienated from* those who are not encompassed within our borders.

It is not just that such categories describe us in some physically observable way (e.g., gender, skin color, age), but that we have learned to give them existential significance. They go to the essence of how we think of ourselves. We may identify ourselves by the color of our skin, but not of our eyes, because our minds have attached meaning to one set of abstract distinctions but not others. It would not be an exaggeration to suggest that, for most of us, our identities are our lives. If you doubt this, try describing yourself without making use of any collective abstractions. In the words of the caterpillar in *Alice in Wonderland*, "who are you?"

Ego-boundary thinking, another expression of our dualistic way of organizing our experiences, has collectivized our minds and created our world of institutionally-directed conflict and disorder. By identifying ourselves with any category of persons, we necessarily separate ourselves from those who are not part of our group. Being *other* than us, they become *less* than us. When the interests of one group come into contact with those of another, particularly along the boundary lines that divide one group from another, conflicts easily arise.

Political institutions thrive by encouraging the development of various group identities. Insisting upon maintaining the clear distinctions of our collective boundary lines, they help to foment conflicts among such groups and then offer to mediate the very differences it has been in the state's interests to foster! It is a racket, which, if engaged in by private parties, would result in long prison sentences. Look at how easily governments have been able to mobilize their citizens into wars against other nations, or to create discord between "consumers" and "retailers," "employers" and "employees," "environmentalists" and "lumber companies," "parents" and "school officials," "gays" and "straights," "immigrants" and "native-born," along with racial, ethnic, religious, gender, and other sub-groupings of people. As the state expands the range of its decision making over our property, it necessarily enlarges the boundaries that separate us from one another while increasing the likelihood of personal and social conflict. The dispute that I might have with my neighbor over a fence line is, by its nature, localized. Given the personal, rather than abstract, nature of our relationship, our differences are likely to be resolved amicably. However, as we become drawn into politically generated quarrels with abstract categories of people whose existence may span the globe, the boundaries of our interests not only become more depersonalized, but take on global dimensions. Doesn't this describe the deadly confrontations that set strangers against one another for no other reason than their being members of opposing nation-states or political or religious factions?

As our thinking becomes more abstract and institutionally centered, we tend to deprive ourselves of the qualities that make us human. The abstract differs from the concrete. Human beings function on the basis of blood, emotions, pain, fears, and dreams, while institutions—such as the state or corporations—tend to operate upon such abstractions as statistics, collective trends, and chain-of-command decision-making. The same person who can feel sadness over the death of an unknown child can, when identifying himself with the state, feel a sense of indifference to statistical reports of the wartime deaths of hundreds of thousands of civilians.

A moment's reflection should make us aware of how our "ego-boundary" practices are based on the same dynamics as those at work in property. Each provides a way of asserting our will upon the world, to the end that we may develop and express our sense of who we are. One can think of ego identification as a form of claim staking in the world of collective identities. The patriot who reacts to the defiling of his nation's flag; or the religious believer who takes angry offense at a cartoon that ridicules a man he regards as sacred, experiences every bit —if not more—the sense of being trespassed as is felt by a homeowner who has been the victim of a burglary. Perls has characterized the conflict that arises from such identity disputes as *boundary* clashes, which are more likely to occur along boundary lines than at a distance. For this reason, he adds, India is more likely to go to war with China, than with Finland.[13]

Ego-boundary trespasses abound in such areas as political and religious behavior. One very emotional, property-related issue has to do with the burning of an American flag as a form of political protest. The arguments on behalf of making flag burning a crime emphasize the state's interest in protecting an *image*, a *symbol* that is used to mobilize people to identify with the nation-state. But how does one describe and locate an image or a symbol? What are its boundaries? Is it simply the *cloth* from which the flag was made? A reading of flag desecration statutes extends the offense to any representation of the flag, including a photograph or a school-child's drawing thereof. Furthermore, the burning of an old flag is the institutionally accepted way of disposing of it, meaning that the state of mind of the burner defines the offense!

In order to have a trespass there must be a boundary to be trespassed. But when dealing with ego-boundaries, such qualities are the products of the mind; visions, impressions, sentiments, and other emotions fashioned, in a multitude of forms and meanings, from the unique experiences of each person. The flag burning issue is but one more illustration of the fallacy that politics *unites* people into a harmonious whole. Any nation is, after all, composed of millions of unique personalities, with diverse tastes, values, dreams, and opinions. We are simply too

---

[13]Perls, *Gestalt Therapy Verbatim*, p. 13.

varied to permit an easy consolidation under collective images to which we attach a common meaning. To a war veteran, the flag may represent the virtue of obedience to authority, or a symbol of a sense of duty. To a war protester, it may represent either a symbol of collective violence or a nation's commitment to an unrestrained freedom of individual expression. A dollar sign symbolizes totally different values to a follower of Ayn Rand than it does to an idealistic ascetic, just as a swastika conjures up divergent images and emotions to Jews, neo-Nazis, Buddhists, Tibetans, and American Indians.

Just how muddled most of us are with notions of property was expressed by a lawyer who defended flag desecration laws by arguing that, if burning the flag was an exercise of free speech, one would have to defend the painting of swastikas on synagogues as free speech. Such disordered thinking arises from a failure to clearly define one's conceptual boundaries, adding to the general confusion over the meaning of property. A person who paints a swastika—or, for that matter, street-gang graffiti, or the phrase "John loves Mary"—on a building owned by another, is not engaging in free speech, but committing a trespass upon that property. It is the violation of the synagogue's *property* boundaries—not the swastika itself—that makes this a trespass. Such an act extends one's decision making beyond one's own property boundaries and invades the boundaries of another—if a man chooses to paint a swastika on his own house, that would be an expression of free speech.

The example of the defiled synagogue would be more apropos to a situation in which an individual, without the permission of the owner, burns a flag owned by another. If Smith burned a flag owned by Jones, this would amount to a property trespass, as would Smith's burning of Jones' car. But flag desecration statutes are not designed to protect the property interests of flag owners, but the imagery through which political institutions function. Since images and symbolism, like art or pornography, have meaning and existence only within the minds of individuals, the state cannot identify any clear boundary that would give it a property interest in such imagery. For the state to insist upon the power to "protect" the inviolability of such images is to assert a property interest in the content of our minds.

One also finds such boundary line disputes in the phenomenon of philosophical, religious, or ideological allies engaging in more ferocious infighting with one another than they do with diametrically opposed groups. Marxists and lesser socialists, for instance, have often had more heated conflicts with one another than with the defenders of private capitalism. Likewise, one finds contemporary libertarians and conservatives reserving some of their most quarrelsome rhetoric for one another, rather than for their socialist opposition. The reason for this appears to be related to the fact that minor differences may blur boundary line distinctions and, in the process, cloud one's sense of identity. Both *ego* and *property* boundaries require a continuing clarity of definition, particularly in an inconstant environment. When such definitions become unclear, as they always are when such abstract boundaries as race, religion, nationality, ideology, or politics are involved; or when your neighbor insists that the property line is two feet closer to your house than you believe it to be, conflict is likely to erupt. Nor should we be surprised to discover that, as political and social turbulence calls into question the future of existing systems, many people become eager supporters of the efforts of the state to resist such changes by the most repressive and violent means.

Ego-boundaries, like property boundaries, segregate us from one another. The overstepping of either can evoke anger and violence against the transgressor, although our reaction is likely to be subdued when a neighbor with whom we have regular, face-to-face dealings, walks across our lawn. But should an outsider intrude upon our ego-boundaries, the more abstract nature of the trespass may engender more intense violence, as one sees in wartime. Such are the energies prevailing along boundary lines that can erupt when violated.

Because ego-boundary conflicts are quite abstract, and often involve millions of people with little face-to-face contact, their violence is far more destructive than the more localized and transient nature of boundary disputes by owners. This fact, alone, should illustrate the advantages of decentralizing decision making away from political institutions and into the hands of individual property owners.

Whether we are differentiating the meanings of words, expanding the boundaries of our understanding, trying to reconcile seemingly contradictory experiences, fighting with a neighbor, or confronting our conflict-laden "ego-boundaries," there is tremendous energy associated with activity along boundary lines. If we can begin to understand the nature of the energy contained within the boundary concept, we may gain valuable insights into the role that the inviolability of property boundaries plays in maintaining both free and orderly social systems. We may discover that much of the destructive energy that is regularly released into our world as conflict and violence is the product of the systematic disrespect for property boundaries in a variety of settings.

There is, admittedly, a paradoxical quality to property as it relates to social conflict. On the one hand, privately owned property provides what may be the most important mechanism for avoiding intra-species conflict. The biological and social purpose served by property boundaries is to recognize the existential significance of each person not only as his or her own purpose for being, but also as a means for the survival of the species. This is accomplished by separating those resources over which each of us will exercise our respective control. It is not simply an ideological preference, but a fact of nature, that no organism can survive without exclusive space to occupy and resources to consume. On the other hand, to claim a resource for oneself, to the exclusion of everyone else, is to divide oneself from others. Conflict is produced by division and yet property ownership seems to both *produce* and *alleviate* conflict.

This introduces us to another phenomenon that may further help us transcend the divisions generated by our dualistic thinking. There is an interrelated quality apparent to opposites which, when closely examined, provides intuitive glimpses of a more holistic universe. The seemingly irreconcilable but interdependent nature of the two aspects of a magnet, which introduces "polarization" into our vocabularies, clouds a unity that is immediately revealed when the magnet is cut in half to produce two magnets, each with a "north" and a "south" pole. One sees this unity of opposites in marketplace behavior. A free market involves the energetic pursuit of individual self-interest while, at the same time, it is dependent upon participants respecting the property interests of others. Buyers and sellers commit only their own resources, often with great risks involved, and absorb their *own* costs associated with their individual pursuits. In spite of all this self-serving activity, market participants end up benefiting others, even without intending to do so!

I suspect that when we encounter seemingly irresolvable discrepancies such as this, we may be straddling the boundary lines that our dualistic thinking employs to divide our experiences into discrete, manageable categories. Such ambivalence may provide us with the opportunity to see the world more holographically—to move beyond our divisive methods of thinking.[14] William Blake's "Contraries" come to mind. "Attraction and Repulsion, Reason and Energy, Love and Hate, are necessary to Human existence."[15]

A paradox may only be our mind's intuitive grasping of this fundamental interconnectedness. Niels Bohr's "complementarity principle," addressing the phenomenon of wave-particle duality in quantum mechanics, may have a social analogy to help us understand the seemingly paradoxical qualities of our individual and social behavior as reciprocal, symmetrical expressions of wholeness, rather than division. It is at boundaries that

---

[14]We have seen this phenomenon elsewhere, one of the better examples arising from the study of quantum physics with its conundrum of whether subatomic particles are exhibiting *mass* or *energy*, the implications of which are expressed in Einstein's classic "$E=mc^2$." "Superstring" theory extended the metaphor by positing that fundamental units of matter may consist not of particles, but of loops of vibrating energy. See Brian Greene, *The Elegant Universe* (New York: W.W. Norton & Company, 1999), pp. 142–46.

[15]William Blake, "The Marriage of Heaven and Hell" (1790), in David V. Erdman, ed., *The Selected Poetry of Blake* (New York: New American Library, 1976), p. 67.

separation occurs. But it is at the same boundary lines that we have the opportunity to glimpse the integrated nature of the apparent opposites that our mind, alone, has created. With paradoxes, we are able to look across the boundary lines of separation and see our world in a more integrated manner. If this is so, a paradox should be a welcome signal for exploring the implications of our dualistic thinking—to bring about a synthesis of seemingly opposing elements and grasp their wholeness.

We may be assisted in our efforts by approaches taken in Eastern thought. In the philosophy of Taoism, the concepts of Yin and Yang help us transcend dualistic thinking that causes us to understand the universe in terms of mutually-exclusive categories. Such apparently opposing qualities as "hot" and "cold," "day" and "night," "happy" and "sad," or "living" and "dead" can, with a change in perspective, come to be seen as complementary, interconnected characteristics. The concept of "virtue" is meaningless without its partner "sin," just as "truth" and "falsity," "rich" and "poor," and "good" and "evil" have paired dependencies. It is our mind, alone, that insists upon the separation and, in so doing, helps to produce the absolutist mindset that plagues mankind.

As we continue to play with the novelty of holograms, optical illusions, and Escher drawings, we may be able to intuit the wholeness that lies hidden behind boundary lines. We might add to our playthings the Mobius strip—the puzzle created by half-twisting one end of a two-sided strip of paper and attaching it to the other end to create a one-sided surface. Each of these forms of amusement may provide insights into the holistic nature of boundaries that both *separate* us from one another— as an expression of individuality—and, as a consequence, allow us to cooperatively *integrate* ourselves in a sense of community with others.

If, as both Taoism and physics inform us, boundaries are not as precise as we imagine them to be, how do we resolve the paradox that all living things must retain exclusive control over specific space and negentropic resources if they are to survive? Is this an inherent contradiction or a failure to reason clearly, or a paradox whose apparent irreconcilability, like wave-particle duality,[16] suggests that we may be at the frontier of a more profound social discovery? Contrary to collectivist thinking that is grounded in the divisive proposition that the lives of some may be sacrificed for the benefit of others, the private property principle may be the expression of a more holistic premise that could help extricate humanity from its collective destructiveness.

Because our individuality and need for autonomy is what each of us has in common with one another, is it not evident that only a system of personally owned property is consistent with both our personal and social interest to be free of conflict? Doesn't the apparent conflict between individual and societal purposes—fashioned by ideologues as a rationale for state power—evaporate once we grasp the simple fact that conflict is a byproduct of boundary trespasses? As we endeavor to understand the significance of new models of social organization in which interconnectedness, autonomy, and autopoeisis are the principal characteristics, we would do well to consider the role of property boundaries as information systems through which we maintain our needs for both community and individuality. Such boundaries function much like DNA: to communicate the boundaries of our individual uniqueness even while continuing the life of the species itself.

The influence of boundaries is also at work in the development of our personalities. Because we are social beings, you and I learn "who" we are largely in terms of our relationships with one another. We do a lot of bumping into one another as

---

[16]The classic "two-slit" experiments in quantum physics may provide insight in helping us circumvent our paradoxical thinking. These experiments suggest that, in testing for whether an electron or a photon behaves as a *wave* or as a *particle*, the outcome depends upon the intentions of the experimenter: behaving like a particle when testing for particle responses, and like a wave when wave activity is being sought. (See, e.g., John Gribbin, *In Search of Schrodinger's Cat* (New York: Bantam Books, 1984), pp. 163–76, 210–12; Gary Zukav, *The Dancing Wu Li Masters* (New York: William Morrow & Company, Inc., 1979), pp. 85–102, 117–18, 298–99; Paul Davies, *Superforce* (New York: Simon & Schuster, Inc., 1984), pp. 28–30.

we grow up, and learn from each other's reactions the propriety of our respective actions. The realm of "manners" consists of informal attempts to define "proper" behavior—a term with obvious property connotations. We often employ property language to inform others that their behavior has gone too far: "don't crowd me," "give me my space," and "keep your hands to yourself," have become fence-lines we employ in our social claim-staking for what we regard as ours. As we respond to others, and experience their responses to us, we contribute to the development of one another's sense of "self." Thus who you and I are, and what is yours or mine to control, are determined by related processes of negotiation for our boundaries with one another.

A society in which peace and liberty prevail is dependent upon this mutually-exclusive nature of property boundaries. Because institutional interests depend upon confusion in our minds as to what decisions are or are not for us to personally make, it is not surprising that we should succumb to the idea that our individual interests could be inherently in conflict. Because boundary lines separate what is "yours" from what is "mine" to control, recognition of, and respect for, boundaries set the limits of our individual actions and, in the process, provide a functional basis for harmonious social behavior. Without a concept of individual ownership of property, human activity is inherently conflict-ridden, with most of us reduced to competing for the control of resources on the basis of violence. That such social discord accompanies the expansion of state power, with its inherent contempt for privately-owned property, should not amaze us. Every political system is nothing more than a mechanism that allows some to benefit at the expense of the many through violent takings of property. Modern society provides a clear reflection of the destructive consequences of failing to observe the inviolability of private interests. Only by describing and respecting separate and exclusive areas for each of us to control can such discord be eliminated in our world.

The significance of property boundaries is not confined to human behavior. Those who regard "property" interests as nothing more than a human invention to maintain existing interests in the world, must come to grips with the fact that various life forms—animal and plant alike—identify and defend the boundaries of their territorial interests. In landmark works that have helped to expand an awareness of the territorial nature of many other species—be they fish, birds, or mammals—Konrad Lorenz,[17] Robert Ardrey,[18] and Edward O. Wilson,[19] provided empirical evidence for the role that respect for territorial boundaries plays in reducing conflict within various species. Members of a particular species will stake out a territorial claim, with their boundaries marked by urine, or the range of one's warble or trumpet. Even molds and bacteria assert their territorial claims to fruits and vegetables by creating toxic substances to discourage trespassers.[20] Boundaries operate as barriers that tend to discourage trespasses by outsiders, and thus give to the owner an exclusive realm within which to function. A trespass will invite a defensive response from the claimant, with the interesting result of the claimant being able to successfully resist the intrusion in the overwhelming majority of cases. As Ardrey has observed:

> We may also say that in all territorial species, without exception, possession of a territory lends enhanced energy to the proprietor. Students of animal behavior cannot agree as to why this should be, but the challenger is almost invariably defeated, the intruder expelled. In part, there seems some mysterious flow of energy and resolve, which invests a proprietor on his home grounds. But likewise, so marked is the inhibition lying on the intruder, so evident his sense of trespass, we may be permitted to wonder if in all territorial species

---

[17]Konrad Lorenz, *On Aggression* (New York: Harcourt, Brace & World, Inc., 1966).

[18]Robert Ardrey, *The Territorial Imperative* (New York: Atheneum Publishers, 1966).

[19]Edward O. Wilson, *Sociobiology* (Cambridge, Mass.: The Belknap Press of Harvard University Press, 1975).

[20]Barlow, *The Ghosts of Evolution*, p. 198.

there does not exist, more profound than simple learning, some universal recognition of territorial rights.[21]

This overwhelming tendency for the territorial occupier to
prevail against an intruder has also been acknowledged by Wilson, Lorenz, and others.[22] Who has not witnessed this phenomenon in even the smallest dog's indignant barking that wards off
the invasion of its property by a much larger and stronger dog?
Perhaps this disposition helps to account for the "home field
advantage" in sports,[23] or contributed to the American government's difficulties in its wars against the Vietnamese and Iraqis,
the Soviet Union's problems in Afghanistan, and the Israeli government's troubles in Lebanon.

This social role of property was noted, as early as 1878, by
T.E. Cliffe Leslie:

> A dog, it has been said, shows an elementary proprietary
> sentiment when he hides a bone, or keeps watch over his
> master's goods. But property has not its root in the love
> of possession. All living beings like and desire certain
> things, and if nature has armed them with any weapons
> are prone to use them in order to get and keep what they
> want. *What requires explanation is not the want or desire
> of certain things on the part of individuals, but the fact that
> other individuals, with similar wants and desires, should leave
> them in undisturbed possession*, or allot to them a share,

---

[21] Ardrey, *The Territorial Imperative*, p. 3.

[22] Wilson, *Sociobiology*, pp. 259–60; Lorenz, *On Aggression*, p. 35ff.; James R.
Carey and Catherine Gruenfelder, "Population Biology of the Elderly," in Ken-
neth W. Wachter and Caleb E. Finch, eds., *Between Zeus and the Salmon: The
Biodemography of Longevity* (Washington, D.C.: Commission on Behavioral and
Social Sciences and Education, 1997), chap. 8, p. 133.

[23] See, e.g., Barry Schwartz and Stephen Barsky, "The Home Advantage,"
Social Forces 55: 641–61; Donald L. Greer, "Spectator Booing and the Home
Advantage: A Study of Social Influence in the Basketball Arena," *Social Psy-
chology Quarterly* 46, no. 3 (September 1983): 252–61; Eric M. Leifer, "Perverse
Effects of Social Support: Publics and Performance in Major League Sports,"
Social Forces 74, no. 1 (September 1995): 81–121.

of such things. It is the conduct of the community, not the inclination of individuals, that needs investigation.[24]

Again, as Ardrey writes, most territorial contests are restricted to members of the same species. "A squirrel," for instance, "does not regard a mouse as a trespasser."[25] For much the same reasons, we humans would tend to not look upon a bird as a trespasser if it built a nest in our bushes, but would be inclined to regard a homeless person as a trespasser if he took up residence in those same bushes.

There is an interesting photograph of a dozen or more male mouthbrooder fish, each occupying a hexagonally shaped territory whose boundaries are delineated in the sand of an outdoor tank of water. When one sees the efficiency with which these fish have gotten the maximum amount of usable space from what was available to them, and then compares this arrangement with the patterns we humans have created in subdividing our territories into housing developments, the parallels are remarkable.[26]

Those who insist that privately-owned property is nothing more than a fiction created by humans, or the creature of political and legal institutions, would do well to examine the behavior of other life forms. Such an anthropocentric vision expresses a fundamental ignorance of the nature of all living things to occupy and consume resources. Territory is the most fundamental fact of existence. Even plants, trees, and corals stake out and defend individual territorial boundaries. Other species have no known governments or laws and yet maintain a very high degree of respect for the territorial claims established by other members of their species. The territorial boundary not only informs others of the area within which the claimant intends to be the sole owner and occupier, but also determines where another may traverse without causing conflict.

---

[24]T.E. Cliffe Leslie, Introduction to Emile de Laveleye, *Primitive Property* (London: Macmillan, 1878); emphasis added.

[25]Ardrey, *The Territorial Imperative*, p. 3.

[26]See Wilson, *Sociobiology*, p. 272.

Perhaps the violent, angry, and stagnant quality of life in many larger cities reflects our failure to understand the importance of individualized space and the need to respect one another's boundaries in a crowded world. The study of astronomy informs us that it is the vast amount of space existing among galaxies, stars, and planets that prevents a destructive, gravity-driven collision of such bodies. Our cities may provide us the social equivalent of such insights, namely, that without a sufficient respect for the space that separates us, conditions may become too catastrophic to sustain life.

Since we use the boundary concept to inform one another of what we claim as ours to own and control, one of the first boundaries we ought to consider defining involves our most basic property interest: the ownership of our individual selves. If you and I do own ourselves, *what* is it that we own? At the most basic level, the boundaries of our selves can be defined in much the same way we describe other material entities, namely, by the three-dimensional nature of our bodies. There may be some debate as to whether these boundaries begin and end at the epidermis, or whether they might also consist of some hazily-defined "aura." Nonetheless, the implicit recognition of the physical dimensions of the body as representing the minimal boundaries of self-ownership finds support not only in common speech ("your rights end where my nose begins"), but in the standard common law definition of a "battery" as "the least touching of another in anger."[27] Questions concerning abortion; the right to commit suicide, use drugs, decide whether or not to wear seat belts or a motorcycle helmet, or select one's health practices; or whether a person continues to own his or her bodily organs once they have been removed from their body[28] (an issue to which we shall return later) show that the question of how we define our personal boundaries is far from being resolved.

---

[27]See, e.g., *Cole v. Turner*, at Nisi Prius, coram Holt, C.J. (1704), 6 Mod. p. 149.

[28]*Moore v. Regents of the University of California*, 793 P2nd 479 (Cal., 1990), cert. denied 499 U.S. 936 (1991).

Similar problems of definitional uncertainty—largely the leg-
acy of feudal thinking and early court decisions—are found in
the law. In defining the boundaries of real property, the extent
of "air rights" and "subsurface rights" are not subject to precise
measurement. The old common law definition, untested by earlier technologies, was that rights to land extended from the center of the earth outward into infinite space. This concept never
did satisfy the functional meanings of property ownership and
has undergone great transformation as a result of such inventions as the airplane, radio and television, and space satellites.

As we have seen, it is a reflection of the social nature of property that each of us can freely negotiate with one another to redefine our boundaries, a practice which has even been observed
in the territorial behavior of animals. While territorial claimants will be the most aggressive when a trespasser intrudes to
the center of another's claim, a greater tendency for boundary
negotiation occurs at the periphery, where one animal's territorial claim abuts a neighbor's.[29] Even on an informal level, our
personal boundaries can have a flexible quality to them. We
have each had the experience of being on a crowded elevator,
with strangers shoving and pressing against us without a sense
of being trespassed. But suppose that you are alone on an elevator, and a stranger gets on and presses up against you. You will
now likely regard your boundaries to be trespassed, and even
treat his intrusion as a personal threat.

In addition to self-ownership and real property interests,
there are other tangible, personal property interests called *chattels*. Automobiles, clothing, furniture, cameras, computers, and
books have spatial boundaries that are synonymous with the
chattel itself (e.g., the boundary of a chair or a watch is the chair
or watch itself). The physical nature of land is such that it is
continuous and, thus, if we wish to claim ownership of some
parcel we must create artificial boundaries as to what is ours,
such as by putting a fence around it. With a chattel, on the other
hand, the chattel and its boundaries are self-defining. They are

---

[29]Lorenz, *On Aggression*, pp. 36ff.

one and the same unless, as we saw in the example of the car encumbered with a chattel mortgage, a bank also has a property interest. We can thus think of the boundaries of the car, itself, as self-defining while, at the same time, the boundaries of the respective ownership interests are more abstractly described.

It is when we are considering those interests that do not have a visible, material nature to them—what we call *intangible* property—that the boundaries are much more abstract and, therefore, more difficult to conceptualize and identify. Nevertheless, the same principles are at work here as they are with more tangible forms of property. Intangible property consists of such interests as patents, copyrights, contract rights, mortgages, bank accounts, corporate stock, promissory notes, computer systems and programs, electronically transmitted information, and the like. Does a bank, having secured a promissory note from you with a mortgage on your house, have a property interest in this arrangement? Yes, both as to the note and the mortgage.

As mentioned earlier, technological change has, for centuries, been creating new forms and systems that challenge the prevailing definitions of what can be owned. Computers are making their contributions to the uncertainties of the boundaries separating the tangible from the intangible. The ownership of computer programs was fairly easy to resolve in terms of traditional copyright principles. But the emergence of what is known as "virtual property" is forcing a rethinking of the boundary lines between what is "real" and what is "fantasy."

Various complex online computer games make use of an intricate array of characters, objects, currencies, memberships, and other interests, with which a multitude of players compete to accomplish the game's objective. In the course of doing so, players accumulate certain of the above categories of assets. Like the board-game of "Monopoly," these assets might consist of the equivalent of a hotel on "Boardwalk." Unlike the board-game, however, these online games create the unintended opportunity for players to go to a website, such as eBay, and auction one or more of their assets for real money. This practice has raised such questions as whether income taxes must be paid on the revenues so generated or whether, if the game should be discontinued before the purchaser of one of these assets has been able to exploit it in the game, a cause of action might lie against either (a) the seller of the asset, and/or (b) those responsible for shutting down the game.[30]

Because our industrialized culture places such an emphasis on material interests, we have a tendency to objectify intangible property interests by equating them with some physical manifestation, or memorandum, of their existence. But since the purpose of boundaries is to define the scope of the property interests we claim as our own, and since many of these interests have no three-dimensional quality to them, it should not confuse us to discover that the boundaries of intangible interests are, themselves, intangible. They consist almost entirely of *words* which, as we have seen, have an inherent fuzziness to them that must be interpreted.

Even the boundaries of our property interests in a bank account—one of our most valued assets—are difficult to identify in any material way. When, as a nine-year old, I opened a savings account for earnings from my paper-route, I imagined that the currency I deposited with the bank was being placed in a personal drawer or box, and should I wish to withdraw any of these funds, the bank would take the money from this container. Modern bank accounts consist largely of a series of "1" and "0" entries in a computer, with secondary evidence of such property provided by periodic bank statements.

Because of our fixation on materiality, it is a common mistake to assume that the stock certificate, or the signed contract, or the patent certificate, or the deed to real estate, is the property interest. While such documents are important, in a legal sense, as *evidence* of a property interest, they do not constitute the interest itself. Our common law system recognizes this fact. For instance, the loss of an insurance policy, or the destruction

---

[30]Julian Dibbell, "Unreal Real Estate Boom," *Wired* (October 2002). See also Richard Bartle, "Pitfalls of Virtual Property." The Themis Group white paper, April 2004, at http://mud.co.uk/richard/povp.pdf.

of a stock certificate or warranty deed, does not extinguish the underlying interest that such documents represent. A lost stock certificate, for instance, will be replaced by the issuing corporation. On the other hand, if the ownership interest were synonymous with the written instrument, it would be correct to classify the document as a *chattel* (e.g., old gold mining stock certificates of now defunct corporations may have collectors' value, even though they no longer represent an ownership interest in the corporation). If a chattel is destroyed (e.g., a painting), the ownership interest is also destroyed, even though one may retain a property claim against the insurance company that had insured the value of that interest. Likewise, currency or a "bearer bond" is treated as an item of property in itself, which will not be replaced if it becomes lost or stolen.

The boundaries of our claims may also be defined temporally. A leasehold interest is of a fixed duration; a life estate terminates upon the death of its owner; while so-called "determinable estates" may last until the happening of a specific event or, in the absence of such limiting occurrence, may run indefinitely. The Shasta Indian tribes of northern California allowed families to claim exclusive rights to tobacco plots, but for only one season.[31] Likewise, among the Somalis, a herdsman who is the first to bring his animals to a pasture or watering site is entitled to the exclusive possession of same until such time as he leaves that location.[32] In this same temporal vein, courts have awarded commodities investment firms property claims in the information they wire to their clients for a period of a few minutes[33] The underlying assumption of such a holding was that, by the end of that time period, the information would have spread throughout the market, depriving it of its unique, exclusive boundaries.

---

[31]Linda S. Parker, *Native American Estate: The Struggle Over Indian and Hawaiian Lands* (Honolulu: University of Hawaii Press, 1989), p. 18.

[32]Van Notten, *The Law of the Somalis*, pp. 27, 52.

[33]*Board of Trade of City of Chicago v. Christie Grain & Stock Co.*, 198 U.S. 236 (1905).

I am fond of asking my students if they have ever "seen" or "signed" a contract, and almost all answer affirmatively. I then inform them that none of them has ever seen, or will ever see, or draft, or sign a contract, because a contract is a nonmaterial account of some presumed identical *states of mind* between or among two or more persons. While the contract, as an agreement, is real, it has no material nature to it, except as one can identify its electro-chemical constituency in the brain. But as a "thing" to be signed, or photocopied, or locked away in a safe, a contract has no physical existence. The written forms that we write up, sign, and have notarized are what lawyers themselves, often call a "memorandum of agreement," and a memorandum is generally understood to be "an informal record of something that one wishes to remember."[34] The written memorandum becomes a chattel interest, but not the agreement itself. The boundary of a contract, then, is the presumed coalescence of the states of mind of the parties agreeing to it. It is this distinction that allows courts to "reform" the written expression of the contract where drafting mistakes have occurred that do not reflect the actual intentions of the parties.

Just as we strive for as much clarity as possible in defining the boundaries of the words we employ, we try to describe our property interests with great precision. Nevertheless, boundaries are simply another information system, an abstraction of reality. As such, they are as subject to Korzybski's admonition as any of the other expressions of our mind. Still, the inherent haziness of all boundaries—particularly at the edges of what we seek to define—should not dissuade us from our efforts to make clear descriptions. We are creatures of language, and are bound to relate to and negotiate with our fellow humans through the use of words. Increased clarity in language is important in our efforts to reduce conflict. The inherent imprecision in such undertakings should, however, impress upon us the importance of a sense of humility, particularly when we are

---

[34]*Webster's Third New International Dictionary*, p. 1408.

staring across the boundaries of what we regard as ours, into the face of another.

A number of years ago, in the city in which I live, two neighbors got into a boundary dispute. One man was trimming a hedge along the property line separating their respective lands. The second man thought the first was trimming rose bushes that were on his side of the boundary line. It is not clear whether this was so or not but, if true, it would have amounted to a trespass. What is clear is that, in a flash of anger, one man pushed the other to the ground, which was a trespass (battery) upon the man so attacked. The man who had been pushed called the police and had his neighbor arrested for criminal assault. The man, so charged, was later found guilty and given a fine. The man who had been pushed to the ground organized a neighborhood party to celebrate the conviction of the attacker, at which the attacker showed up with a rifle and shot a number of the revelers, killing some.

While one can find a number of boundary trespasses in this incident, including the killings, and while an insistence upon one's inviolability is a worthy stance to take, the more important lesson for both men—as well as the neighbors—would have been to be a bit more humble in insisting upon the micro-measured specificity of their respective boundaries. Perhaps, if we can learn to have respect for one another's ownership interests, we can also learn to more easily tolerate the errors and miscalculations of others.

Boundaries express both the divisions that separate us from one another, as well as the respect for our separatism that minimizes the conflict that would otherwise result therefrom. As such, boundaries represent a paradox that disguises deeper patterns of harmonizing truth. It is not just our ideas or motives that inject a sense of differentiation among us, but the entropic nature of our existence. Each of us must be able to exclude others from the use and consumption of resources necessary for our survival. This fact of nature includes the ability to consume other living things. Perhaps in being sensitive to the fact that what we have in common are our individual needs for negentropic behavior, we may discover why respecting one another's boundaries may be the only peaceful—and most productive—way of resolving this dilemma.

It is well to remember the dualistic nature of property boundaries. When respected, individuals will be free not only from the trespasses of others, but to do as they will, regarding what is theirs. When disrespected, however, conflict and violence ensue and liberty is diminished. We should also heed Fritz Perls's warnings about the potential for disputes to arise along boundary lines. If we fail to pay attention to the conflict-generating implications of our actions, we may find ourselves in deadly conflicts even as we go about trimming our rose bushes.

Chapter Five
Claim: The Will to Own

Private property began the instant somebody had a mind of his own.

— e.e. cummings

aving considered the *physical* nature of property, our attention now turns to its *social* implications. Contrary to the assumptions of our politically conditioned thinking, is it possible for a system of privately owned property to maximize, without contradiction or conflict, both individual *liberty* and societal *order*? Why do such forms of entropy as victimizing crime, political oppression, and the unintended injuries we inflict upon one another, ultimately reduce themselves to conflicts over property? To explore such questions, we must look at the interplay of the two elements of property that are rarely understood, even in our materialistic, industrialized culture: the *claim* of ownership to, and the exercise of *control* over those interests we call "property." To comprehend the meaning and importance of these concepts is to understand how respect for the inviolability of our lives and other property interests is what human liberty and social order are all about, and why all political systems are at war with individuals concerning these factors.

The element of "claim" is the most philosophically controversial feature of property ownership. This is because all property, in order to be owned, must be claimed by someone, whether they be *private* persons (e.g., an individual, a corporation) or a *political* entity (e.g., the state). To claim ownership is to assert a right to decision-making control over an item of property. But, contrary to our materialistic assumptions, a claim of ownership does not involve our relationship to an item of property (e.g., a car) but to our *neighbor* concerning that item of property. Which of us will have the authority to decide the use—or even the destruction—of the car? Upon examination, the idea of having a relationship with your house, or car, or a painting, borders on silliness. It is to others that our claims are directed, something we would not need to do if we were the only human being on earth.

Because property ownership is a social concept, a consideration of the claim element must begin within the context of societal definitions and practices. A claim of ownership is the assertion of one's will, addressed to others, to be the exclusive decision-maker over oneself or some resource; to have what one claims be immune from trespasses by other persons.

Political and other social systems are defined by how property is owned within them. Every political system owes its existence to some degree of collective claim over property, for each form of government is only a variation on the theme of how authority over property is to be exercised by the state. The claim element is murky for one major reason: the state could not exist in an environment that recognized an unrestrained right of private ownership. Politics is unthinkable without property trespasses and takings. For the sake of their very survival, political systems must convince us that "property rights are not absolute." On the other hand, the authority of the state to define the limits of our ownership interests *is* regarded as absolute! As we shall discover, *all* property interests are, by the nature of ownership, absolute, it being only a matter of determining whether individuals or the state will have the ultimate claim of authority.

Feudalism is a politically structured system of land owner-ship, wherein all feudal lands are ultimately owned by a ruler—such as a king—who grants rights to such lands in exchange for continuing duties and services (e.g., participation in fighting wars, which was that system's principal purpose).

In a *communist* system, the state nationalizes the ownership claims of all the means of production. Other factions of state *socialism* part company with the Marxists over the question of what types of privately owned property are to be brought under state ownership (e.g., steel mills, mines, or railroads, as opposed to small farms or retail shops). In each of these sys-tems, the state confiscates both the "title" (i.e., legally recog-nized ownership interest) and the "control" (i.e., effective deci-sion-making power) of the property in question.

Welfare state systems operate on the premise that a portion of private property will be confiscated from its owners, through taxation, and redistributed to others whom the state chooses as beneficiaries of such programs, be they "poor" persons or "rich" corporations.

Under a system of *fascism*, the title to property remains in private hands, but the state exercises actual decision-making authority (i.e., *control*) over the use of such property.[1]

This helps to explain why increasing numbers of people cor-rectly intuit that there are no fundamental differences among major political parties: at their core, each embraces the authority of the state to regulate how property will be owned and used. That the modern neo-conservative movement has been greatly

---

[1]One dictionary offers this definition of "fascism": "the retention of pri-vate ownership of the means of production under centralized governmental control" *Webster's New Universal Unabridged Dictionary*, 2nd ed. (New York: New World Dictionaries/Simon and Schuster, 1983), p. 665; while an econom-ics dictionary defines "fascism" as "In its economic aspects, a plan by which the institution of private property and the private production of goods and services is retained, but is made subject to extensive control by government." Harold S. Sloan and Arnold J. Zurcher, *A Dictionary of Economics*, 4th ed. (New York: Barnes & Noble, Inc., 1961), p. 126.

influenced, if not dominated, by socialists and ex-Marxists,[2] dramatically illustrates the collectivist nature of all political systems. To the extent that James Burnham's "managerial state"— or the modern "corporate state"—has supplanted political ideologies, the scope of its power is nonetheless measured in terms of control over property. Collectivism is a generic concept, not restricted to partisan usage of either the "Left" or "Right." Since control is the very essence of ownership, one can begin to understand how disingenuous it is to pose "socialism" and "fascism" as polar opposites along a continuum. Each system involves a coercive taking of private ownership, a truth not lost on Adolf Hitler who gave the name "National Socialist German Workers Party"—or "National Socialism"—to his fascist regime.

By contrast, a *stateless* society is one in which the ownership and control of property remains in the hands of individuals or voluntarily-constituted associations.

Because every political system is grounded in certain assumptions about how property is to be owned and controlled, how we resolve the claim question tells us whether our lives are to be *individually* or *collectively* directed. This, in turn, defines the extent of personal liberty in a given society. To the degree control over property is *decentralized* among individuals, we can be said to have a free society while, conversely, a society in which such authority is *centralized* in the state is, to that degree, a nonfree society. Liberty, then, is defined not in terms of how much *property* you own, but how much *authority* you exercise over what you do own.

At this point, collectivists can be expected to object to any individual's claim of ownership. Citing Proudhon's self-contradictory phrase that "property is theft,"[3] they would interject a presumed collective claim on behalf of all mankind. But what is the historic or principled basis for such a claim? Given the diversity of preferences, tastes, values, and other interests

---

[2]See, e.g., Justin Raimondo, *Reclaiming the American Right* (Burlingame, Calif.: Center for Libertarian Studies, 1993).

[3]Pierre-Joseph Proudhon, *Qu'est-ce que la propriete* (1840).

that distinguish one person from another, is it conceivable for an abstract "mankind" to express a common will concerning the employment of resources? If it is, is there any evidence that a collective humanity has ever asserted a prior claim to such resources and, if so, against whom was such a claim addressed? Upon what basis can those who exercise political authority allegedly on behalf of such a collective will be assured that they know of what that common understanding consists? Does this proposition amount to anything more than a preference for *collective* thinking—upon which all political-systems depend—over *individual* behavior? This is a topic to which we shall return in chapter nine.

An analysis of the claim of ownership question begins with the most basic of inquiries: do you own yourself? Because of the central importance that the question of self-ownership has to an understanding not only of property, but to the nature of a free and peaceful society, the first case I have my students read for their first day of law school is *Dred Scott v. Sandford*.[4] Scott challenged his legal status as a slave on the grounds that when Congress enacted a statute prohibiting slavery in the Northwest territories, he had obtained his freedom when his master took him into that region. The United States Supreme Court refused his claim in part on the grounds that he was not a "person"—and thus could not seek redress in the courts—but remained the "property" of his master, an ownership interest that could not be lost by a person taking his property from one state into another.

This case has far more profound meaning than its racial implications, going to the question of whether the state should be in the position of conferring legally recognized "person-hood" upon human beings. Self-ownership and other private property principles have long been denied by governmental regulation of transactions among people. In 1861, Henry Maine addressed this problem in an essay concerning the locus of authority for determining the sources of the rights and duties

---

[4]*Dred Scott v. Sandford*, 61 U.S. (19 How.) 393 (1857).

of individuals.[5] Were such matters to be decreed by traditional, family-based definitions, or by agreements entered into by individuals? Maine characterized such rights and obligations as deriving either from "status" (e.g., family birth order, gender, caste) or from freely-negotiated "contracts," adding that "the movement of the progressive societies has hitherto been a movement from *Status* to *Contract*."[6] By this, he meant that, historically, the determination of one's rights and obligations had moved away from legally defined *status* to those based upon voluntary *contracts*.

While Maine focused on family-generated expectations in his discussion of "status," these competing concepts also apply to politically-imposed versus individually bargained-for relationships. To illustrate the point: a legal system may prohibit married women or minors from owning property or entering into contracts on their own behalf. This is not because such persons had *agreed* to such arrangements, but because they were *imposed* upon them by virtue of their legally-defined "status" (i.e., "married woman," or "minor"). A legal system operating upon such principles is, to the extent of such imposed restraints, *status-based*. On the other hand, if these same individuals are able to freely bind themselves, their rights would reflect a *contract-based* system. Minimum wage laws, rent control ordinances, and government mandated product standards, are a few more examples of how status-based rights conflict with those freely contracted for by employers and employees, landlords and tenants, or retailers and customers.

Dred Scott was challenging the practice of state-conferred "status" that defined him as the property of another instead of recognizing his claim to be an owner. From its very inception, this nation's history has been characterized by a profound disrespect for claims of self-ownership. The institution of slavery and the despoiling of the lives, lands, and cultures of many

---

[5]Sir Henry Maine, *Ancient Law,* 10th ed. (New York: Henry Holt and Company, 1884).

[6]Ibid., p. 165; emphasis in original.

American Indians, represent a form of entropy that our society has still not managed to work out of its system. While such practices have been attributed to racist inclinations—which is certainly true—what has been overlooked in the assessment of such brutalities was the implicit denial of the principle of self-ownership. While almost all thoughtful men and women now condemn these earlier practices, there has been little awakening to the importance of asserting the case for self-ownership. To the extent that we deny our own self-ownership, we have not ended slavery, but only redefined it. By subjecting our lives to the control and management of institutional authorities—particularly the state—we have done little more than transfer our allegiances to new masters. Since the ability to overcome entropy is essential to survival, and since external resources are the only means available to any living thing trying to overcome entropy, state control of any sort has anti-life implications.

How you answer the self-ownership question has profound implications, for control over your life will be exercised by someone, be it you or another. If you are unwilling to assert a claim to your own life, you can be assured that there are others who are prepared to do so in order to further their interests. The question of whether *you* or the *state* is to have the ultimate control over your life underlies most political and legal issues.

While there are no objectively "right" or "wrong" answers to the self-ownership question, there are consequences that flow from how we answer it. How the question gets resolved—or whether it even gets asked—goes to the essence of what is meant by a claim of self-ownership: the assertion of one's will to have exclusive power and control over one's life. As we explore this question, we get a sense of how deeply it cuts into our lives—whether we think of ourselves as self-controlling, and, therefore, self-responsible individuals, or as subjugated and dependent members of an undifferentiated mass.

Social conflict arises out of a sense that one's interests have been trespassed by another. As we have seen, the extent of our ownership interests is defined by the boundaries of what we claim. Since it is not an expression of our liberty to transgress the boundaries of others, our decision-making authority necessarily ends at our boundary lines. If each of us confined our actions to what is ours to own and control, conflict with others would cease. This is why *peace* and *liberty* are compatible only when considered within the self-limiting context of property ownership. Can we imagine a violent act that is not a trespass to some property interest? Can we imagine a peaceful act that is a trespass? Only when each of us enjoys an absolute authority to determine what we will and will not do with what is ours—insisting upon the boundary line that assures both our inviolability by others and confining the reach of our own actions—will we enjoy what political systems deny: a community of mutually self-respecting men and women.

It may be easy to agree with such an idea when it is offered only as an abstract proposition. How such a concept plays itself out in a social setting, however, is dependent upon whether, and under what circumstances, any of us can assert a property claim that others are bound to respect. Does the urban gang member whose sense of territorial integrity is violated by another gang's graffiti have a property claim that should be honored and, if so, by whom? Along related lines, is an offense to one's "ego-boundary" identity, such as in the uttering of a racial slur, or the burning of his or her nation's flag, or denying the existence of a god to a religious person, worthy of being considered a trespass or, in the alternative, should such acts be respected as the behavior of a property owner? What about a local retailer who resents a competitor moving into "his" neighborhood and attracting away "his" customers? How free, peaceful, productive, and orderly would a society be if property claims were not considered inviolable, but could be taken from the owner by force? In order to answer such questions, how do we assess the basis of one another's claims of ownership? Is there a principle to which we can resort that rises higher than the childish refrain "I want what I want when I want it?"

In a culture that dotes on material values, the "claim" element appears to have mystical qualities. It has certainly been the most difficult concept for my students to fathom. But there is nothing any more mysterious about human beings proclaiming themselves to be the owners of things than there is for wolves to urinate, birds to sing, or elk to bellow *their* respective territorial claims. While the "right" of individuals to acquire and maintain control over property has been articulated by numerous "natural rights" advocates, the claim element does not depend upon ideological commitments. The need of all living things to occupy space and ingest energy from their external world offers an adequate explanation, and justification, for their assertion of exclusive interests in property. Because we are social beings who can sustain ourselves only by the individual consumption of resources, the property principle is at the core of our well-being.

Another basic question relates to *what it is that may be owned.* Over what may I make a claim of ownership? Do I own my children? My pet animals? My organs once they have been removed from my body? My thoughts? My reputation in my community, such that I should be able to maintain libel or slander actions against those who make false statements about me? May I own another human being and, if you answer "no," upon what is your response based?

Thomas Pynchon has stated that, "If they can get you asking the wrong questions, they don't have to worry about answers."[7] It has been our failure to ask relevant questions that has generated so much confusion in our thinking. This is evident from the question: do we own our children? If we answer "yes," we are left in the uncomfortable position of acknowledging the right of a parent to do whatever he or she wants with their child, regardless of the degree of harm involved. Because ownership is manifested in decision-making control, the owner (i.e., the parent) is free to do anything with that property interest, so long as it doesn't involve a trespass on another person's property interests. Brutal beatings of the child, or even taking its life, would seem justified if, indeed, the parent is the owner.

---

[7]Thomas Pynchon, *Gravity's Rainbow* (New York: Penguin Books, 1987), p. 251.

On the other hand, if you answer "no" to this question, how do you respond to the person who insists on taking "your" child away from you for their own purposes? What if a neighbor used candy to persuade your child to come live with him: if you do *not* own this child, what claim would you have to regain your custody?

What if we rephrased the question to read: "do you have a property interest in an exclusive decision-making *relationship* with your child?" In much the same way that a husband and wife, or an employer and an employee, have property interests in contractual associations with one another, a parent could be said to have a property interest in a continuing relationship with the child. The parent does not *own* the child—any more than an employer owns an employee—but has an inviolable interest in raising and caring for the child, at least until he or she has developed to the point of being able to exercise self-control.

Our culture retains so many after-effects of the vulgar practice of slavery that we tend to answer with a reflexive "no" to the question of whether or not we can own another human being. But let us consider the matter more analytically. Slavery has existed in so many cultures throughout the world and over such prolonged periods of time that we need more than moral outrage to react to the practice. Using a property-based analysis, the principal criticism of slavery rests on its denial of an individual's claim to self-ownership.

It may be argued that a particular slave made no claim to self-ownership and, therefore, no property violation had occurred as to him. Such a contention, however, overlooks the fact that few of us have ever expressed such a claim. This argument presumes a claim to rest on a *formal* declaration, whereas such should be inferred from the autonomous, self-directed nature of one's actions. That force may be resorted to by others—including the state—to secure our participation in their undertakings, is an implicit recognition of a claim to immunity from trespass having to be overcome by threats of violence.

Once an ownership interest has attached to any item, including ourselves, a respect for property claims requires those of us who wish to make use of such property to secure, by contract, the right to do so. Thus, if I am a respecter of property claims, and I would like Smith to come to work for me, I would need to secure a claim to his services from his present owner, Smith. To try to force him into my service, without his consent, would be to take his property interest by an act of *theft*, rather than respecting the property interest of the claimant. Such are the implications of Maine's important distinction between legal rights premised on "status" as opposed to "contract."

Likewise, if I desire to exercise some control over your property, such as using your land for some limited purpose, I may purchase from you, by contract, a portion of your authority, as an owner, to exclude me. This is why governmental takings, whether through eminent domain, taxation, conscription, asset forfeiture, or other involuntary means, amount to acts of plunder: the owner's claim is not contracted for by the state. It is also why those who characterize a contract of employment as "wage slavery" do a great disservice to the need for clarity in our use of words. Those who do not know the difference between a coercive system of involuntary servitude, and a voluntary system of contractual employment, deserve to find out.

Can we claim ownership over other living things, such as animals? The animal-rights advocates would answer "no," declaring that nonhuman creatures are as entitled to their lives and self-control as are we. But why limit such protections to animals? What about *vegetables*, or *viruses* (are they living microorganisms, or chemical agents?)? If we extend coverage to all living things, upon what shall we feed in order to reduce entropy in our lives and survive? The need for living things to survive at the expense of other living things, effectively destroys the so-called "natural rights" and "animal rights" arguments. After all, if we acknowledge all living things to have "rights" to their lives, each of us would have to content ourselves with such limited food sources as milk, beans, unfertilized eggs, fruits, nuts, and seeds—and only then until someone else came along to remind us that these products of living things are also life forms entitled to protection.

Life, as we know it, is both carbon-based and contains DNA, meaning that even what we might regard as the lowest form of life is a distant cousin of each of us. As we came to understand that the entire universe is alive, including the subatomic particles that exhibit so much of what appears to be free will, we would even have to give up these food sources. If human beings, or any other species, actually tried living by such a premise, it would not be for long. They would face starvation, as such restrictions on food sources could not provide enough protein to support many people.

Restricting the sense of personhood to humans, alone, does find support in the behavior of other species, which may suggest a genetic basis for such a distinction. This is why the insistence, by other life forms, on respect for territorial boundaries tends to be confined to members of the same species, ignoring the intrusions of members of other species. For the lioness to respect the personhood of the aforesaid wildebeest would be as fatal to the lioness as it would be to the wildebeest making the same concession to the grasses. This might suggest to us a biological basis for our exclusion of nonhumans from the "rights" equation.[8]

Whether or not we continue to have an ownership interest in our bodily organs, once removed from our bodies, is answerable in the same way as any other item of property in which we are no longer in possession. If I have a claim to the ownership of my car, do I lose it to a thief simply because, at the time he took it, I was not in control of it? Or, if a repairman removes the CD player from my car to work on it, have I lost my ownership interest in the player? The answer to this question necessitates our revisiting the "boundary" element, as well as going to the very essence of what is meant by a claim of ownership.

---

[8]The animal-rights position suffers from another major flaw which its advocates tend to overlook. If other animals have "rights," are they also entitled to vote in elections and hold office? Would "separate but equal" treatment be acceptable to our modern thinking? Would a nuisance judgment against a neighbor whose dog barked incessantly amount to a violation of the dog's First Amendment rights?

"Ownership" is not the same as "possession." The latter amounts to being in physical control of an item, while the former is based upon the assertion of one's will over the item. It is the owner's sense of *personality*—not his or her physical power—that attaches to the item as a claim of ownership. While a claim may include a right to possession—unless that right has been contracted away by the owner, as in a landlord-tenant relationship—it transcends a mere possessory interest. This is why, when we speak of purchasing property from another, we are not buying the "property," but the owner's *claim* to the property.

Every contract amounts to nothing more than an agreement, by two or more property owners, to transfer their respective claims of property ownership to one another. The property involved may be realty, a chattel, an intangible interest (e.g., a copyright), or one's personal services. If you and I enter into an agreement by which I am to sell you my car for $5,000, I am promising to do more than provide you with possession of the automobile: I am agreeing to convey my ownership claim to the car, just as you are agreeing to transfer your ownership claim to the $5,000. Thus, if I have not transferred, or abandoned, my claim to the ownership of any item of property of mine—be it a removed organ, or my car, or a CD player—I have not lost my ownership interest in any of such items.

The continuing recognition by others of an owner's claim even when he or she is no longer in possession, is a rather sophisticated practice. Other life forms do not seem to exhibit this trait. It is an attitude that is essential to any complex, long-term system of economic production and exchange. A hunting-and-gathering society, for instance, might not have need for such a principle. If an owner's being out of possession was an invitation for others to take control of his interests, significant investment in either the creation or employment of tools would be unlikely to occur.

This is not to disparage possessory interests in property. One who possesses the property of another, whether rightfully or wrongfully obtained, has a sufficient ownership interest that the courts will protect against anyone other than a person with a superior claim. There have even been cases in which *thieves* have been able to recover their stolen property from another thief,[9] the rationale being that a man who has been forcibly deprived of a possessory interest might not always be able to prove his right to same, providing wrongdoers with a field day for expropriation. The legal doctrine that possession gives a presumption of ownership that another claimant must overcome—the basis of the popular saying that "possession is nine points of the law"—is intended to prevent the disorder that would arise from property interests being taken by force.

This is why, other than forced takings by the state, an act of theft does not deprive an owner of his or her legally recognized claim. Only a willful act by which the owner no longer chooses to be an owner can accomplish this. Apart from state takings, the common law courts have taken a fairly consistent position: one does not lose his or her ownership claim by silence or inaction. An owner must make a conscious choice to either *sell* the claim (for consideration), or make a *gift* of it (without consideration), or *abandon* it. Even the concept of "adverse possession" has been rationalized by the courts as either an "abandonment" of ownership by the record owner, or the product of a "lost grant," either of which would explain the prior owner's longstanding disinterest in the land.

We abandon our claims to property with far greater frequency than either selling or giving them away. We make a daily habit of abandoning our property claims through the practice of disposing of "garbage" (i.e., unwanted claims). We purchase a grocer's ownership claim to a bottle of soda, drink the beverage, then throw the empty bottle—and our claim thereto—into a trash container, which my students learn to define as a "claim abandonment center." We engage in this practice with such frequency that, once a week, trash collectors come through our neighborhoods to collect our abandoned property claims and transport them to dumpsites (i.e., larger claim abandonment

---

[9]See, e.g., *Anderson v. Gouldberg*, 51 Minn. 294, 53 N.W. 636 (1892).

centers). In the language of chaos, we can think of trash containers and dumpsites as "attractors" for the disposal of property claims.

While we are unable to transfer more than what we own to others, we may transfer *lesser* amounts of our total claims. In such a case, we reconfigure the boundaries of our property interests so as to conform to what we are transferring and retaining. Thus, a woman who owns a parcel of land in "fee simple absolute" (i.e., the highest estate, free of any limitations) may convey a lesser interest, such as a "life estate", and retain a "reversion" in herself. The redefined claims would, if combined, recreate the original fee simple absolute interest. The land, itself, would reveal no transformation to an observer by virtue of such a conveyance, reminding us that it is not the physical property that is being transferred, but only the claim of ownership.

In each of these examples, the owner is expressing his or her *will* to no longer be a claimant—or a sole claimant—to an item of property. In anticipation of death, we then arrange for the disposition of our ownership claims through a document we call our "last will." In it, we proclaim to exercise our "last will" over what we own by having our claims transferred, upon death, to various designated persons.

Having explored this issue, a number of other questions arise: how will this claim of ownership be established? To whom is the claim addressed? May one properly assert a claim of ownership over property presently claimed by another and, if not, why not? Over what may I claim an ownership interest? There are four principal means that have been employed to answer such questions: the formal *legal* means, the *philosophical* means, the *biological* means, and the informal *social* means.

From the perspective of a legal positivist, a recognizable claim is defined by whatever criteria the formal political/legal system recognizes and defends through state enforcement (e.g., judicial action). This approach constitutes what most of us regard as our "rights" in any matter (i.e., whatever the government considers our rights to be). At any given point in time, the existing political system has determined who would and who would not be entitled to assert a legally-recognizable claim to the ownership of a property interest. Slaves were denied their claims of self-ownership and were, in fact, determined by the formal legal system to be the property of their masters. The American Indian tribes' claims to the ownership of their lands were legally invalid because the political/legal system did not choose to recognize them. Likewise, there was a time when males could rightfully claim ownership of property, but married women could not. Upon her marriage, a woman's property claim automatically transferred, as a matter of law, to her husband, yet another example of Maine's "status" defined rights. Other would-be property claimants, e.g., minors, persons lacking mental capacity, et. al., continue to be denied legal ownership rights because of the refusal of the state's legal structure to recognize them. There has been a continuing political jockeying for a redefinition of these categories (e.g., the abortion issue is based on the same question as the slavery debate: is the fetus a self-owning person, or the property of the mother?), with the legal outcome turning on the age-old question: *who gets to make decisions about what?*

The principal shortcoming of a formal political definition of ownership interests lies in the coercive, conflict-ridden nature of all political systems. Contrary to our high school civics class understanding, political processes do not consist of principled or rational inquiries into the kinds of profound philosophical questions that stirred the minds of Socrates, Aristotle, Thomas Aquinas, John Locke, or John Stuart Mill. As modern experiences with violent coups, political assassinations, genocides, bloody repressions of dissent, and massive levels of warfare attest, having recourse to politics as a means of determining the "rights" of parties, is always a resort to legalized violence. Because the concept of a legal "right" derives from notions of formal state power, it necessarily implies a coercive authority to define such standards. Furthermore, the state's power to confer or deny ownership interests to anyone is always at the expense of somebody else, a somebody whose talents for mobilizing the forces of realpolitik are less developed than those of their more successful rivals. Since the state generates no property interests on its own, but can only despoil the property interests of others, and since the state has no power to confer a capacity for ownership upon any of us that was not already present within our self-seeking natures, the tendencies for political institutions to produce anything other than social conflict should be evident.

As an alternative to the legal positivist position, a number of political thinkers have advanced the idea that there are certain philosophical principles—usually spoken of in terms of "natural law"—that transcend the formal authority of the state and condition an individual's legal duty of obedience to legal mandates. John Locke made a respectable effort to formulate such a natural law explanation for the origin of individual rights to property. Beginning with the assumption that each person has a property interest in his or her self, Locke employed the "labor theory" of ownership to extend one's ownership of *self* to include the right to acquire ownership of various resources in nature. In his view, a claim of ownership arose when a person "mixed his labour" with some previously unowned resource such as land and, in so doing, incorporated his will into the property.[10] The labor theory of ownership is certainly compatible with the idea that private property is necessitated by the entropic nature of life. Since we can overcome entropy only by consuming external sources of energy, our existence depends upon the exertion of our will upon the material world.

While the natural law approach has a certain emotional and logical appeal to it—assuming one accepts its premises—it suffers from the major shortcoming of all normative thinking: how does one discover the *content* of these principles? How do we distinguish one person's identification of a transcendent "moral principle" from another person's expression of a private prejudice? Are the natural rights theorists doing anything more than projecting their subjective preferences onto the universe and

---

[10]John Locke, "Two Treatises of Government" (1690), in William Ebenstein, *Great Political Thinkers* (New York: Rinehart and Company, 2nd ed., 1956), p. 378.

then characterizing them as "eternal principles?" Do moralistic debates amount to anything more than sophisticated shouting matches for the rationalization of a speaker's biases? How do we verify that we have a natural law principle before us? Is it possible to do so without translating such ideas through our own prior experiences and thoughts? How can *normative* propositions be made subject to *empirical* proof? Furthermore, is not the insistence upon justifying liberty as an imperative emanating from "God" or "nature," simply another example of our traditional, pyramidal-based thinking that assumes our affairs to be governed by higher authorities; that our claims to immunity from coercion must be conferred by external forces?

The "natural law" theory also suffers from a failure to identify causal relationships associated with their violation. If someone speaks to me of Newton's "second law of motion," I can set up an experiment to test its validity. While one may justifiably quarrel over the propriety of speaking of *regularities* in nature as *"laws,"* one can at least identify a relatively clear cause-and-effect connection. But if I argue that I have a "natural law" right to my property, and my neighbors proceed to violate my interests, what will occur? Will the forces of nature suddenly turn upon them—perhaps by suspending the principle of gravitation —causing them to no longer be able to function in the world? And if the inviolability of my property is mandated by the laws of nature, how could my neighbors succeed in despoiling me in the first place? If their actions violated "natural law" they could not, by definition, carry out their act. The "natural law" advocates have another difficulty to overcome: given that most of the land on Earth has, throughout recent human history, been under a claim of authority from some political power—and that stateless societies today are the great exception rather than the rule—the idea that state systems are "unnatural" is rather difficult to defend. How, after all, can *anything* that happens within nature be considered to be in violation of nature's laws?

When it becomes evident that the so-called natural law or moral principles being advocated by someone just happen to coincide with the speaker's preferences, the self-serving nature of such rationalizing becomes even clearer. I say this as one who continues to be attracted to much of the thinking of Locke and other "natural law" theorists. It is not that their understanding of the importance of private property is *invalid*: quite the contrary. Human society would function much more peacefully were we to live in accordance with such principles. But having said that only confirms the subjective nature of all belief systems.

As I suggested earlier, there is little doubt in my mind that the world has an objective existence, but I can only surmise that subjectively, as an opinion derived from my experiences. My views regarding the desirability of certain social attitudes and practices are no less the product of my experiences and other subjective influence than are yours, or those of Thomas Hobbes, John Locke, or Karl Marx. That I embrace my opinions with great intensity is no justification for my regarding them as any more than deeply-held sentiments. Any attempt to elevate my opinions to the level of eternal moral truths would be but to engage in self-delusion, no matter how valid I may consider my views to be. Such efforts amount to intellectual devices for deceiving ourselves that our opinions have a ring of certainty to them. They also serve to manipulate the thinking of others in order to get them to behave as we want them to behave. At the same time, in believing that externally-derived ideas and moral philosophies are essential to living as a free individual, and that one's claim to be free from the trespasses of others must be founded upon something greater than the expression of one's will, we reinforce the sentiment that we are incomplete within ourselves; that we lack integrated wholeness. To delude ourselves that our preferences for liberty depend upon forces beyond our will is to acknowledge our fundamental unworthiness as autonomous individuals.

One of the principal debates arising out of the "legal" versus "philosophical" explanations for the origin of property rights has been whether such interests *preceded* or *followed* the establishment of governments. John Locke embraced the former proposition, while John Stuart Mill and Jeremy Bentham espoused the latter point of view. Bentham was rather succinct in stating that, "property is entirely the creature of law."[11] He then reiterated one of the central articles of faith of every legal positivist: "Before the laws, there was no property: take away the laws, all property ceases."[12] Again, we see an expression of the pyramidal model of social order: the conditions necessary for the very existence of life had to be conferred by the state! That human beings survived for hundreds of thousands of years before settling down into the agricultural communities that preceded the development of any political institutions, and that property must have existed *before* those institutions would have had anything to tax and regulate, should be apparent. Furthermore, because life itself is dependent upon the existence of property (i.e., space to occupy and resources to consume, to the exclusion of everyone else), Bentham's absurd proposition presumes that legal systems preexisted *life itself*! Thomas Hodgskin has offered one of the more poetic critiques of the view that property rights were created by governments:

> we must believe that men had naturally no right to pick up cockles on the beach, or gather berries from the hedge—no right to cultivate the earth, to invent and make comfortable clothing, to use instruments to provide more easily for their enjoyments—no right to improve and adorn their habitations—nay, no right to have habitations—no right to buy or sell, or move from place to place—till the benevolent and wise law-giver conferred all these rights on them. If the principle be true in one case it must be universally true; and, according to it, parents had no right to the love and respect of their offspring, and infants no right to draw nourishment from the breasts of their mothers, until the legislator—foreseeing, fore calculating the immense advantages to the human race of establishing the long list of rights and

[11]Jeremy Bentham, "Principles of the Civil Code," (1802) in John Bowring, ed., *The Works of Jeremy Bentham* (New York: Russell & Russell, Inc., 1962), vol. 1, p. 308.

[12]Ibid., 309.

duties which grow out of our affections, and constitute
our happiness—had established them by his decree.[13]

One recalls from the previous chapter the works of Ardrey,
Lorenz, and others regarding the sense of territoriality exhibited by other animal and plant species who, as best we can tell,
had no state apparatus to confer such "rights!" These interests—reflective of the purely physical needs for property that
all living things require for their survival—express the biological rationale for ownership. So widespread is the role of territoriality throughout nature, that one is tempted to characterize
it as a "natural law," with all the subjective baggage that such a
term entails.

As our social systems continue their divergent transformations, the question arises as to how private claims to property might be established. If state systems were no longer in a
position to confer or acknowledge ownership interests, might
another means be available for protecting such rights? How, in
other words, might our interests be protected in a society operating upon what might be thought of as a holographic model of
organization?

The variable and unpredictable nature of a world of six billion people makes it absurd for anyone to propose utopian
blueprints for humanity. I suspect that thousands of alternatives may be experimented with by different groups of people.
Still, a suggestion can be made as to one way in which some
might choose to respond in a decentralized world. In what
I would call an informal *social* means of recognizing claims
to property, a marketplace approach could be employed. In
much the same way that any economic transaction occurs,
we and our neighbors express our respective expectations of
one another regarding our claims to property. Through our
neighbors' responses to our behavior and stated intentions, we
informally seek their respect for our claims.

---

[13]Thomas Hodgskin, *The Natural and Artificial Right of Property Contrasted*
(Clifton, N.J.: Augustus M. Kelley, 1973), pp. 19–20; originally published in
1832.

Upon what basis might such claims be asserted? As with other social and economic transactions, might we not be expected to appeal to the values, preferences, beliefs, and other interests of our neighbors? For listeners of a pragmatic disposition, appeal might be had to utilitarian arguments that respect for our claims would benefit not only ourselves but also the rest of the community. For those with a legal perspective, resort might be had to common law property principles and case law. If the audience were religiously or philosophically attuned, we might insist upon our "God-given" or "natural law" right to our claims. Just as the marketplace is comprised of men and women bargaining for the buying and selling of claims to goods and services, members of a community can confer recognition for one another's respective claims to be exclusive decision-makers over some resource. The community's recognition of such a claim could be said to confer upon the claimant a "right" to the property, meaning a claim to immunity from being trespassed. The process could work in much the same way that "consensus" techniques work in such places as were discussed in chapter one. Most of us might be inclined to do so in the hope that, should some other party forcibly intrude upon our interests, our neighbors would be inclined to come to our defense.

The following hypothetical may help illustrate the social, or informal transactional approach to property claims. Suppose that twenty of us are marooned on a previously deserted island, and that I manage to locate—and lay claim to—the only source of fresh water on the island. Perhaps I erect a fence around the area I am claiming, in the expectation that those with a Lockean perspective might regard this act as a sufficient mixing of my labor with the land. Having asserted my claim, I now await your decisions as to whether to respect it or not. In an effort to persuade you to do so, I may try to rationalize my claim by appealing to what I perceive to be your religious or philosophical dispositions, or only the felt need for territory that motivates other species. Whatever argument I employ has no inherent substance to it, being important only as a sales argument designed to help convince the rest of you to acknowledge and respect my claim. Will you be likely to do so?

If you are inclined toward Locke's view, you might insist that I do more than put up a sign; that I should extend my labor to improving or preserving the water source itself. Socialists among us might deny the validity of my claim en toto, on the grounds that individual claims to productive lands ought to be denied in favor of collective ownership. An environmentalist might object to my claim, believing that my control of the fresh water supply might disturb wildlife presently living on the island. There may be a sizeable number of persons who don't care, one way or the other, whether the water should be privately or collectively owned, as long as they are assured of an adequate supply.

Whether my claim will be respected or not may depend not upon the persuasiveness of my abstract argument, but on how I behave toward the rest of you regarding the water. If I deal with the water as a valuable resource, for whose use I would be willing to make contractual exchanges—such as for food or shelter—and the rest of you perceive that I am developing and caring for this resource in a way that benefits our community,[14] my claim might well be respected by the rest of you. Should one or more of you try to forcibly dislodge me from my claim to exclusive control, the rest of you might be counted upon to help defend my interests against such an attack. Furthermore, when my claim is recognized by the rest of you—as something to which you have contributed—there is harmony generated between myself and my neighbors: the claim has not created division within the community. To the contrary, the rest of you are more likely to feel that you have a vested interest in supporting my claim because your willingness to respect it has given it strength.

---

[14] I am using the word "community" not in any political sense, but to refer to a group of individuals who regularly interact with one another in a social setting.

On the other hand, should I deny access to the water to everyone—either by an outright prohibition of its use, or by demanding an exceptionally high price for its consumption—the rest of
you would likely not respect my claim, particularly since your
lives depended upon its use. I would then experience conflict
with the rest of you—no matter how strongly I believe in the
legitimacy of my claim—and my ownership would be difficult
to maintain without a continuing confrontation with others.
Thus, if one or more of you should try to forcibly take some of
my water, it is unlikely that the rest of you would come to the
defense of my claim. If that should prove to be the case, I might
be able to defend my interests by myself—just as any of us are
free to try to satisfy all of our economic wants without trading with others. But without the support of my neighbors, the
security of my claim will never be any stronger than my level
of constant vigilance in its defense. I might have to mount a
twenty-four-hour-a-day defense of my property, which I could
likely not maintain for more than a day or so. In a short time,
my property claim would probably be overrun and, worse, I
might come to be regarded as a pariah with whom the rest of
you might choose to have no further dealings. The advantage,
to me, of behaving reasonably toward the rest of you in order
to have my claim respected, should be evident. By relying upon
the respect accorded my claim by the community, my own
time would be freed from having to maintain a constant vigil,
thus allowing me to pursue other interests and to trade, to my
benefit, with the rest of you. Such are the dynamics by which
marketplace transactions—grounded in liberty and respect for
property interests—generate individual and social well-being.
    But in the real neighborhood in which I live, why would
any of my neighbors have an interest in defending my ownership claims should my interests be threatened by a wrongdoer?
Why would they be motivated to get involved in any way? In a
world in which we have become content to allow political and
legal processes to define our interests and resolve our disputes,
we have forgotten the capacity of informal systems, such as
neighborhoods and communities, to provide for social order.

Whereas the interests of political systems are separated from those of the rest of us, within the neighborhood there tends to be an interconnectedness among neighbors, born of face-to-face relationships, that fosters mutual support and protection.

Because neighbors are less inclined to separate their interests from one another, they have a common fate in matters involving societal relationships. What this means, with respect to property questions, is that each of us has an interest in supporting those claims to property, made by our neighbors, that are consistent with the property claims we want to assert. In other words, our neighbors have an incentive to support what they perceive as our valid property claims, as a way of reinforcing the community recognition of their own claims. This is how our personal and social interests are fundamentally harmonious: respect for *my* claim depends upon my respecting *yours*. At the same time, our neighbors have a motivation to reject what they see as the invalid claim of an interloper who has ousted a recognized owner, so that the rest of the community may be inclined to come to the assistance of one who is faced with a "claim jumper." There is more than just a theoretical rationale for such practices, as early gold-mining claims in California were established in such informal agreements among neighbors.[15]The ways in which we bargain with others for recognition of our claims are not as formal as when we engage in buying a house or obtaining employment. Rather, they tend to be quite informal, a part of the socialization process that begins in infancy and continues throughout our lifetimes. Anyone who has raised children has observed their need to understand the appropriate range of their behavior. They want to discover principles that help them define the limits of their actions, and so they keep testing the boundary lines of what they may and may not do. They continue to ask us "why?" as they struggle for explanations to provide them with a rational and predictable basis for identifying these boundaries. They almost beg us

---

[15]See Shinn, *Mining Camps*, pp. 221–46.

for this information, and we often do a poor job helping *them* because we haven't discovered such principles for *ourselves*.

Children continue this negotiation process with their peers, particularly when they are at play with one another. Jean Piaget's studies of children's playgroups are most illuminating here.[16] The spontaneous and usually peaceful manner in which children informally bargain amongst themselves for the modification of rules to make a game more competitive or beneficial to all players, tells us much about ourselves that we have forgotten. Such child-directed practices should remind us of the developmental importance of allowing children to control their own play, rather than having it organized and directed by well-meaning adults who, without intending to do so, help their children learn how to be managed by others.

One expression of this informal process has arisen around ATM machines, in which people, without any formal direction, have developed the practice of standing a number of feet behind the person using the machine, so as to allow him privacy in his transaction. Contrary to the "social contract" fictions through which we fantasize the creation of massive nation-states, these informal processes have an authentic quality about them: they arise out of face-to-face dealings between and among people who may be total strangers to one another, and who bargain with the glance of an eye or the wave of a hand.

The prospect of bargaining with one's neighbors for a recognition of property interests may sound unfamiliar to most of us but, on the other hand, we must already negotiate with the formal *legal* system for a determination of such rights. When we go into a court of law, we are trying to persuade a judge to confer upon us a "right" to some legally-protected interest. Lobbyists are also employed by various interest groups in an effort to convince legislators to enact statutes that will confer desired benefits upon their clients. The question now before

---

[16]Jean Piaget and Barbel Inhelder, *The Psychology of the Child* (New York: Basic Books, 1969); Jean Piaget, *Play, Dreams and Imitation in Childhood* (New York: W.W. Norton, 1951).

us, in a decentralizing society, is whether our lives will be better served by having to deal with a representative of the state, or with our neighbors, for a determination of our interests. The process is the same in either instance: it is simply a matter of determining to which audience we wish to make our case. Our experiences with both the state and the marketplace, however, ought to apprise us as to where more abundant personal benefits and capacities to control our interests are to be found.

Some may suggest that it doesn't matter whether we are appealing to the state or to a community of our neighbors for acknowledgment of our claims, that in either event, we are relying upon the judgments of others. But social negotiation for the recognition of property claims differs from politically recognized claims in one important respect: in the former system, there is no coercive, institutionalized means of enforcing one's claim. They arise not out of a fear of being trespassed, but from the social need to relate to one another. Political systems are, by their nature, intrusive; their officials desire to advance their interests by expanding the range of their authority, an appetite that necessarily places them in conflict with our lives and property interests. Such conduct arises not from a need for genuine relationships with other persons but from the need to compress all of humanity into abstract categories so as to make them manageable for the system's societally-defined ambitions. The distinction between the marketplace-focused study of *micro*economics, and the politically-collectivized nature of *macro*economics, comes to mind.

The ultimate "bargaining" tool of the state is the threat of *violence*—which its devotees believe is the cement that holds society together. To the extent political mandates conflict with the expectations of members of the community to have their property claims respected, social discord will ensue. Over time, a politically-grounded society infects the community in destructive ways, as fear, force, confrontation, punishments, and other socially discordant practices manage to trickle down into all levels of social conduct.

By contrast, the thinking and behavior of our neighbors—
when they are not organized politically—tend to be more
conciliatory and respectful of one another's interests. Vol-
untariness, negotiation, and cooperation, practices that are
reflective of mutual respect for one another's inviolability
become disseminated throughout a community of people
who regard themselves as *neighbors* rather than *citizens*. As
with other transactions in the marketplace, there is no assur-
ance of a sufficient support among one's neighbors on behalf
of one's claim. Some may choose to acknowledge the claim,
and some may not. But in a non-politicized setting, such as
one sees among the Amish, for example, the refusal to respect
another's claim is more likely to be expressed in terms of
a withholding of respect, or of ostracism, neither of which
involves a trespassory intrusion upon the life or property of
the other. We may not be able to count on the support of all
our neighbors, but, unlike our experiences with the state, we
will be less likely to have to fear their violent intrusions upon
us.

It is such lack of general support that bothers many people,
who look to the state to provide through its judiciary, consistent and standardized enforcement for such claims. But political definitions, and enforcement, of claims fosters a uniformity
of thought and behavior whose standardizing influences, as
we have seen, may prove to be detrimental to the well-being of
both individuals and civilizations. As with marketplace transactions in general, decentralized rules of conduct—as negotiated
within contracts—are more suited to the diversity of behavior
inherent in individual tastes and preferences.

Because we are so accustomed to thinking of our "rights"
as some fixed set of objectively-defined categories—rather than
a plea for our subjective preferences that we try to get others
to respect—we are uncomfortable considering that they may
derive from the same processes as our economic interests. Just
as we are able to satisfy our demands in the marketplace without the participation of everyone else, the strength of our property claims depends only upon enough of our neighbors being

willing to respect and support such claims. In the same way that our neighbors help to determine the prices of goods and services in economic transactions, they also determine the value of our property claims by the intensity of their willingness to recognize them. I have no "natural law" right to insist upon your goods or services, no matter how important to my interests I may regard them. In order to obtain such a right, I must negotiate with you. That such a transactional approach is consistent with human history is confirmed by anthropologist E. Adamson Hoebel, who observed:

> although an individual may be the possessor of some valued object, . . . that object does not become property until the members of the society agree, tacitly or explicitly, to bestow the property attribute upon the object by regulating their behavior with respect to it in a self-limiting manner.[17]

The idea of negotiating with our neighbors for a definition of our respective rights—rather than relying upon the state for such a determination—is no more implausible than the established practice of negotiating in the marketplace for our economic interests, instead of having the state make such decisions on our behalf.

Those who insist upon a politically-based structuring of property rights, out of a sense that formal, legal standards will be more certain, should be aware that state enforcement of claims is anything *but* consistent in either defining the criteria for claims, or applying such standards to a given set of facts. The state does not resolve the problem of inconstant support for property claims. For example, a court of law that laid down a principle recognizing A's right to divert water from a river onto his land, might have its opinion reversed on appeal. Or, this principle might be overturned, years later, by another court, or be repealed by a statute enacted by the legislature. All that

---

[17]E. Adamson Hoebel, *The Law of Primitive Man* (New York: Atheneum, 1968), p. 58.

political enforcement adds to the recognition of claims is the coercive backing of the state to protect the claimant. While the property owners who benefit from such protection are happy over the result, those whose claims were denied by such decisions are upset. It is simplistic to believe that a political determination of rights assures any consensus or uniformity as to the propriety of such claims.

Nor ought we to forget that many troublesome practices in our society, including the defense of slavery, the denial of land claims acquired from Indian tribes, and the abortion issue, have been grounded in the formal, legal definition of property claims in spite of varying degrees of public controversy regarding the propriety of such holdings. Those who are inclined to celebrate the virtues of legal positivism should recall that the atrocities of Nazi Germany and the Soviet Union were carried out pursuant to legally defined criteria and mandates. We too often assume, to our later regret, that state enforcement of values and the protection of interests will necessarily and permanently result in our values and interests being upheld.

The same process of social negotiation takes place in our adult relationships with family members, friends, neighbors, work colleagues, or total strangers. We negotiate with one another for space on freeways, elevators, or checkout lines in grocery stores; we assert claims upon those who try to crowd into a line at a movie theater, or whose cell-phone rings during an operatic performance. We usually find it sufficient to enforce our demands with little more than a glance that conveys to the other person the message that he or she has transgressed some established social norm.

We learn so much about ourselves from the responses others have to us. We know, also, the psychological problems experienced by persons who are kept in isolation. Sociopaths (e.g., serial killers, terrorists) are frequently described by neighbors as "loners." Perhaps by living in isolation, such people have not maintained sufficient, continuing negotiations with others that will help them identify the boundary lines of proper behavior. We may also wonder whether the state's efforts to expand the range of regulations over our lives, both as children and as adults, short-circuits these negotiating processes. When the propriety of our conduct is defined *not* by transactions we personally conduct with others, but by rules coercively imposed by institutional authorities, we may become socially isolated from one another, members of what David Riesman termed "the lonely crowd."[18]

Many of our social difficulties arise from our failure to understand the importance of insisting upon the inviolability of both our *own* and others' ownership claims, an attitude into which we are conditioned from early childhood on by repeated admonitions against "selfishness." The pursuit of self-interest is the fundamental nature of all living beings, and yet we have been taught to deny this characteristic, a lesson that fosters an inner conflict that gets projected into our social relationships. We have been trained to put aside our personal interests and cooperate with others, unaware that true cooperation can occur only among people who respect one another's inviolability. As marketplace economics continues to demonstrate, it is in our respective self-interest to cooperate with one another, a truth whose broader implications have been explored in Robert Axelrod's study illustrating the beneficial strategies of cooperation.[19]

My youngest daughter witnessed an interesting example of this complementary interplay of selfishness and cooperation, with respect for property claims providing the catalyst. She was helping at a party for young children when she saw a small boy, between two and three years of age, playing with some toys of his own that he had brought to the party. A small girl was attracted to these toys, and when she reached out for them the boy grabbed the toys and said "mine!" The boy's father, who was seated nearby, assured his son that "you don't have

---

[18]David Riesman, with Nathan Glazer and Reuel Denney, *The Lonely Crowd* (New Haven, Conn.: Yale University Press, 1950).

[19]Robert Axelrod, *The Evolution of Cooperation* (New York: Basic Books, 1984).

to share your toys if you don't want to; they are your toys and you can do what you want with them. It's up to you." The little girl wandered away and began playing by herself. A few minutes later, this boy took his toys over to the girl, sat down and began placing them in front of her, and the two started playing together.

I cannot know what the boy might have been thinking, but I suspect that, being secure in the recognition of his own claim of ownership, he had nothing to fear from sharing his toys with the girl. There was no separation, no contradiction between the boy's *ownership* and his *authority* over his property. Contrast this example with that of so many children who, after having been browbeaten by their parents into not being selfish, can only clutch or hide their toys from others in an effort to protect the property interests that others have not respected. When we are allowed to express our self-interest, we are more willing to share; when we are compelled to share, our resentment intensifies into conflict-ridden greediness.

I mentioned this incident in one of my seminars, and a woman student of mine said: "I'd have whacked the little boy across his backside for not sharing," an attitude that doubtless reflected her own upbringing. Other students immediately responded, pointing out that (a) such an act would have interfered with the boy's ownership interest, and (b) the boy did eventually share his toys with the girl, voluntarily, without feeling resentment at having been forced to do so. The first student then said: "but if he was going to share, anyway, how would it have hurt to force him to do what he eventually did?" I asked her if she saw any fundamental difference between "rape" and "seduction," which seemed to make the point clearer. The assumption, in her remarks, was that the *result* was all that mattered; not recognizing that the *process* leading to the result is not only what truly matters, but in a world of wholeness, *is* the result.

The incident involving these two young children provides a microcosmic illustration of our basic nature: we are social beings who have a fundamental need for cooperation with one another. But the price of our cooperation is in knowing that we have nothing to lose in doing so. As the experience of this young boy teaches us, what we really expect from having our property claims respected is not so much the exclusion of others from the use of what we regard as ours, but only to have others acknowledge the inviolability of our sense of personhood. When we are able to freely negotiate our interests and differences with one another, we retain the power over our lives that which is lost when the state intervenes. Each of us, I suspect, is far more amenable to cooperate and compromise with others when we are approached peacefully and with respect for our being, than we are when confronted with threats of force and violence.

To claim personal ownership of anything is to express a sense of existential worthiness one expects others to respect. It is to assert to the rest of the world a claim to something of far greater significance than a given item of property, namely, one's inviolability. It is a claim to have the self-interested and self-directed nature of our being acknowledged by others, as we endeavor to sustain ourselves through the exercise of autonomous control over some portion of the world. It amounts to an insistence upon our rightful authority to exclude all others from making decisions about the use of such property interests unless consented to by the owner.

The spiritual undertones to this inquiry into the question of self-ownership go to the essence of how we conceive of human life. Is it the nature of life to express itself as variation, diversity, autonomy, and spontaneity, or as permanence, uniformity, and restraint? Is each one of us a sufficient reason for being, for pursuit of our own individual purposes; or are we simply resources for others to employ in furtherance of their self-interested objectives? Do we regard one another's lives as having a fundamental sanctity, a respect essential to any decent and peaceful society, or do we look upon each other, mechanistically and materially, as only so much protoplasm to be exploited for our purposes?

As important as our industrial and commercial productivity has been to our *physical* well-being, it has been of little significance in satisfying our inner needs for *spiritual* fulfillment. We have learned to accept monetarily-defined values as a substitute for *transcendent* ones, and are no longer aware that we gave up the latter for the former. It is little wonder that, in our world of material comforts and resplendent wealth, so many of us confront an inner bankruptcy.

Despite the foot-dragging of socialists to admit to the fact, mankind has figured out how to maximize human well-being. The empirical record of performance by free-market economic systems, compared with the stultifying consequences of state-socialism, has resolved the pragmatic question of how best to satisfy our material needs. As thoroughly as the heliocentric model replaced the geocentric one, socialism retains its viability only within the minds of ideologues. Indeed, I suspect that it is our having answered the pragmatic material question that is giving rise to an examination of our inner, spiritual sense of being. Who are we?

Are we little more than organic matter to be fed, watered, and maintained so as to remain serviceable to others, or is each of us an expression of a more encompassing life force, a sacred center that is nonetheless *ubiquitous*? Our claim to self-ownership, in its fullest meaning, is the assertion of our will to become and remain spontaneous and autonomous in our individual efforts to discover and experience transcendence. Such an intuitive sense of awareness will not arise out of the mouthing of new platitudes, but requires the integration of our outer and inner being. Stoicism provides a necessary reminder of the importance of listening to the voices that speak to us from deep within, but it is not sufficient for living the transcendent life. One will never find a sense of wholeness in a fragmented life, wherein either the material or spiritual become subordinated to one another. To dissolve the boundaries that separate such expressions requires us to insist upon the inviolability of our claim to a place in the world.

There are others, of course—most notably those in control of political institutions—who regard the rest of us not as self-justifying, autonomous beings, but as resources to be exhausted on behalf of *their* interests. In order to overcome our self-interested nature, they have helped condition us in the alleged virtue of being "selfless"—of placing the interests of *others* ahead of our own. Political systems, organized religions, and ideologies, have been the principal exponents of this pernicious and demeaning doctrine. A friend of mine told me that he had been lecturing his young son on the importance of this belief: "we are here to serve others," he informed the boy. The father was awakened to the absurdity of such a proposition by his son's asking: "then what are *other* people here for?"

Trying to harmonize the irreconcilable notions of "selflessness" and "self-interest" creates a sense of division and conflict within the individual. Having been rendered weak and confused by an idea whose substance we had not bothered to explore, we are left without a clear sense of direction in our lives. In the renunciation of the primacy of our own sense of our self, we look to the state, or a church, or an ideology, to restore the wholeness that only we are capable of discovering. So spiritually and morally corrupting is the doctrine of "selflessness," that many of us learn to accept our dismemberment on a battlefield as the essence of a "heroic" life, or to regard the act of tax evasion as "cheating" the state!

Whatever the nature of the social system in which we live, our claims to various "rights" are the products of our relationships with others. If those "others" are political or judicial officials of the state, the power to determine our interests will be *centralized* in those who enjoy a privilege that we and our neighbors do not, namely, of enforcing their preferences by coercive means. On the other hand, if those "others" are our *neighbors*, who enjoy no greater power over us than we do over them, then social power has been effectively *decentralized* into the hands of individuals. The contrast between command economies and the marketplace offers more than just an analogy. It expresses the fundamental choice we must always make between violent and peaceful systems of social behavior.

For people who have become accustomed to having most of their social questions dealt with through political means, rediscovering the informal, social means of establishing claims may take some effort. Not unlike the experiences of many tourists who, accustomed to dealing with the administered pricing practices in shopping malls, feel discomfort in haggling with merchants in third-world countries, there may be some initial anxiety in taking direct control over one's affairs. Just as new technologies cause us to redefine how we deal with one another, learning how to negotiate for our interests will involve a good deal of trial and error. But as we learn to give to the opinions of our neighbors, with whom we share common interests and a sense of existential equality, the same regard we now have for the edicts of political authorities, who presume to command us, we may discover our lives becoming more peaceful, free, and cooperative, and more individually empowered.

Chapter Six
Control as Ownership

*Everything that emancipates the spirit without giving us
control over ourselves is harmful.*

— Johann Wolfgang von Goethe

Ownership is a practical concept, having less to do with abstract philosophic principles than it does with decision-making power. For this reason, the essence of ownership is found not in certificates of title, sales receipts, or recorded documents; but in the socially recognized authority to exercise *control* over an item of property, i.e., to direct what will or will not be done with it. When we are able to identify the person(s) whose will, according to the consensus of the community, is to prevail in determining the use or disposition to be made of any entity, we will have discovered who the actual owner is. But what is meant by "control?"

Control goes to the essence of ownership. To be an owner of anything, whether a chattel, real estate, an intangible interest, or yourself, is to be the effective decision-maker over such an item of property. The owner is the person whose will can be exercised over a property interest without having such control subject to veto by another. In a principled approach to property ownership, the element of control is inextricably tied to the claim concept. A claim of ownership derives its validity from a recognition by others, of the inherent worthiness of an individual to act to sustain himself or herself through negentropic action in the world. To have one's will respecting one's own property subject to preemption by another, whether an individual or the state, is to deny the existential significance of each of us, and to elevate such preempting authorities to the status of our owners. Once we acknowledge others to have rightful control over us, we become mere resources to their ends. To have any functional meaning in the world, our negentropic efforts must be directed to resources that can be converted into the energy necessary to achieving such ends.

It is this capacity to control a property interest that makes a claim of ownership meaningful. What is it, for instance, that prevents me from laying claim to the ownership of the moon, and to have others respect my claim? There is nothing any more unique about owning the moon than for our ancestors to have laid claim to previously unowned land on the North American continent. The moon certainly has a boundary: it is a self-contained entity. If no one else has already done so, I could run newspaper ads throughout the world asserting my claim to the moon's ownership. But no one would be expected to respect my claim because I am not in a position to exercise decision-making control over the moon. Standing down here on Earth, there is no way that I can exert my will over the moon to have it reflect my purposes. Because property is essential to us as a pragmatic means of extending our will over some portion of the world in order to reduce entropy in our lives, the inability to exert such control over a given entity renders such a claim pointless. And yet, were I to actually go to the moon and stake out my claim to some portion of it, over which I could have such control, my claim would be entitled to respect by the same principles of discovery and claim that produced much of the post-Columbian settlement of North America. This distinction underlies Locke's thinking as to when a claim is entitled to the respect of others. On the other hand, collectivist thinking has led a small handful of nations to ratify an international "Moon Treaty" which would, if more widely adopted, ban legal ownership of any portion of the moon by any "organization or person" unless such organization is an international governmental body. The old mindset of government agents sticking flags in the ground and claiming ownership and control of the great outdoors now threatens outer space as well.

A similar problem existed with the old legal maxim that landed property rights extended from the center of the earth into the indefinite reaches of space above the land. As I am unable to exercise any control over space some ten million light years beyond the surface of my land, it is meaningless for me to claim such an interest. The courts have long since recognized the extent of air rights as being measured by the nature of the use being made of the land. The extent of one's ownership of the space above the land (i.e., the control one exercises over the surface) helps define the boundary of the property. Thus, a wheat farmer's air rights would be less than the rights of an owner of a one-hundred-story office building. For this reason, I would have no justifiable claim—either in law or by the nature of property—against airlines flying their planes some thirty thousand feet above my house. Because the airlines *do* control such space (i.e., by regularly flying their planes through a spe-cifically bounded area), they would enjoy such a property inter-est. On the other hand, if I have been operating an observatory on my land since before the airlines began flying through such space, my claim should prevail over theirs. My control over the surface might then be said to conform to the ancient maxim that my air rights extended into the endless space above my land.

To bring the issue down to earth—pardon the pun—what would prevent me from laying claim to the Earth's atmo-sphere? Again, the atmosphere is bounded—albeit at increas-ingly thinner dimensions as one approaches outer space—and I am declaring my claim to its ownership. When I ask my first year law students this question, I usually get an empty response along the lines of "because everyone needs to breathe air." "Then they'd better start coming up with some money to pay me for the privilege," I tell them. I remind them that everyone also needs to occupy space, and consume food and water, and yet private ownership of these resources has not been rejected for such a reason. The grocery business is dependent upon the grocer's owning such food whose claims he or she later sells to customers. It is the very importance of such resources to our personal survival that requires us to be free to claim and control them, and generates markets for the suppliers and consumers of such commodities. If I am to effectively reduce entropy in order to sustain myself, I must be able to consume energy from our world—including air—to the exclusion of every other person on this planet.

At this point, I usually get a student asking: "but how could any person get control of the atmosphere?" When I remind them that some people *do* extract oxygen from the atmosphere, put it into oxygen tanks, and sell it to the public, they begin to see that there is a principled way to address such issues. They also begin to see how the question of ownership is tied to the capacity to exert control over a specific subject matter of property. It is the ability to capture free oxygen and confine it within the boundaries of a tank that gives meaning to a claim of ownership. Should any of the oxygen escape from the tank, the ownership interest in the free oxygen would probably be lost because, while the oxygen would continue to have a molecular existence, it would no longer exist in a form that could be differentiated from previously unowned oxygen molecules. As such, the oxygen would have lost both its *boundary* and the erstwhile owner's capacity to *control* it, thus depriving the owner of a *claim* entitled to the respect of others. My inability to reduce the atmosphere to my control in order to exercise my will over it would make my claim as meaningless as my claim to the planet Neptune. Furthermore—as with my earlier hypothetical example in chapter five of claiming ownership of the island's fresh water supply— even if it were possible for me to control the atmosphere, the likely refusal of others to respect my claim to the air would render it indefensible.

The control factor is what makes patents and copyrights difficult to reconcile with property principles. If one writes a poem,

novel, or other literary work, and retains possession of the manuscript, one's claim and control—hence, ownership—remains
intact. But when the author chooses to release that work to others, his or her control is lost and, like the hypothetical of oxygen
released from a tank, so is the claim to exclusive decision-making. The common law courts have followed just such reasoning,
recognizing a writer's "common law copyright" in unpublished
work that ends when the author "publishes" (i.e., makes public)
its content. If a writer or inventor were to enter into a contract
with each purchaser to not reproduce his or her work, its creator
would retain a property interest in the terms of the contract. But
this is not the way the present system works. Instead, the state
has enacted patent and copyright legislation that, by fiat, provides authors and inventors with property interests for which
they have neither contracted nor otherwise retained control.

A question that is invariably raised by critics of privately
owned property has to do with the quantity of property one
might claim. "In early American history, what would have kept
one individual from laying claim to all the land that had not
previously been owned by others?" is the usual form of such
an inquiry. The fear that a few individuals might amass large
landholdings seems quite misplaced in a society in which property is privately owned. In the first place, such a fear appears
to be a carryover from feudalism, when wealth and status were
synonymous with state-conferred and enforced ownership of
land. Secondly, as history has shown, it has been *governments*,
not private individuals, that have laid claim to entire continents
by placing flags in the ground. The largest landholder by far in
present day America is not some billionaire industrialist, or a
"Fortune 500" corporate giant, but the federal government.

Historically, individuals tended to claim only as much land
as they could reasonably manage and control. The *state* might
have the resources—extracted from taxpayers—to control vast
quantities of real estate, but *individuals* rarely do. As long as
one's claim of ownership is effectively limited to what that person can control—an expression of the Lockean "labor theory"
of ownership—the quantity of land claimed by private persons

would tend to be minimal. Furthermore, if the strength of ownership claims ultimately rests on the willingness of one's neighbors to recognize and respect such claims, a person would have to test the limits of his or her claim within the community. Is it likely that a claim to a ten-acre tract would be respected? Probably so. Would similar respect be accorded a claim to half the North American continent? Probably not.

Under any system of property, the claim of ownership issue always comes down to the question of who is to exercise ultimate control. How, and by whom, will authority be exercised in our lives? Will decision making be decentralized into the hands of individuals, or centralized in institutional hierarchies, particularly the state? Because control is the defining factor in identifying both ownership and the locus of authority over our lives, such questions raise a deeper inquiry into where the ownership of our lives resides. Whether or not we choose to claim that ownership has more than simply an abstract, arcane significance. It goes to the very essence of what it means to be a human being. *Individual liberty* and *self-ownership* are synonymous concepts; we enjoy liberty only insofar as we insist upon the exclusive authority to control our own lives. For liberty to prevail, we must claim—and our neighbors must acknowledge—our self ownership.

These are the kinds of inquiries we have never been encouraged to undertake. In our highly structured world, such authority is centralized in the state. Because we are comfortable allowing established authorities to formulate our questions (and answers) for us, and because such entities have no interest in having us question the existing arrangements, many readers may be inclined to regard the inquiries I am suggesting with suspicion or anger. Such a response will also come from the institutional question-keepers, who have always preferred that we not ask troublesome questions. But centralized authority necessarily carries with it centralized control over the lives and property of us all. To the degree our personal decision-making has been preempted, we have lost the control—hence, the effective ownership—of our lives. If we are to live freely, intelligently, and responsibly, we must become aware of the implications of the dynamics of both centralized and decentralized systems.

In a system of *privately* owned property, there is no confusion—and no conflict—in the matter because claim and control will be integrated into a specific owner. Conflicts will arise only from a failure to either *identify* or *respect* separate property boundaries and the claims implicit therein. Stated another way, conflict is generated when *control* over property is severed from *ownership*. As we saw earlier, an owner may create multiple interests in what he or she owns—as, for example, a deed of trust, easement, or leasehold—but, as such interests are defined by contract as expressions of the will of the owner, conflicts will tend to be minimal and resolvable by the language of the agreement.

But in *political* systems, which are distinguished from one another in terms of how property is owned and controlled, contradiction, confusion, and conflict will always ensue. A woman who is prevented from putting an addition onto her home because local housing codes prohibit it, or a farmer who is legally precluded from plowing a portion of his land because it is the habitat of an "endangered species", or a person who is compelled by a court to submit to a medical procedure he does not want, are anecdotal instances of the more pervasive conflict that is consuming our lives. Like the fractal patterns observed in the study of chaos and complexity, individualized conflicts experienced by these owners get enlarged into the more pervasive hostilities found in zoning laws, urban renewal projects, and eminent domain practices. War, itself, becomes the exaggerated expression of the conflict model that inheres in any systematic trespass of property interests.

Furthermore, because the existence of the state is inherently incompatible with a system of private property, language must be twisted and corrupted to disguise the nature of governmental action. In the American political system, which still pays lip service to the concept of private ownership of property, a candid admission of the confiscatory nature of government regulation might prove unsettling. Consequently, the courts have historically resorted to the meaningless distinction between "control" and "ownership," or between "regulation" and a "taking." Whatever the degree of interference with an owner's decision-making, however, all forms of state regulation amount to some taking of a property interest. If you have $100 in your pocket, and the state forcibly deprives you of the right to use $10 of that amount as you choose, is such regulation any less a taking of your property because it has left you—at least for the time being—with control over the remaining $90?

In furtherance of such subterfuges, and consistent with the divisive premises upon which political systems are founded, our formal political/legal system has fragmented ownership into the subcategories of "title" and "control." The purpose in doing so is to disguise the state's regulation of private property as something other than a taking of ownership interests. The word "title" relates to "official authority or power,"[1] and generally implies the kind of ownership that a court of law would recognize as valid. When the state presumes to define, and thus legitimize, claims to property ownership, such authority necessarily carries with it those limitations on private control that are mandated by legislative or judicial power. If one insists upon using his property in ways that violate such governmental restrictions, he runs the risk of losing title to that property.

Government regulation not only usurps the authority of owners to control the use of their property, but the power to transfer their claims of ownership via contracts with others. As we have seen, a contract is but an agreement, by two or more persons, to exchange claims to the ownership of their respective property interests. Thus, when the state, through its regulatory practices, intervenes to alter the terms of this contract, or to decree, under statutes defining legal status, who can be contracting parties, it is denying people control over their property interests. Extended to its logical conclusion, such regulations amount to a denial of the self-ownership of the contract-

---

[1]Eric Partridge, *Origins: A Short Etymological Dictionary of Modern English* (New York: Greenwich House, 1983), p. 723.

ing parties, as they are denied the liberty of controlling their own efforts and resources to sustain themselves.

It does not require a law school degree to understand that there has been a decided movement away from contractually defined rights and duties and back to having such standards determined by legislative, judicial, or administrative bodies. Doctrines of "unconscionability," "fairness," "unequal bargaining power," and "equity," have been employed, along with outright prohibitions on certain types of transactions, or the prices to which parties may agree, to greatly diminish the control individuals may exercise over their lives and property. In a contract-based system, such control is *decentralized* into the hands of individuals who freely enter—or choose not to enter—into agreements with others, with each party assessing their own interests and risks. But decentralist tendencies are incompatible with politically-directed systems that thrive on forced uniformity and standardization. Today, there is scarcely a realm of human activity over which the state does not demand the powers of micromanagement.

A review of the case law confirms that our legal system has failed to embrace any clear or consistent principles when it comes to the property question. If a court wishes to deny the state's power to intrude upon privately owned land, it will speak of such verities as, "every man's home is his castle." If, on the other hand, this same court desires to uphold some state regulation, it will remind us that, "property rights are not absolute." Of course, at the same time that the state denies the inviolability of *private* property interests, it insists upon the inviolability of its *own*! If you doubt this, try entering a military base, national park, or government office building, and see how the state—like a feudal lord of the manor—insists upon an absolute respect for its property holdings in defending them from trespassers and poachers (i.e., you and me). When the state erects walls or fences around such facilities, it is—like a landowner—asserting a claim of ownership to all these boundaries contain. Likewise, when it builds walls or fences around an entire *nation*, the state makes an ownership claim to all within such borders.

All property rights are absolute: some person or persons must exercise ultimate control over things to be owned. The only question relates to the identity of such parties, an inquiry that was as relevant on the early American frontier as it was in the Soviet Union. If we were to identify all of the persons entitled to exercise some degree of control over a given parcel or item of property, and if the interests of all those persons could be purchased by one person, that buyer would, by definition, be entitled to do *anything* regarding that property, including destroying it, because there would be no other party entitled to exercise control over it. This is the reason that title searches to real property are done, and that title insurance is purchased to assure the state of the title that is revealed: to identify any other persons whose interests must be obtained if the new owner wants an unlimited power over a piece of land.

The ways in which political systems usurp control over property have been rather subtle, and their implications still manage to escape even most lawyers. Because most of us do not understand that property ownership is a reflection of decision-making authority over things that can be owned, we fail to see the contradictions inherent in the judicial system's separation of "control" and "ownership." Like the denizens of George Orwell's *Animal Farm*, we take uneasy comfort in the legalistic corruption of language played at the expense of our ignorance (e.g., "all animals are equal, but some are more equal than others"), and content ourselves that ownership—including that of our own lives—is little more than a state-conferred, defined, controlled, and limited "title." Having become thoroughly politicized, we fail to ask the fundamental question: upon what basis does the state presume to restrict our claims of ownership to within boundaries it has decreed, and without our consent?

Every property is, by definition, subject to the absolute and unrestricted control of someone. This is what is implicit in a "claim of ownership." Of course, this absolute authority need not be in just one person. An owner might convey his or her ownership interest to a husband and wife, or business partners who, as new owners, would then exercise joint control

over some item of property. But the point is that *some* person—
or persons—must have the final word regarding what is to be
done with any given property interest. This is why the ultimate
test of ownership comes down to the question: who can decide,
without having to get the permission of another, to *destroy* this
property? If a man has great quantities of food left over after
a sumptuous banquet, and he chooses to destroy such remains
while starving children look on hoping he will give the food to
them, will his liberty to destroy the food be respected? This is
not to suggest that an owner *must* make such a decision, or that
he might not be held in contempt by others for his denial of
their request; only that the owner is the one who can rightfully
make such a choice. If this man's decision is forcibly over-rid-
den by others, then they, and not he, must be regarded as the
owner. Ownership resides in the person(s) whose arbitrariness
in decision-making will be recognized by others as supreme.
This principle is as true for property in a communist regime as
it is in a society founded upon private ownership. Regardless
of the system, it is the nature of property ownership that there
must be someone who will be acknowledged as having such
ultimate authority. Having this authority in the hands of private individuals is what troubles the defenders of state power,
who continue to preach the catechism that "property rights are
not absolute."

The authority of government officials depends, in part, upon
our continuing to believe in the myth that "we" have an ownership interest in what is really state-owned property. They have
no illusions about genuine ownership control residing in any of
us. The distinction—as well as the inherent contradiction in the
idea of "collective ownership"—was clearly expressed in a sign
I saw in a park in Niagara Falls, Ontario: "The parks are yours
to enjoy, not to destroy."

Any particular item of property may, as we saw in the
examples from mining in chapter four, be subject to various
ownership claims. Nevertheless, if our thinking remains clear,
and we don't confuse the boundaries of a parcel of land with
the boundaries of each property interest in the land, every

such claim can be identified as a separate ownership interest subject to separate control. The following hypothetical may illustrate the point. Suppose that I own a parcel of land containing an old house. Suppose, further, that I desire to set fire to this house and burn it to the ground. Am I entitled to do so? If the answer is "no," then I am *not* the owner of the property, but the person or entity whose permission I require is. Let us suppose that a bank has a mortgage on the property to secure payment of a loan obligation. Let us further suppose that I had put a new roof on the house last year, for which I have not paid the contractor, who has since filed a lien on the property. Let us also assume that I have rented this house to a tenant, who still has one year remaining on her lease. Let us also assume that I have a fire insurance policy on the house and, further, a neighbor who does not want me to burn down my house. Finally, let us assume that the city in which this house is located has an ordinance designed to preserve (i.e., to prevent the modification or destruction of) historic buildings, and that my house has been so designated. If I wish to proceed with the destruction of the house, need I secure the approval of any of these parties and, if so, why?

In terms of *legally* defined property claims, it is likely that each of these parties enjoys a sufficient interest in this property to entitle them to exercise some degree of control over it by securing judicial remedies to thwart my plans. As with the earlier example of an automobile purchased with a loan secured by a chattel mortgage, the bank could claim a property interest in my house, the boundaries of which are defined by the contract it entered into with me. It would be entitled to exercise control over the property insofar as was necessary to protect the security interest I had created in the bank. This would entitle the bank to keep me from destroying the house, but would not permit it to restrict my repainting of the house or whom I might choose to invite onto the property. Since I, as the owner, had created this interest in the bank by contract, its interests would be consistent with both the *legal* and *transactional* definitions of ownership.

What about the lien interest of the contractor? Like the bank's mortgage interest, the lien-holder has a legally protected security interest in the house, limited to the extent of its unpaid bill for the roof. Unlike the bank, however, it is unclear whether the lien interest was created by the terms of my contract with the roofer—which would satisfy the transactional definition of ownership—or imposed upon me by operation of law—which would be an intrusion upon my property interests.

The interests of my tenant are clearly protected under either a legal or transactional analysis. My contract with her has created a property interest in the house (i.e., the right to the "quiet use and possession" of the property) for the term of the lease. She *owns* a possessory interest in the house, and my act of burning down the house during the lease period would violate her ownership rights.

The interests of the fire insurance company require clarification. Its interest is not so much in the property that it is insuring, as in the contract between the company and myself. Thus, the insurance company doesn't have an interest in my not burning down the house, but does have an interest in my not destroying the house for the purpose of submitting a fraudulent claim for its loss. Since the insurance company and I have both contracted regarding our respective property interests (i.e., my payment of premiums and the commitment of their assets), the company's interest in the property would be—depending upon the terms of our agreement—consistent with a transactional approach to property. If I were to submit a fraudulent claim, I would be violating the insurance company's property interests in this *contract*.

As to my neighbor's objections, unless he could show that he had acquired a transactionally-based interest in my not destroying my house (e.g., a restrictive covenant by which I had agreed, with my neighbors, not to burn down my house)—an interest that the courts would enforce—he could assert a legal claim to prevent my burning of the house under either a *nuisance* or *trespass* theory. If smoke or flames were to cross my boundary lines onto his, I would be engaged in a trespass, which could be actionable under either a legal or a social definition of property. As my rightful decision making, as an owner, ends at my property boundaries, such a trespass would be a violation of my neighbor's property interests.

But without an identifiable trespass, which will be discussed more thoroughly in chapter seven, an action premised on *nuisance* would be a denial of my property interests. If my neighbor's objection to my proposed action was only grounded in aesthetic considerations, or living next door to a vacant lot, or any other concern for which he and I had no agreement, his nuisance action would amount to his trespassing my interests, by extending his decision making, through judicial action, onto my land.

Finally, as to the interests of the city, a clear conflict exists between the legal and social/transactional definitions of property interests. Since the courts will enforce the ordinance against me, the city can be said to have a legal interest in my property, at least to the extent of being able to prevent my destruction of the house. While the courts would never be so frank as to declare that the city had usurped my property interests—preferring the phrase "regulatory interest under the police powers"—it does amount to a legally protected interest every bit as much as the bank's mortgage interest. The city's interest fails to satisfy the transactional definition of property, however, in that its interest was not acquired through any contract with me, in which the city gave up a property interest it had in exchange for what I had given up. As in all governmental action, the city simply *imposed* the restriction on me and other property owners covered by the ordinance, without negotiating with us regarding our acquiring an interest owned by the city.

In a purely functional sense, because the person who has ultimate control over an item of property is the effective owner, and because all forms of government regulation create a division between *ownership* and *control*, politics *always* generates personal and social conflict (i.e., the purported owner is restrained in the exercise of his or her control by a state agency). I desire to use my property in a particular way (e.g., to burn down my house), but the city ordinance prohibits this. Control of this property is now divided between the incompatible preferences of myself and the city, thus creating a conflict in ownership.

Anyone who has ever given two children joint ownership of a toy, or observed the division of jointly-owned property during a divorce, can attest to the dissonant nature of two owners each desirous of controlling the same item in inconsistent ways. Such conflicts can easily be resolved by the owners contracting with one another (e.g., child A gets to make decisions on odd-numbered days, child B makes decisions on even-numbered days). At first glance, it might be supposed that the city's ordinance qualifies as such a contractual compromise. However, since a contract requires the giving up of some property interest (e.g., one's money, land, personal services) in exchange for the other party doing the same thing, and since, as we have seen, the city is giving up no property interest of its own in exchange for my obligation not to burn down my house, such regulations fail this test. Like the playground bully who promises to not beat you up in exchange for your lunch money, the government restriction is nothing more than an act of plunder.

In a society that has replaced concerns for individual liberty with notions of due process of law, the idea that arbitrariness is not only a permissible but an essential element of property ownership will be troubling and ring of absoluteness. Such a response reflects an ignorance of the realities of power and authority. It is the nature of every kind of human action that some person, or group of persons, will ultimately make a decision concerning a specific course of action, based upon their preferences, from which no appeal will be taken. If you and a group of friends are trying to decide whether to have dinner in an Italian or a Szechuan restaurant, you will debate the alternatives and, at some point, make a discretionary choice. No matter how much a decision-maker tries to be reasonable, or consistent with prior decisions, or tries to accommodate the views of all interested persons, his or her decision will *always* come down to a choice that is not subject to review by anyone. If there is some other party who can override this decision, then *that* person is the ultimate decision-maker. There is nothing remarkable in this: it is only a reflection of the nature of *all* decision making that someone must ultimately say "yes" or "no", to make a quantum jump from one state of mind to another.

When such authority is exercised over property, the person who can make that final decision is the de facto owner, regardless of where "title" may reside. This is what is meant by "arbitrariness" herein. It refers to the *locus* of the decision-making authority, *not* to the *quality* of the decision itself. For example, a developer wishes to cut down an aged tree on his land in order to make way for a residential development. Another person who objects to this act chains herself to the tree in an effort to get the courts to intervene to save the tree. In this situation, the tree's future will be determined by somebody. Whether the developer or the court prevails tells us who the de facto owner of the tree is. This is what the concept of property entails, and there is no way of avoiding the issue, regardless of the nature of the political system involved.

The intertwined nature of control and ownership also helps to explain why economies grounded in private ownership have been far more productive than socialistic systems. Because an owner is able to reap the benefits of his or her decision making over property, an incentive exists for creative, productive activity. No matter how well-intended I may be, my motivation for productiveness will be greater if I am the *owner* of what I am able to generate than if I am only a *manager* of another's property interests, a truth continually made evident in the collective factories and farms of communist systems. As we saw earlier in Joseph Schumpeter's contrast between *owner*-controlled and *manager*-controlled business firms, an owner tends to have a longer-term perspective in decision making than do most managers, whose outlooks become more akin to those of employees. I first encountered this phenomenon in law practice, where clients who owned their own businesses tended to be more determined to resist government regulatory practices than did the managers of firms I represented. The former seemed to have a sense that a bad decision might prove harmful to the business they envisioned their children and grandchildren owning one day. Managers, on the other hand, seemed more concerned with how their decisions would affect their careers within the next few months or years.

One also witnesses the motivational benefits arising from control in the workplace. It has long been evident in the study of managerial styles that unstructured and less formalized systems can be far more creative and productive than systems based on the pyramidal, authoritarian model. The traditional organizational structure of top-down management, with its emphasis on centralized decision making, close supervision, and rigid externalized discipline grounded in fear and threats, has proven less rewarding to both the firm and its workers than a more decentralized approach.[2] Conventional managerial thinking has been built on the same assumptions we find in political systems, namely, that one has "an inherent dislike of work" and "will avoid it if he can." Because of this, it is presumed, "people must be coerced, controlled, directed, [and] threatened with punishment" to get them to work on behalf of organizational purposes. More recent management thinking, however, rejects such premises in favor of a diffused authority—sometimes referred to as "participatory management"—which has been shown to increase both productivity and job satisfaction among employees who enjoy increased decisional control over their work environments.[3] Consistent with Schumpeter's insights, it is no coincidence that such decentralist arrangements are often analogized to workers having a "property" interest in *how* their work is to be performed.

Property is also a system for defining and allocating *responsibility* within society. The person who controls the property is responsible for the consequences of his or her actions regarding such property *because* they were the one exercising such control.

---

[2]See, e.g., Douglas McGregor, *The Human Side of Enterprise* (New York: McGraw-Hill Book Company, 1960); Robert A. Sutermeister, *People and Productivity* (New York: McGraw-Hill Book Company, 1963).

[3]McGregor, *The Human Side of Enterprise*, pp. 33–34.

This responsibility follows not from some a *priori* moral imperative, but from the purely functional consideration that one who
directs the exercise of his or her will has, thereby, produced
the effects attributed to such control. I am responsible for my
actions *not* because the state so mandates, or because some religion or moral philosophy has so proclaimed, but because *I* am
the one who makes and acts upon the choices available to me.
By my exercise of control over what I own, I cause that property to produce its effects. In the same causal, nonjudgmen-
tal sense in which a tornado can be said to be responsible for
destroying Smith's barn, I am responsible for what I do in the
exercise of my will.

If we are able to live without contradiction—with our stated
principles and our actions providing a precise Indra's Net
reflection of one another—our causal and moral responsibilities
will be in symmetry. But when our behavior exceeds the limitations prescribed by our principles—e.g., extending our decision
making beyond our property boundaries—division and conflict
arise. At this point, we bifurcate our sense of responsibility, and
seek comfort for the adverse consequences of our conduct in
explanations that absolve us of personal accountability (e.g., we
lack free will, we were abused as children, "the devil made me
do it," etc.)

Freedom and responsibility are thus inseparable aspects of
control. Because I, alone, control the exercise of my energies, I
am free to decide how I shall act. Since there is no one else who
can direct my brain cells, my muscles, or my emotions, there is
no other person who can be held to account for what I do. I am
responsible for my actions because I control them. The realization of this simple fact is what is meant by being "free." At the
same time, the failure to understand this inseparable nature of
freedom and responsibility is what makes mob behavior and
other forms of mass-mindedness so destructive. By seeming to
lose control over our individual will within the will of the collective, we separate our behavior from any sense of personal
responsibility for our actions. The state, whether functioning as the military, police or prison systems, or bureaucratic

departments, provides the clearest example of how collective authority diffuses responsibility, allowing individuals to conceal accountability for their actions in the shadows of monoliths. Words attributed to Rose Wilder Lane express this essential duality: *"freedom is self-control, no more, no less."* The owner is free to control what *is* his, and in confining his actions to what is his, he behaves responsibly and "properly" (i.e., consistent with the property principle). The popular phrase "with freedom comes responsibility" is a clumsy way of recognizing that we are responsible for the consequences of our actions. The clumsiness of the phrase arises from its generally being used without its connection to the property concept. When such words are employed to justify the state imposing duties upon us, the element of "freedom" is severed from our actions, turning "responsibility" (as a *causal* factor) into an "obligation" (i.e., something we are compelled to do).

Most of us have remarkably little understanding of the interrelated nature of our individual liberty and personal responsibility. It has become commonplace for politicians and members of the media to publicly decry the lack of "responsibility" exhibited by modern teenagers. Children are criticized for using drugs and alcohol, for their lack of initiative in school or work, for their preoccupation with the pursuit of sensual pleasures, or for their poor judgments in making decisions. But responsibility is a function of control. How can we expect children to become responsible when they have been denied control over their own lives? They are compelled, by law, to attend schools that look and function like penitentiaries where they are subjected to often mindless curricula that have no apparent meaning to their lives. Those who exhibit any independence in the classroom are labeled "hyperactive" or victims of "attention deficit disorder"—meaning they have their own agendas that differ from the teachers—and are legally drugged into more compliant behavior.

Minimum wage and child labor laws greatly restrict teenagers' opportunities for employment, and we then wonder why so many of them turn to the sale of drugs or to prostitution as ways of earning the money they hope will give them more decision-making power in their lives. Emulating the methods of the state, which has taken away so much control over their lives, many have set up their own military structures, in the form of street-corner gangs, in an attempt to exert their authority through violence. We also cannot understand why teenagers are so preoccupied with their cars. If we thought about it, we might realize that the automobile represents, to the teenager, the one part of life that is under *their* direct control, which responds to *their* commands, and takes them where *they* want to go. One of the advocates of the previously mentioned practice of abandoning traffic signs in various European cities has observed: "[t]he greater the number of prescriptions, the more people's sense of personal responsibility dwindles."[4]

Someone once defined "hell" as a place where you are *responsible* for what happens, but have no *control* over matters. Is this not what we have created for ourselves by separating control from responsibility in modern society? The state continues to expand the scope of its control over our lives and property and we then wonder why people have become increasingly irresponsible in their behavior. Responsible men and women bear the costs of their actions, confine their decision making to their own property interests, and do not impose burdens upon others. Political institutions, on the other hand, are the epitome of irresponsibility *because* their very nature consists in violating property boundaries. How easily does the state provide others a role model for avoiding responsibility for their actions? In the spirit of "victimhood" that now pervades our culture, men and women are able to project onto tobacco companies the responsibility for lung ailments brought on by their choices to smoke. Distillers and drug dealers—not alcoholics and addicts—are blamed for the miseries people bring onto themselves through their habits. Many of us prefer such explanations to the more troublesome task of confining our expectations of others to

---

[4]www.spiegel.de/international/spiegel/0,1518,448747,00.html.

respecting our property boundaries, as well as accepting the sense of personal responsibility that inheres in self-ownership.

If we are to move beyond the misery and viciousness of our politicized world, each of us must be willing to confront our own thinking, for at the core of most of our problems is our fear of personal responsibility. To be *responsible* is to be held *accountable* for the consequences of our actions. Such fear is what Walter Kaufmann so poignantly labeled "decidophobia,"[5] i.e., the "fear of autonomy."[6] What we fear the most is not the judgments of *others*, but our *own*. In the words of Epictetus: "It is impossible for that which is free by nature to be disturbed or hindered by anything but itself. It is a man's own judgments which disturb him."[7] To avoid such self-judgments, most of us allow others to bear this responsibility that, in turn, necessitates our turning over control of our lives and property interests to those who become our authorities. But such abandonment of autonomy begins with our *thinking*. In exchange for giving up our liberties, we gain the comforting illusion, carried on from childhood, of being relieved of our responsibility. If things do not go well for us, we can always hold *others* accountable: our employer, our parents, our teachers, the politicians—those parties to whom we long ago learned to abdicate control over our lives.

The division between self-ownership and personal responsibility is also expressed in the idea that men and women are not responsible for their actions; that the causes of violent crime, for instance, lie not in the choices people freely make, but in poverty, racism, drugs, sexism, guns, alcohol, television programming, or motion pictures, to name but a few. Such mechanistic explanations for human behavior are most comforting to those who fear their own sense of responsibility, and are quite

---

[5] Walter Kaufmann, *Without Guilt and Justice: From Decidophobia to Autonomy* (New York: Peter H. Wyden, 1973).

[6] Ibid., p. 3.

[7] From *The Discourses and the Manual*, in Ebenstein, *Great Political Thinkers*, p. 147.

content to surrender the control of their lives to political systems in exchange for a state of dependency and release of personal responsibility. There is a childlike quality in attributing consciousness and sense of purpose to inanimate objects, while denying responsibility for one's own acts. Having become dependent upon the decisions and actions of others, they can then posture as *victims* of what other people or things do to them, an attitude that keeps personal injury lawyers and politicians in business. But it is an illusion for us to pretend that we can abandon responsibility for our thoughts and actions by transferring such accountability to others. No matter how much others may threaten or try to seduce us to comply with their demands, each of us remains in control of our energies, and must choose to either resist or comply. The choice we ultimately make reduces itself to a matter of will.

To such "decidophobes" liberty, which finds expression in private ownership, is a terrifying specter. I suspect that this is a major reason why so many men and women in the 1960s and 1970s played around with notions of "self-liberation"—a concept inseparable from self-control—but then, seeing the personal responsibility implications quickly abandoned introspective efforts in favor of political and ideological proselytizing and the drafting of codes of "political correctness": activities directed toward changing *other* people's thinking and behavior. The concept of self-ownership can be very disturbing once we discover its connections to personal responsibility. Minds conditioned to a dependency upon the authority of others are not likely to be heard demanding the reclamation of control over their own lives.

We will not become "free" by attacking or overthrowing the authorities in our lives, but only by taking back what, in fact, we were never truly able to give up: the responsibility for our thinking and actions. Likewise, recommitting ourselves to political or religious systems is but to perpetuate the illusion that others are in control of our lives, and that we must content ourselves with obsequious efforts to influence their policies in our favor. To live as both free and responsible men and women is to be *self*-controlling, not obedient. Such a condition can arise only from a fundamental change in our thinking, and will find expression only within a system in which each of us exercises an unrestrained authority over what is *ours* to control. Our failure to insist upon a system of privately owned property, and to bear the personal responsibility that goes with it, has been a major contributor to what mankind has become.

The interconnectedness between "control" and a claim of self-ownership is reflected in the legal debate over whether a person should have a right to commit suicide. With the increasing sophistication in medical technology, more and more terminally ill or severely injured people face the question of whether they wish to be kept alive at all costs, or have their lives terminated. For many doctors, judges, legislators, clergymen, and moral busybodies, however, this is not a decision they want to allow the patient to make. On the surface, it might appear that the concern of such parties is simply the preservation of human life. But there is more to it than that. The same judge who, while reflecting upon his proclaimed sentiments for life, refuses a patient's request to be taken *off* life-support systems, may later sentence a convicted murderer to the gas chamber. Or, members of Congress who support legislation making it more difficult for people to end their own lives—all in the guise of upholding the sanctity of life—can nevertheless be counted upon to support the expenditure of hundreds of billions of dollars to send soldiers and weapons into wars that kill hundreds of thousands of people.

What really troubles institutional officials about the right to commit suicide is the implicit recognition of the ultimate ownership authority—i.e., of self-control—being in the hands of the individual. We once again confront the ownership issue: who can destroy the property without asking the permission of another? The judge who decides to grant a patient's request to be allowed to die, isn't really concerned about life or death of the patient, or of upholding the patient's choice in the matter. He is, however, very much concerned about *who* is to have such decisional power: the *individual* or the *state*. Randolph Bourne's observation that "war is the health of the state"[8] reflects the state's need to monopolize the exercise of the power to inflict death, or what one observer has referred to as the "nationalization of the right to kill."[9] The religious leader who condemns suicide as a "sin" recognizes, implicitly, that if men and women begin to insist upon the authority to control their own *existence*, churches will have lost all power over their *souls*. Those who would deny individuals the authority to commit suicide on the grounds of "respect for life," are only expressing a mechanistic, materialistic view of life. Such thinking overlooks the fact that life is respected only when the living are permitted to remain autonomous. If you and I are understood to have such ultimate authority over our very existence—a power that goes to the essence of self-ownership—think of all the *other* questions we might begin to ask regarding who should have control over other aspects of our lives! As I tell my students on their first day of my class on property, the question of whether they own and control themselves has profoundly subversive implications.

The utter confusion about the central role property plays in decision making in a society of free men and women is illustrated in a further issue in the euthanasia debate: the role of the medical profession in helping a patient commit suicide. That most doctors and hospitals have not maintained any consistency regarding a patient's claim of self-ownership is evident from a long line of cases. Patients compelled by court orders, often secured by their doctors, to submit to surgeries, blood transfusions, and even amputations; mental patients forced to undergo drug or shock treatment or lobotomies; compulsory vaccinations of children; and the medical profession's leadership in procuring legislation making it a crime for anyone to provide alternative health care that is opposed by the medical establishment, are just a few examples of how doctors and hospitals eagerly participate in violating people's wills regarding their own lives.

---

[8] Randolph Bourne, *War and the Intellectuals* (New York: Harper & Row, 1964), p. 71.

[9] Will Durant, *The Life of Greece* (New York: Simon & Schuster, 1939), p. 50.

The willingness to use state power to advance one's interests at the expense of others proves infectious. Members of the medical profession might, in the future, find themselves targets of proposed legislation requiring them to perform abortions, even though the physicians may have moral objections to doing so. Upon what basis might doctors resist such a government mandate? They may now have incentive to move beyond weak appeals to their "Hippocratic oath" and try to discover a principle that will protect both doctor and patient from unwanted, intrusive practices. Perhaps in the radical idea that a *patient* has the ultimate authority to determine what treatment he will or will not receive, and that the *doctor* has the final determination of what treatment or procedure she is willing to perform, we can find the mutual respect that we have lost in our willingness to force our wills upon one another. If individual self-ownership is to be respected, the physician is just as entitled to refuse his or her services in performing an abortion or any other medical procedure as the patient is in trying to obtain the voluntary assistance of another in his or her efforts.

Such a principle reflects both the self-limiting, yet individually sovereign, nature of property-based behavior. In restraining the over-reaching of *both* the doctor and the patient, such a principle fosters peaceful and orderly social practices. Without acquiring an understanding of this basic fact, we may very well find decision making about our health taken over by the modern *state*, which will tell us that we *must* submit to its mandated practices, as has been done by other tyrannical regimes. Unless we discover how our freedom is manifested in the authority we exercise over our own lives we may, like the feminists who wish to extend the state's power of military conscription to include women, find ourselves mouthing the new catechism that state-compelled medical treatment is a "fundamental right!"

To understand how liberty, peace, order, and private property coalesce to produce social integrity, necessitates an inquiry into the nature of *control*. How property is controlled within a given society tells us whether the well-being of *individuals* or of *institutions* will have central importance; which will be regarded as their own reason for being. To control property is to control life itself. The remaining question is—as it was in the *Dred Scott* case—whether the living are to be considered their own property, or only the resources of others. Contrary to the habits formed from our materialistic and mechanistic culture, such questions will force us to begin inner conversations with the spiritual nature of our being. As social creatures, such inquiries will also require us to bring into the discussion our fellow humans, with whom we have long been in deadly and destructive conflict as a consequence of our mania to control one another's lives. Once we learn the deeper significance of respecting the inviolability of our neighbors' boundaries, we may discover a richer dimension to our humanity.

Chapter Seven
Private Property and Social Order

Every thing that tends to insulate the individual- to surround
him with barriers of natural respect, so that each man shall feel
the world is his, and man shall treat with man as a sovereign state
with a sovereign state;—tends to true union as well as greatness.

— Ralph Waldo Emerson[1]

B ecause life is dependent upon the use and consumption of property, it is the nature of any property system—whether private or collective in form—to generate divisions between those who will, and those
who will not, be entitled to the enjoyment of various resources.
It is the entropic nature of life itself, not some belief system,
that dictates such harsh realities. The competition that invariably exists among all living things for negentropic resources
injects an element of conflict into the life process that cannot
be wholly excised. There will also be disappointments or even
hard feelings over the outcomes of such contests. Nothing in
the holographic model of social systems suggests that billions
of people will suddenly develop a collective mindset, and agree
to allocate resources in a manner that reflects a cheerful unanimity. Such illusions of group-think are what have turned the

---

[1] Ralph Waldo Emerson, "The American Scholar" (1837), in Brooks Atkin-
son, ed., *The Selected Writings of Ralph Waldo Emerson* (New York: The Modern
Library, 1950), p. 62.

dreams of utopian thinkers into the nightmares under which others have suffered and died. Society will become more peaceful and cooperative only as individuals transform the nature of their conduct with others. Such changes will arise marginally, at the boundaries where people transact their relationships and exchanges with one another. Like the young boy at the party chaperoned by my daughter, such individual transformations in consciousness are more likely to arise in an environment in which one's claims to ownership are respected by others. As a means of harmonizing our needs for both self-centered activity and social cooperation, a system of private ownership allows us to experience the deeper meaning of being human.

Again, what is being proposed here is not a utopian ideology, in which humanity will miraculously march off together, in lockstep cadence, to yet another visionary millennium. Utopian thinking is premised on the delusion of universally shared preferences, as well as the idea of a fixed end state. But a creative and vibrant society is a continuously changing one, comprised of people with a multitude of varied tastes, preferences, ambitions, and skills. And as history has demonstrated, creative change is not necessarily favorable to all mankind. There were many contemporaries for whom the Renaissance or the Industrial Revolution were not beneficial. The Luddite riots, for instance, were greatly influenced by the reaction of many artisans to the threats that industrialization posed to their established economic interests.

Regardless of the form of the social or political system under which we live, it is unavoidable that each of us will be entitled to use and consume particular resources to the exclusion of everyone else. This is but a fact of existence. Again, we witness the interrelatedness of apparent opposites: both individual liberty and social order depend upon a system grounded in the division that inheres in the nature of property. But lest any be inclined to treat this only as a paradoxical feature of *privately* owned property, it must be noted that *collective* ownership fosters the same divisiveness, but without a concomitant benefit to our sense of individuality, a topic to be explored more fully in chapter nine. Whether we live in the most ideologically repressive Marxist state, with its insistence upon state owner-ship of all productive property, or in a stateless community of cooperative, uncoerced individuals, some method will have to be arrived at for determining the answer to the question: *who gets to make decisions about what resources?* Whether the process involves voluntary, marketplace negotiations among compet-ing interests, or the arbitrary determinations of bureaucratic agencies, the use of a given item of property will be enjoyed by some to the exclusion of others.

Given the nature of property, there must be some arrange-ments for deciding who gets to stand or sleep or work or play within a given space and period of time, and who gets to con-sume what resources to the exclusion of everyone else, in our efforts to sustain ourselves. One thing is clear: all five billion of us cannot sleep in one bed at the same time, or eat the same hamburger. Whether I decide—by my act of asserting a claim to and taking control of previously unowned resources, or by purchasing the claim of another—where I am to live and sleep, or whether this decision is imposed upon me by some state bureaucrat, the inescapable fact remains that I will end up *some-place*, if only by default, and to the exclusion of everyone else on the planet. What this means is that *any* method of making such decisions will always separate the "occupier" or the "con-sumer" from the "non-occupier" or "non-consumer," the best intentions of the market participants or the noblest state hous-ing commissar to the contrary notwithstanding.

Whether property is to be controlled *privately* by individuals, or *collectively* by the state, tells us much about our existential sense of being. Are human beings ends in themselves, or only means to the ends of others? Do we regard ourselves as unique individuals, or as undifferentiated parts in some giant piece of social machinery? Are our individual interests to be considered inviolate, or subject to preemption by those who enjoy power?

Private property, as a system of social order, reflects the extent to which we are willing to acknowledge one another's autonomy and to limit the range of our own activities. Private property is the operating principle that makes real Immanuel Kant's admonition: "Act so that you treat humanity, whether in your own person or in that of another, always as an end and never as a means only."[2] It is a tenet that not only diffuses authority in society, but helps us reconcile our seemingly contradictory natures as self-seeking individuals who, at the same time, require some form of social organization in order to survive. Such a system of social individualism reflects the paradoxical nature of reality, in which self-interest finds expression in cooperation with others.

Respecting the inviolability of the boundaries that enclose our neighbors' property claims accords them our respect for the autonomy that is essential to any meaningful form of individual expression. In acknowledging one another's realms of unimpeded activity, we not only confirm our sense of their self-justifying existence but, in so doing, dissolve the barriers of distrust that separate us. Only in a condition of such mutual respect can we expect to find a reasonable basis for social harmony. Knowing that our claims to immunity from trespass are likely to be respected, and being aware of the advantages of cooperation, we are more inclined to organize ourselves in peaceful and productive ways than we are when, as now, organization tends to be grounded in fear and the violent and divisive assumptions of coercive power.

The property principle operates as a buffer, separating the realm of your decision making from mine. We need to have our will free of coercion, and the inviolability of our sense of self acknowledged, before we will feel comfortable enough to cooperate with others and feel safe within groups. Our social organizations must reflect these qualities with a sense of wholeness and integrity before we can live in harmony with our neighbors, instead of the counterfeit forms offered by the state. It is only within systems in which each of us enjoys the unrestrained

---

[2]Immanuel Kant, *Critique of Practical Reason and Other Writings in Moral Philosophy*, trans. and ed. by Lewis White Beck (Chicago: University of Chicago Press, 1949), p. 87.

autonomy to act in furtherance of our individual interests that our personal and social interests can merge. When decision-making is decentralized into a system of privately owned property, individual self-interest and cooperation coalesce to maximize personal liberty and social harmony. With authority diffused into the hands of individuals, each of us enjoys control over some portion of the world within which we can pursue our interests in our own way. What we share in common are our individual needs for a sphere of action in which we can be as autonomous, spontaneous, arbitrary, self-indulgent, and as unanswerable to others as we care to be, without being subject to any coercive preemption by others. At the same time, cooperation with others is premised upon sharing or exchanging with one another that which belongs to each of us (e.g., our personal energies or our material resources).

The decentralization of decision-making that is implicit in a system of privately-owned property provides another instance of the unity that inheres in apparent opposites. By distributing authority widely rather than narrowly, private property provides a greater flexibility allowing individuals to voluntarily join with others in concentrated communities in which they can choose to associate with others in pursuit of shared interests. The Silicon Valley, artists colonies, Detroit automobile manufacturing, Hollywood film production companies, and religious communes, are just a handful of examples of the interrelated dynamics of decentralized and concentrated activity.

Whether our relationships with others will be increasingly based upon state-driven *coercion*, or will find a more creative expression in *agreements*, depends upon our attitudes about the inviolability of property claims. When we acknowledge property boundary lines, rather than statutes or court decisions, as confining the range of our personal actions, mutual respect for one another's boundaries integrates our individual and social needs and, as a consequence, generates liberty and order in society.

One need not rely on hypotheticals or theoretical analyses to demonstrate the social, or transactional, negotiation for property claims. There is an emerging field of study in law regarding the role played by social norms—enforced informally by interpersonal pressures rather than coercive state power—in maintaining peaceful and orderly behavior. The Amish have used such methods for decades to provide for an orderly, productive, and mutually-supportive society.[3] In Northern Ireland, a nation bloodied by political and religious divisiveness, many of those desiring to end such violence have taken to publicly shaming the participants into changing their ways.[4]

There is a well-documented history of the respect accorded to property and contract rights along the overland trails in nineteenth-century America. In a harsh and uncertain environment in which there were no courts, judges, prisons, administrative agencies, or other government law enforcement officials, emigrants freely and peacefully negotiated with one another over claims to all kinds of chattels and intangible property interests. High levels of respect were accorded the property claims of both acquaintances and total strangers, even in situations in which scarcity existed. Such negotiated rights were sometimes so sophisticated as to provide for contract terms designed to benefit future wagon trains. In one such case, a wagon train had built a raft for use in fording a river. Upon completion of its crossing, the wagon train company sold the raft to the next wagon train, with the understanding that it would later be sold to subsequent trains at a price no higher than that agreed to by the original contracting parties. When a much later wagon train tried to sell the raft to its successor at a higher price than the original one, the successor was able to successfully invoke the terms of the initial contract to which neither group had

---

[3]See, e.g., John A. Hostetler, *Amish Society*, 3rd ed. (Baltimore: The Johns Hopkins University Press, 1980); Steven M. Nolt, *A History of the Amish* (Intercourse, Penn.: Good Books, 1992); Donald B. Kraybill, ed., *The Amish and the State* (Baltimore: The Johns Hopkins University Press, 1993).

[4]See, e.g., David Barash, *The Survival Game: How Game Theory Explains the Biology of Cooperation* (New York: Macmillan, 2003), p. 98.

been a party.[5] Such an example attests not only to the power of social respect for property interests, but to the effectiveness of information systems, even on the undeveloped frontier, in communicating terms of agreements to unknown strangers!

A more recent study involves residents of Shasta County, California and their methods for dealing with damage done to farmers' lands by ranchers' cattle. Some parts of this agricultural county were legally defined as "open range," and other parts were designated "closed range" territories. In open range areas, cattlemen were lawfully free to allow their livestock to wander freely, without being legally responsible for damages that might accrue to the crops of neighboring farmers. If the farmers wanted to prevent such trespasses, they would be expected to build fences to keep out the offending cattle. In closed range areas, by contrast, the cattlemen had the legal duty to fence in their cattle, and would be liable for damages done to neighboring property owners should the fences not keep their animals in.

Those trained in purely positivist definitions of proper behavior would intuit that, if X's cattle got off his property and wandered onto Y's land and did damage, the question of X's liability would depend upon which legally defined area was implicated. It did not. The residents of this county had their *own* understanding of the rights and obligations of property ownership totally apart from what the formal legal system dictated. It was understood, both by the cattlemen and the farmers, that if X's cattle caused damage to Y's property, X was obligated to compensate Y for his loss, even though, in an open range district, he would not have any *legally enforceable* duty to do so. Because such expectations were contrary to formal legal requirements, the residents developed their own informal, nonviolent ways of enforcing these community standards upon the occasional recalcitrant cattleman. Subtle methods of communication, informal accounting practices, and economic inducements,

---

[5]John Phillip Reid, *Law for the Elephant: Property and Social Behavior on the Overland Trail* (San Marino, Calif.: The Huntington Library, 1980), pp. 300–01.

helped provide the social pressures to keep this system working.[6] These examples illustrate how peaceful, long-term systems of order can be voluntarily maintained, not only in the *absence* of state rules, but in *spite* of them.

Nowhere was the order produced through mutual respect for property claims more vivid than in the early gold mining camps in the western states. So prevalent was the regard for one another's property interests that miners' gold, bank deposits, and even gambling stakes could be freely left in the open by their absent owners without fear of loss. One early scholar observed:

> The miners needed no criminal code. It is simply   and literally true that there was a short time in California, in 1848, when crime was almost absolutely unknown, when pounds and pints of gold were left unguarded in tents and cabins, or thrown down on the hillside, or handed about through a crowd for inspection. . . . Men have told me that they have known as much as a washbasinful of gold-dust to be left on the table in an open tent while the owners were at work in their claim a mile distant. . . . There was no theft, and no disorder; few troublesome disputes occurred about boundaries and water-rights.[7]

A writer from that period, Sarah Royce, stated: "I had seen with my own eyes, buckskin purses half full of gold-dust, lying on a rock near the road-side, while the owners were working some distance off. So I was not afraid of robbery."[8] Based upon his personal experiences, an Idaho attorney from this period declared that "life was safe, property was safe" in the mining camps.[9]

---

[6]Robert C. Ellickson, *Order Without Law: How Neighbors Settle Disputes* (Cambridge, Mass.: Harvard University Press, 1991).

[7]Shinn, *Mining Camps*, pp. 111, 112; also quoted in Vardis Fisher and Opel Laurel Holmes, *Gold Rushes and Mining Camps of the Early American West* (Caldwell, Idaho: The Caxton Printers, Ltd., 1968), p. 275.

[8]Fisher and Holmes, ibid.

[9]Ibid.

Although another student suggested that widespread honesty among the miners was brought about by a respect for "the summary justice likely to be dispensed by the crowd,"[10] such presumed fears did not seem to dissuade the criminal types who swarmed into California following the discovery of new gold fields in 1849. The divergent behavior of the early miners and the plunderers was more likely due to dissimilarities in character of the two groups, as is reflected in the observation of one contemporary that the latter group "were a different kind of people; more of the brute order."[11] Such behavior differences demonstrate, as Carl Jung and others have insisted,[12] that the quality of life in any society is the consequence of the character of the people who comprise it—that social order is a product not of the fear of punishment, but of the respect neighbors accord one another's interests. In our dealings with the state, we do not negotiate from the position of an uncoerced free will, but are compelled by threats of violence to our interests. In contrast, our informal, social negotiations are premised upon a mutuality of respect for our individualities.

Such examples provide evidence of how individual liberty, social harmony, and responsible behavior are measured by the respect we accord to one another's property interests. Likewise, tyranny, social disorder, and irresponsible conduct derive from property violations, which become formalized as the *modus operandi* of all political systems.

If we are to learn to live responsibly, we must begin by understanding that the "wrongs" others perpetrate upon us, and from which we desire protection, are nothing more than trespasses to our property interests. A peaceful social order consists, in major part, of men and women conducting their

---

[10] J.D. Borthwick, *Three Years in California*, Joseph Gaer, ed. (Edinburgh and London: William Blackwood & Sons, 1857); quoted in Fisher and Holmes, ibid., p. 276.

[11] Daniel Knower, *The Adventures of a Forty-Niner* (Albany, N.Y.: Weed-Parsons Printing, 1894), quoted in Fisher and Holmes, ibid., p. 276.

[12] C.G. Jung, *Psychological Reflections* (Princeton, N.J.: Princeton University Press, 1970), p. 178.

affairs without causing injury to one another, an end that requires us to focus our attention on understanding the social implications of property. Such crimes as murder, rape, assault and battery, and kidnapping, are *not*—despite the pronouncements of government officials—wrongs committed against an amorphous, collectively-defined "society," but violent *trespasses* against the property interest the victim has in his or her person. When we declare such actions to be "crimes against the state," we are implicitly recognizing the state's claim to the ownership of our person.[13] Likewise, acts of burglary, theft, embezzlement, arson, forgery, and shoplifting, are not offenses against the state, even though the state brings the criminal action against the accused, but invasions of the real or personal property interests of an *owner*.

It is the distinction between crimes in which there are property trespasses, and those in which such trespasses do not occur, that constitutes the difference between "victimizing" and "victimless" crimes (once again, a failure to heed Pynchon's warning about the adverse consequences of asking the wrong questions). So accustomed have we become to blurring the meaning of property in our lives that we have reduced the distinction to a vague abstraction that begs the question of what kinds of acts these are. Stated in property terms, a *victimless* crime (e.g., drug use, gambling, prostitution, pornography, smuggling, etc.) is one in which the state, for reasons of its own, chooses to criminalize conduct that would not otherwise amount to a property trespass against another. Criminalizing such conduct, in fact, violates the property interests of the purported criminal as well as his customers by depriving them of the legal right to exercise control over their own property.

---

[13]Lest any doubt that government regulation amounts to the state's claiming an ownership interest in people, consider Justice Harlan's dissenting opinion in *Lochner v. New York* (198 U.S. 45 (1905)), a case striking down state legislation limiting the number of hours employees could work in bakeries. In Harlan's view, long hours "may endanger the health and shorten the lives of the workmen, thereby *diminishing their physical and mental capacity to serve the state* and to provide for those dependent upon them" (p. 72; emphasis added).

The same analysis can be applied to other types of injuries. The tort of injuring another through the negligent operation of an automobile, for instance, amounts to a trespass to the boundaries of the victim, as well as to other interests (e.g., the victim's car) damaged by the defendant's act. The defendant's wrong was not that he had been driving in a negligent or reckless manner—even though such behavior may have produced the injury—but that he had failed to control his property in such a way as to prevent a trespass upon the interests of his victim. A world organized on the principle of the inviolability of property interests is a world that reduces injuries to others. Responsible behavior is thus encouraged, as the scope of one's liberty to act ends at his or her property boundaries.

Likewise, a breach of contract action arises out of an alleged violation of a property interest. A and B enter into an agreement by which A is to sell B her claim to the ownership of a new television set, and B agrees to pay A $500 for the set. When it comes time to perform, A delivers B a *used* television set. Because a contract is nothing more than an agreement to transfer ownership claims, B has not received the ownership claim for the agreed upon property.

Most of our societal problems arise from a failure to stay out of one another's way. Schools interfere with children's learning, not only by thwarting their wills, but in replacing intellectually significant learning with politically-based indoctrination; government agencies impede our lives by economic regulations that increase production costs which, in turn, generate higher prices and increased unemployment and, as a consequence, foster greater tendencies toward concentration that accelerate entropic processes;[14] state-licensed medical professions and the Food and Drug Administration

---

[14]See, Walter Adams, "The Military-Industrial Complex and the New Industrial State," *American Economic Review* 58 (May, 1968): 652–65; reprinted in Ralph Andreano, ed., *Superconcentration/Supercorporation* (Andover, Mass.: Warner Modular Publications, 1973), R-337-2; Murray L. Weidenbaum, *Government-Mandated Price Increases: A Neglected Aspect of Inflation* (Washington, D.C.: American Enterprise Institute for Public Policy Research, 1975).

dictate what health care services we may lawfully select, and what treatments and medications we may consume; governments hinder the free expression of ideas and lifestyles; and countless coveys of people-pushers demand legislation mandating standards of personal behavior ranging from child-rearing practices to smoking, to the kinds of food and other substances we may ingest, to our safety, to our bodily weight, to how we speak to one another, to whether we can own guns, and other practices that are regularly added. This madness has gone so far as to produce a bill in the California legislature making it a crime punishable by as much as a one-year prison sentence to spank a child.[15] Whether as parents, or in social relationships, or in efforts to make the world better, we insist on getting in one another's way because we have not learned that most important of social graces: respecting the inviolability of one another's boundaries. Like young puppies, most of us are not housebroken. We babble our bromides about the insignificance of property principles, because to do otherwise would limit our ambitions to control the lives of others and reveal our mutual contempt for one another's independence.

Such attempts to micromanage the daily lives of others seem to be part of the continuing effort by adherents to the vertically-structured social model to maintain its established position. As suggested earlier, the continuing process of change that is bringing about decentralized, horizontal networks poses a threat to members of the institutional order who are disinclined to participate in the transformation. To such people, social systems that run themselves without formal direction and superintendence is not only disturbing to their ambitions for power, but represents a form of fanciful thinking. With an effort that approaches a kind of religious reaffirmation of the old order, the statists resort to a constant repetition of their centralist, coercive methods at ever more detailed levels of human behavior. Such conduct is reminiscent of the behaviors Abraham

---

[15]*San Francisco Chronicle*, January 21, 2007, p. E-7.

Maslow saw exhibited by brain-injured patients who, in their repetitious patterns "manage to maintain their equilibrium by avoiding everything unfamiliar and strange and by ordering their restricted world in such a neat, disciplined, orderly fashion that everything in the world can be counted upon."[16]

Much like Maslow's patients, statists see their world of centralized power structures being enervated by life forces over which they are losing control, and imagine that the rote repetition of familiar patterns will reconfirm its vibrancy. At an unconscious level, perhaps, it may be sensed that if the *ancien regime* is undergoing its decline and fall, the dying model might be revivified—or at least its vital signs made to so appear—by the proliferation of new, centrally-imposed restraints upon the lives of unfettered men and women. Such obsessive efforts seek to reconfirm the validity of an antiquated system that no longer satisfies people's expectations. War, of course, is the most dramatic expression of politically-structured violence as well as being an undertaking that brings fearful people back into a herd mentality, which is why it has become the cornerstone of modern statist efforts to preserve power over people. Perhaps this is why expansions of the war system have been such frequent precursors to the collapse of previous civilizations.

Because the power of the state directly correlates with the extent to which it usurps control over privately-owned property, political and legal systems have little interest in generating a fundamental respect for property principles. As we have seen, alternative rationales (e.g., "health," "safety," "offenses against the state") are offered as the basis for resolving wrongs or disputes that would otherwise be subject to a property analysis. When "reasonableness," the "balancing of interests," "fairness," "justice," and other amorphous vagaries become substituted for an owner's objections to a more clearly defined trespass, it becomes quite easy for people to call upon the state to force a

---

[16]Abraham Maslow, "A Theory of Human Motivation," in *Psychological Review* (1943): 370ff.

neighbor to cease doing what a property principle would otherwise allow him to do.

This is how the violation of property interests underlies most of our social difficulties. Conflict arises from the failure of people to effectively identify or to respect property boundaries. When we regard one another's ownership interests as inviolable, interpersonal conflicts do not arise. But as we have seen, every act of the state involves a forcible intrusion upon the interests of property owners. Whether such governmental action takes the form of regulations that restrict an owner's control of his or her property, or forcibly transfers ownership claims to others (e.g., eminent domain), or amounts to outright confiscation (e.g., taxation), actions by the state invariably produce conflicts between owners who seek to control their property for their own ends and non-owners who use state power to force owners to conform their behavior to their purposes. The state, whether through statutory enactments or judicial holdings, thus introduces contradiction and conflict into society. The peaceful and harmonious relations that would otherwise follow from a respect for property claims, collapse into a formal system of predation, with people organizing into groups to achieve what would otherwise have to depend upon contracts among owners.

Intellectuals, most of whom have their own preferences for political intervention into people's lives for redistributive purposes, have not been very supportive of a system that would extend liberty into the realm where people most need it: the conduct of their daily lives. In the world of *ideas*, where intellectuals are most protective of the inviolability of their boundaries, most accept, as an expression of the essence of liberty, the principle erroneously attributed to Voltaire: "though I disapprove of what you say, I will defend to the death your right to say it." But why are such sentiments so narrowly confined to *intellectual* matters, and rejected when applied to the more mundane *actions* that are central to and comprise so much more of our daily lives? How much freer would both our intellectual and material lives be if we were to modify the aforesaid proposition by telling our neighbor: "though I disapprove of how you conduct your life, as long as you do not violate the property boundaries of others, I shall defend to the death your right to act as you choose"? We might then move beyond the empty bromides by which we feign "love" for our fellow humans while, at the same time, seeking ways to force them to conform to our expectations.[17]

Social order arises not so much from learning to love our neighbor, as in learning to respect him. We do not exhibit such respect when, in order to accomplish our purposes, we insist upon violating his will regarding what is his to control. Neither do our professions of love for others mean much when we are prepared to deny others their existential individuality. There is nothing quite so destructive of social harmony as arrogant, self-righteous men and women mobilizing against the tastes and lifestyles of their neighbors.

When we insist upon the use of legalized force to address what we perceive as social problems, we not only subvert the conflict-resolving role property plays throughout much of nature, but we foreclose any alternative practices. The assumption that only coercive intervention by the state is worthy of practical consideration in such matters ignores the role of informal, interpersonal methods of resolving our differences with one another. Worse still, our resort to force sends a message of contempt to our fellow beings whose purposes we find incompatible with our own, further alienating ourselves from one another and fostering more conflict. We have too often failed to heed the warning of Emerson: "Good men must not obey the

---

[17]If we were to apply such thinking to the realm of learning with as much unfocused facility as we do to economic matters, we would quickly see the absurdity of such ideas. Does *knowledge* come in some fixed quantity, with the more learned having garnered an "unfair" share at the expense of the unlearned? Perhaps it is the function of the government school system to "redistribute" the ignorance, to the end that all can be equally unknowledgeable and operate from a "level playing field." Were the creative geniuses of human history—Aristotle, Copernicus, Shakespeare, Francis Bacon, Dante, Lao Tzu, Newton, Beethoven, the Curies, Leonardo da Vinci, Einstein, Blake, George Washington Carver, Edison, to name but a few—nothing more than pillagers, "robber intellects," who stole from some common storehouse of human inventiveness and insight?

laws too well."[18] We have also overlooked the value of our own life experiences for lessons in resolving disagreements without having to resort to formalized coercion.

As long as we live in society, we will always have a need for standards of conduct, a condition necessitated by the property question. If the inviolability of property boundaries is a civilizing standard that makes for a free, creative, and orderly society, the question arises: how is such a principle to take form in the interactions of people? Historically, we have too often turned to the state to have rules of conduct generated by fiat and enforced by coercive means. But when force is employed, property interests are at once violated. The state becomes the very problem it had, in theory, been created to prevent.

But what if rule-making and enforcement is confined to property owners themselves, beginning with the self-ownership principle? What if our respect for the inviolability of property claims began with the recognition that each person was the sole authority over their respective interests, and was obligated to no one else unless he or she had voluntarily chosen to be bound? What if we recognized that, if I wanted to enjoy some property interest of yours, I would have to enter into a contract with you to do so?

This approach raises the question: what if one party breached the contract, or intentionally or unintentionally trespassed the interests of another? How would the inviolability principle be enforced? Would it be possible to do so without the use of coercion, whether employed by the state or the offended individual? Is it possible to use boycotts, ostracism, marketplace pressures, or other social means—which do not forcibly deprive the offender of his property interests—to persuade him to rectify his wrong? Might we also resort to contracts of insurance to compensate us for our losses? Because we are so unaccustomed to thinking in such non-coercive ways, and regard rule-breaking as

---

[18]Ralph Waldo Emerson, *Politics*, published in 1844 and included in *The Selected Writings of Ralph Waldo Emerson*, p. 427.

an invitation to resort to force, we are apt to dismiss these suggested alternatives as "impractical."

Albert Einstein informed us that "problems . . . cannot
be solved by thinking the way we thought when we created
them."[19] If our prior learning leads us to react with an angry "no"
to the question of seeking alternative practices, let us remember
that such prior learning is what is destroying us! If we are to
resolve our problems before they consume us, we might begin
by taking the responsibility that is inseparable from decision-
making control over our lives. To the degree we insist upon
directing our own conduct, we hasten the decline of the prevailing model of state authority. In the course of doing so, we
may actually generate—rather than just think or talk about—a
system of rule-making and enforcement of horizontal dimensions with no hierarchy of authority, and in which all rules arise
through the peaceful means of contract, custom, and manners.

As suggested earlier, the property concept qualifies as an
informal system of manners, a way of respecting the worthiness and inviolability of others and, in reflection, ourselves.
The word "manners" has a common ancestry with the word
"manage," meaning "to control and direct,"[20] which has property connotations. Perhaps our more distant ancestors understood what we have chosen to ignore at the cost of the conflict
and violence that permeates modern society: namely, that *proper*
and *well-mannered* behavior is intrinsically related to the decision making of property owners.

Each of us experiences trespasses in our life, although
mostly in *de minimis* ways. A neighbor's dog makes a mess in
our yard, or barks incessantly at night; a teenager annoys us
with a "boom-box" turned up as loud as it will play; or we are
bumped and jostled as we get onto a subway or elevator. We
may feel anger at the disrespect shown to us by the other person,

---

[19] Alice Calaprice, ed., *The Expanded Quotable Einstein* (Princeton, N.J.: Princeton University Press, 2000), p. 317.

[20] Partridge, *Origins*, p. 378; *Webster's Third New International Dictionary*, p.
1372.

although an apology—which acknowledges our claim to not be trespassed—usually subdues our reaction. Once again, we see the role played by manners in giving respect to individual boundaries in situations, usually of a transient nature, in which property interests are not clearly defined. Unfortunately, in a culture in which people have internalized the idea that "property rights are not absolute," an appeal to manners often avail us not. We tend to become more confrontational, looking upon every such trespass, no matter how trivial, as a call to more aggressive responses.

Part of learning to live as mature individuals in society consists in our willingness to absorb unintended and relatively insignificant trespasses by others, without developing a self-righteous need for retribution. Implicit in failing to do so is much of what we see in our current world: the breakdown of harmonious interconnectedness as so many treat every slight or encroachment as a cause for angry reaction if not a lawsuit. But how much of such a reflexive response is occasioned by a widespread disrespect for property interests perhaps leading one who has been subject to even a relatively minor intrusion to overreact to its significance?

Because the control of private property and the corruption of language are central to the functioning of political systems, it is not surprising to discover the property concept twisted in ways that make it increasingly difficult for people to distinguish trespasses by others from crude, ill-mannered, or offensive behavior that does not result in a trespass. Herein are found the seeds of "political correctness." More and more of us seem prepared to regard repulsive and contemptible language and behavior as we would a physical trespass. In some instances, there is a willingness to impose harsher penalties upon vulgar or abhorrent conduct than upon physically intrusive offenses. Expressions of racial, ethnic, or gender-based hatred or other forms of bigotry; motorists' "road rage"; or ill-chosen words that do not comport with fashionable attitudes, are often met with demands for punishment that exceed any injury-in-fact.

Personally offensive behavior can generate reactions that, to the recipient, may be more upsetting than a physical trespass. One person may make vulgar comments, or walk down a public street in the nude, greatly annoying others, even though no property violation occurs. It is in such instances that manners have particular application, with non-violent social pressures—such as ostracism being a more effective means of reforming rude behavior than resort to governmental trespasses upon the offending person.

The distorted thinking that conflates trespassing and non-trespassing behavior has reduced the capacity for making critical distinctions in other areas. Thus, at least one prominent feminist has written that "intercourse"—the means by which reproduction takes place among most species—is a "violation of boundaries" of women, who are "forced" to submit to "those who dominate them." She proceeds to analogize women, politically, to "occupied people."[21] Likewise, school administrators have found themselves unable to distinguish between a child bringing a cough drop to school from one bringing heroin; airport security agents periodically bring ridicule upon themselves by failing to differentiate a genuine weapon from fingernail clippers or other harmless items; while the criminal justice system continues to insist that no important distinction exists between *victimizing* and *victimless* crimes. It is the essence of intelligence to be able to discriminate, i.e., to make relevant distinctions between and among various facts and principles and alternative courses of action. Not that many years ago, it was considered a *compliment* to tell another that he or she had a "discriminating" mind. Thanks to the politically generated corruption of language and thought, such a statement now stands as an *accusation*, a generic offense to human decency!

Discrimination is essential to all intelligent thinking and behavior, and depends upon one having clear boundary lines, worthy of the respect of rational minds, that define a speaker's

---

[21]Andrea Dworkin, *Intercourse* (London: Secker & Warburg, 1987), pp. 122–24.

basis for making distinctions. It has been the failure to discriminate amongst the various standards by which people *do* discriminate that produces so much of our social confusion. Is a property owner discriminating—on grounds of which we disapprove—against another being allowed to enjoy access to his property, or is the state doing so when it compels an owner to act in accordance with standards it has mandated? Because the state enjoys a monopoly on the use of force, it has long been thought that its discriminatory acts ought to be kept to a minimum (e.g., criminal statutes that treat murderers, rapists, and thieves differently than non-criminals). But if an owner is the absolute authority over what he or she owns, upon what basis, other than a trespass, can another claim a forceful liberty to enter against the owner's will? Why should a private owner be precluded from denying others the enjoyment of his or her property on any grounds whatever? The intolerance exhibited by one who refuses to associate with those of another race, religion, or lifestyle, is more than matched by others who refuse to tolerate such a bigoted person's decisions regarding his or her own property. As suggested earlier, we pay too little attention in both thought and behavior to the importance of boundary lines. This makes it easy for some to conclude that if a given opinion or act of another is sufficiently offensive, even though not amounting to a trespass, it may be suppressed or punished by the state.

Smoking in public (e.g., in restaurants, airliners, place of employment) is another issue that can most appropriately be seen as raising not *health*, but *trespass* questions. In popular and political discussions on this topic, the issue is usually framed in terms of the smoker's freedom to smoke and the nonsmoker's right to be free of unhealthful substances. Rarely is the question raised as to the restaurant owner's liberty of deciding whether to allow smoking or not. If the restaurateur has a stated policy of permitting people to smoke in his establishment, a customer who is aware of this fact would seem to have contractually agreed to the possibility of breathing unwanted smoke, thus eliminating any trespass claim. When the question is posed in such abstract ways, without any clear lines of definition and limitation, one can understand why the courts and legislative bodies respond by trying to "balance" such "competing" interests. Again, if we rephrase the question, we discover that conflict has been generated because the property principle has been abandoned. If reframed as a property trespass issue, the amorphous and uncertain nature of the invasion is eliminated. As between a smoker and nonsmoker there are no interests to be "balanced" when one person trespasses the boundaries of another.

Suppose you are having dinner in a restaurant, and a patron at the next table begins smoking a cigarette. Her smoke enters your lungs, gets embedded in your hair and clothing, and causes your eyes to water. You object to this. It should be evident that this smoker has committed a trespass upon you. Whether or not second-hand smoke constitutes a health hazard, your claim to be free from such unwanted invasions of what is yours, i.e., your body and clothing, should be a sufficient basis for your objection. For the smoker to suggest that her freedom to smoke encompasses the right to commit such trespasses is to fail to understand that liberty has a principled meaning only insofar as it is grounded in, and defined by, a mutual respect for one another's property boundaries. If an issue of this sort should come to court—and, in our confrontational society it probably will—the only inquiry necessary for a court to make would be a factual one: did the trespass occur? There would be no room for the court to step in and start "assigning" and "balancing"— or, more accurately, confiscating and reassigning—the property rights of individuals.

The same analysis could be applied to what was, a number of years ago, one of the more controversial issues in California: the aerial spraying, with malathion, of entire cities, for the purpose of trying to prevent the spread of the Mediterranean fruit-fly. Those who objected to having their bodies, homes, cars, plants, and pets sprayed with this pesticide had to rest their arguments on presumed *health* problems that might arise. In so doing, the burden of proof shifted to them to show the harm that would result from such spraying, a burden they were unable to meet. Relatively few people saw this as a property trespass issue to be resolved only by a determination of whether an invasion had occurred, not the degree of physical harm suffered by the owner, or whether he or she was being "unreasonable" in making an objection. At the same time, the State of California exhibited its usual confused commitment to mixed premises: in spite of tens of thousands of people expressing strong opposition to such spraying, the state, more attuned to benefiting commercial and agricultural interests, continued to spray. In a clear demonstration of where human beings rank in the state's hierarchy of concerns, the government halted the spraying in a region in which *kangaroo rats* residedx[22]

One sees, in such examples, how the elements of "boundary," "claim," and "control" coalesce to provide a property-based analysis of political issues. Who has the ultimate authority ("claim") to exercise decision-making ("control") over any given item of property ("boundary")? How we answer that question determines whether society will be characterized by peaceful relationships or by conflict.

Politics is the mobilization of property trespasses and despoliation. All political quarrels come down to a failure to identify and/or respect property boundaries. Nowhere is this more evident than in such an emotionally charged issue as *abortion*. This question illustrates, as clearly as any issue, the confusion and conflict that arises from asking the wrong questions. By failing to address the issue in terms of property principles, each side has contributed to an irresolvable—and politically advantageous—conflict.

The abortion debate has pitted the "pro-choice" advocates against "pro-life" supporters, abstract concepts whose inconsistent application further clouds any clear meaning. Most "pro-choice" supporters are nonetheless disposed to deprive people of their right to make decisions in other areas (e.g., to discriminate

---

[22]*Los Angeles Times*, May 3, 1990, Sect. B, p. 12.

against others on a variety of matters, or to support various governmental programs), while most "pro-life" defenders have proven themselves eager supporters of wars and capital punishment. It should not surprise us that such utter confusion has generated much heat but little light in our world.

In an effort to obscure the lethal nature of abortions, and thus make the practice less disturbing to the otherwise humane sentiments of its proponents, most people allow the state to define who is and who is not a "person." History should remind us of the dangers inherent in conferring such authority upon political systems. The American government defined the rights of slaves and Indians out of existence, while greatly restricting those of married women; and twentieth-century tyrannies such as Nazi Germany, China, and the Soviet Union defined whole categories of people out of legal existence. Such historic experiences should inform our intelligence before we become enthusiasts for current listings of non-persons.

It is unfashionable to state, albeit undeniable, that from the moment of conception onward, an embryo is a living being with a distinct DNA of its own, a DNA that derives from, but is other than, that of either parent. Contrary to the reductionists who would debase the embryo as the functional equivalent of a wart or a cyst, it is a genetically unique individual, a fact known to even a first year biology student. Nor should one accept, without examination, the argument that an embryo is still in a "developmental" stage and is, therefore, not a "person." Because of the negentropic nature of life, each of us is in a continuing state of development up until the time of our death. I continue to write, into my seventies, and have recently taken up painting, one way of expressing the changes that continue to occur within me throughout my life. This characterization of embryos by the pro-abortion advocates is but another manifestation of a mechanistic vision of nature.

Attributing "self-ownership" to an embryo may pose some difficulties, however, since it is unlikely that embryos have ever consciously asserted such claims. The same can be said, however, of any infant or, for that matter, most adults: who, among us, has ever made a conscious declaration to be a self-owner? Have you or I done so, if we continue to acknowledge the rightful authority of the state to regulate, tax, and conscript us into its service? When I ask my first year law students whether they own themselves—and whether they understand the implications of whatever answer they give—most sit in stunned silence at the audacity of such an existential question. Thus, if a claim of self-ownership is dependent upon an individual giving conscious voice thereto, the "right" to kill an infant or, perhaps, an adult, could be as justified as the killing of an embryo. It is more plausible, perhaps—and much safer—to presume a claim of self-ownership derived from the self-sustaining, self-controlling actions of each individual, whether embryo or octogenarian.

If we are prepared to acknowledge self-ownership for any genetically identifiable human being, an intentional abortion amounts to an invasion of the embryo's property interest, and the mother and her doctor have trespassed upon that interest. On the other hand, the mother is also a self-owning being, and is entitled to not have her property boundaries trespassed by others (e.g., the state). The pro-abortion advocate would likely argue that the embryo is a trespasser upon the woman, but as almost all pregnancies are occasioned by a volitional act of the woman—and never as the result of a conscious entry by the embryo—such a contention would fail. But even if the embryo were the product of a rape—a non-volitional act by the woman—the embryo is not the wrongdoer but an unintended consequence of the crime. He or she would be, at worst, an unintentional trespasser, to which the question must be answered as to whether a property owner may rightfully take the life of a trespasser. From a property perspective, we are thus left with the seemingly anomalous situation that the embryo, as a self-owning person, is entitled to not be aborted, while the mother, also a self-owning person, is entitled to not have the state trespass upon her in order to restrain the exercise of her decision-making. When abortion becomes a political (i.e., divisive) issue, devoid of respect for property principles, different groups become polarized out of a failure to refine the question. For the state to intervene in the matter in order to enjoin the abortion would constitute a trespass to the mother.

If both the embryo and the mother are persons with separate but necessarily interconnected property interests, and the state's intervention would amount to a trespass of the mother's boundaries, does this mean that, in a society that fully respected property interests, a mother would be *free* to kill this other person? If the answer is "yes," as it applies to a pregnant woman, would it also apply to the rest of us: that we are *free* to kill—or, as a friend of mine used to remind me, free to *try* to do so—another person? *Precisely!* We are free, not because the state, or a religion, or a constitution, or an ideology tells us that we are, but because *each one of us is in control of our energies and conduct*. How each of us chooses to exercise our freedom determines not only the content of our own character, but whether we will live in peace or conflict, cooperation or confrontation, with others. Here again, however, we find ourselves confronted by the fear of being responsible for our own liberty—Kaufmann's "decidophobia"—that causes so many of us to look to constituted "authorities" to render moral decisions for us when we are faced with irresolvable conflicts. As with all property questions, who will make decisions about what?

Social order arises when the values of "peace" and "liberty" are integrated through respect for the inviolability of property boundaries. When social issues are severed into mutually-exclusive categories such as "pro-life" and "pro-choice," the foundations of political division are set in place. Groups compete for control of the coercive machinery of the state in order to enforce their visions upon others. When our thinking is free of conflict and contradiction, however, we are able to discover that "pro-life" and "pro-choice" imply one another. Liberty, exercised within the self-limiting nature of property ownership, is the condition in which individuals are able to make the *choices* upon which the quality of their *lives* depend.

Our daily newspapers are filled with abundant empirical evidence that each of us is free to engage in all kinds of harmful actions, in spite of numerous laws to the contrary. To say that we are *free* to commit injuries upon others does not imply, however, that we are *entitled* to do so, or that such acts are justifiable. Recalling the common origins of the two words, "proper" behavior is that which a "property" owner is entitled to make, i.e., decision-making within the boundaries of what one owns. If we are to be self-owning, self-controlling beings, we must be prepared to acknowledge that our boundaries serve not only to exclude the intrusions of *others*, but to circumscribe the range of *our* actions. Without the concept of property boundaries to define the limits of our actions, our claims become, quite literally, *boundless*. The propriety of our behavior then becomes measured by the constantly shifting fashions of legislation, public opinion polls, cultural tastes, and prejudices formed by unconscious forces.

Perhaps it is time for us all to walk away from both the practice and the self-righteous thinking that presumes the legitimacy of the power of the state to usurp both control over and responsibility for our actions. As people become aware that their responsibility extends to the full range of their actions, and can neither be limited nor increased by the dictates of political fashion, perhaps they will discover their own way to responsible behavior. If not, no amount of political maneuvering or religious/ideological commitment seems capable of forestalling the entropic fate of our civilization.

Herein lies the challenge for all who understand the importance of human freedom: am I able to insist upon the full range of my authority over my own life and, at the same time, respect the inviolability of the boundary lines that distinguish my authority from that of my neighbors? It is the nature of political systems to be dominated by short-term thinking that pays little attention to transcendent principles having no immediate, observable consequences. Violating the will of individuals concerning what is theirs to control is the ultimate default response by the state. Such a mindset is not only incapable of sustaining a productive society but, worse, the failure to see the interconnected nature of respect for property boundaries helps to destroy civilized societies. This is what living in a condition of liberty is all about: making our own choices and accepting the responsibility for those choices, not by participating in state-induced deceptions designed to conceal the consequences of our self-indulgent actions.

Chapter Eight
Property and the Environment

I am in a world which is in me.

— Paul Valery

What are the implications of privately owned property for the world in which we live? In order to demonstrate the pragmatic significance of the principle being developed herein, it might be helpful to focus on one issue that, more than most others, has attracted the attention of thoughtful men and women. Using the environment as an example, how would human behavior differ if decision-making were diffused among each of us as property owners, rather than concentrated in the hands of those who exercise political power? What differences might we observe between social systems premised on *private* ownership rather than *collectivism*?

Protecting the environment has become a major concern in our world, perhaps reflecting Marshall McLuhan's prognosis that the space program, by allowing us to see Earth from space, would cause us to think of the planet as an object, which

we would then want to manage and protect.[1] His prognostication seems to have been born out, perhaps bringing Descartes'
"mind/body" dualistic thinking into the space age. By treating
the planet as an object, environmental thinking has helped separate mankind from the earth, thus creating a state of conflict
between humans and the rest of nature.

There is a legitimate concern for the question of how to
address the problem of people dumping their entropic wastes
into waterways, the atmosphere, and unowned lands. How
does a private property analysis help us with instances of individuals, corporations, or governmental bodies polluting the air
or rivers, or dumping toxic wastes that get into underground
water supplies and cause injury or death to others? We need
to ask ourselves whether the self-interested actions of private
owners of property, dealing with one another in the marketplace, can prevent such problems.

In an age that has rediscovered the importance of mankind
living in harmony with nature, it is often difficult to speak of
the importance of decentralizing authority in society by decentralizing control over property. The fear is often expressed that,
if men and women were free to do with their property as they
saw fit, not only would social conflict escalate—as though society could become even more violent and disorderly—but that
nature itself would be subjected to far greater dangers than at
present. While these are worthwhile concerns, such fears reflect
a total misconception of what is implicit in the decision making
of a property owner.

To begin with, we must carefully define the nature of the
problem. Using the pollution of waterways as an example, it is
not the fact that industrial wastes get put into the water that creates the problem, but the fact that the water in question is generally not owned by the polluter. If, for instance, a manufacturer
has built a totally enclosed lake on its land—with a thick, steel
enforced concrete bottom to prevent seepage—and the manu-

---

[1]Marshall McLuhan and Bruce Powers, *The Global Village* (New York:
Oxford University Press, 1989), pp. 97–98.

facturer pollutes its own lake with sludge, would any injury to others have occurred? To those environmentalists who do not see these issues in any coherent, philosophically principled way, the response may be that there has been a "wrong" done to the water itself. But unless we are prepared to admit other species, trees, waterways, rock formations, the atmosphere, and the rest of nature into that body of legally recognized "persons", a position that would pose serious problems in our efforts to foster our own survival, such arguments will amount to little more than empty tautologies. But if we apply a *property* analysis to the question, we can make clear distinctions between injurious and noninjurious acts.

The environmental problems with which so many people concern themselves represent not the *failure* of private ownership of property, but the failure to live in accordance with such a system by identifying and respecting claims. Landfill problems, the dumping of nuclear or other toxic wastes, the emission of smoke and chemical particulates into the atmosphere have, for the most part, been occasioned either by the *absence* of private ownership, or the refusal to have one's actions governed by such a principle. Who does own the air and waterways, the marshlands and forests, the oceans, mountain ranges, and aquifers? Who is entitled to make decisions as to how these resources are to be utilized, and for what purposes? Are there limits to the range of one's actions and, if so, how are these to be determined? Furthermore, unless one is so innocent as to believe that his or her preferences, alone, are entitled to the respect of reasonably minded people, it must be understood that whether a parcel of land is to be used for the growing of organic vegetables or as a dumpsite for radioactive wastes, is a question that must be answered by *someone*.

Because entropy is a form of energy unavailable for productive use, many of us are inclined to dispose of it in as cost-free a manner as possible. The pollution problem arises from a willingness of the polluter to regard dumping it upon the property of others, rather than his own, as *his* most efficient means of reducing this cost. In Prigogine's and Stenger's model of "dissipative structures", wherein living systems are able to generate a more complex order by dissipating entropy into the environment,[2] the crucial property issue is raised: into whose environment is the entropy to be dispelled?

Most of us operate from the assumption that social order is to be defined in terms of whether the behavior of others is conducive to our ends. As the "war on drugs" and other campaigns against victimless crime activities illustrate, such inquiries rarely distinguish between actions that cause identifiable harm to others, and those that simply annoy our sensibilities or fail to satisfy the expectations we unilaterally project onto others. It is no surprise that such an assumption finds expression in environmental matters. If we can become aware that our values are only *subjective* preferences, rather than *objective* standards, and if we can appreciate the orderly patterns that inhere in complex systems, we may become less self-righteous about the decisions others make for themselves.

If trees are cut down, for instance, orderliness is generated in the paper upon which people may write, and in the lumber used to build houses. Likewise, if trees are not cut down, the ecological orderliness of the forest will be maintained. Whose preferences should prevail, and upon what principles will the making of either choice depend? No matter how strongly we insist upon the primacy of our preferences, no matter how much moral foot-stomping we engage in, the fact remains that our choices are grounded in subjectivity. There are no objectively "correct" decisions to be made, but as with all human action, there are *cost* and *benefit* tradeoffs associated with whatever choices we make. But who is to incur the costs, and who is to enjoy the benefits of human action? It is the private property principle, alone, that allows each of us to pursue our respective preferences, as well as to enjoy the benefits and bear the costs thereof. Through voluntary exchanges in the marketplace, each of us is free to increase the intensity of our demand for one form of usage over another and, thus, try to persuade other

---

[2] Prigogine and Stengers, *Order Out of Chaos*, pp. xv, 12–14.

owners—through the pricing system—to respond to our preferences.

There are, of course, significant consequences associated with the questions of *how*, and by *whom*, decisions regarding property are to be made. Because they will have to bear the costs of the choices they make, owners of property, operating on the basis of the property principle, will be required to take into consideration different factors in their decision making than will non-owners. Owners will always have a more diligent and focused concern regarding their property than will non-owners making decisions over the property of others. Such resources as forests, lakes, mountains, and marshlands are capable of being bounded and controlled by exclusive owners. To the degree such private ownership is established, the owners will have an incentive to protect their value by not allowing their property to be damaged, whether by themselves or others. Such property becomes a producer of resources for future productive use, and self-interest motivations can be relied upon to maximize both present and future benefits to be derived therefrom. The common practice of farmers rotating their crops in order to protect the soil, and of lumbering companies replanting trees on their lands provide such examples. Should one choose to become an owner of land with the intention of preserving its undeveloped character, the property principle would support that decision as well.

But to the degree any of these resources are not capable of being privately owned (e.g., an entire river or river system, the ocean, or the atmosphere), and/or have been collectively claimed by the state on behalf of the "public," (e.g., national parks and forests), confusion of ownership will result. As we shall see in chapter nine, belief in the idea of a collective ownership in unowned or state owned property gives rise to implicit assumptions about the personal use of such resources. If I should think of myself as one of a multitude of co-owners of a major river, or the atmosphere, or forest land, why *wouldn't* I be inclined to regard it as being within my collective "rights" to use such resources for whatever purposes served my interests?

To proclaim collective ownership creates, in the mind of a listener, the mistaken assumption that he or she is an owner and, thereby, entitled to control the property for their purposes. As with so many other examples of state action, this practice generates unintended consequences that are often contradictory to their stated purposes.

The confusion of control brought about by the idea of collective ownership, has been a major contributor not only to environmental problems, but to the conflicts that necessarily arise whenever government agencies act to further policies about which there is widespread disagreement among men and women who like to imagine that such entities are "theirs" to direct. Isn't this confusion what has turned government schools into attractors for conflict over whether such schools will or will not employ bilingual education, or teach sex education, or teach creationism rather than Darwinism—a confusion that tends not to arise in *privately* owned schools? Whether the redwoods are to be preserved or harvested; whether "public" lands are or are not to be used for nuclear weapons testing or for nuclear waste disposal; what types of radio or television programming are to be permitted on so-called "public airwaves"; whether rivers are to be used for toxic waste disposal, are just a few of the irreconcilable conflicts arising from a commitment to collective ownership.

Given the general confusion as to the nature of property and the widespread disrespect for private property, and given that almost all of us have less of an interest in protecting other people's property than we do our own, it should come as no surprise that many of us regard the property of others as appropriate sites for the disposal of wastes. Let us suppose that the United Updike Company has dumped toxic wastes into the ground, and emitted noxious fumes from its factory smokestacks. Is it not clear that the company has failed to control its property (i.e., its byproducts) so as to prevent trespasses to others—that it has allowed the range of its decision making to exceed the boundaries of what it owns? If those toxic substances seep into the water supply of the neighboring town, and a child drinks that water and becomes ill, is it not evident that the company committed a trespass upon that child? Likewise, when the fumes from the smokestacks are breathed into the lungs of a young woman, or the toxic wastes that get into a nearby river end up in fish that are later eaten by her, has the company not trespassed upon her?

In a culture in which the nature of privately owned property is neither generally understood nor respected, such polluting practices tend to be referred to as "environmental" or "health" problems. But, in fact, they represent what economists call "externalities"—i.e., the failure of an actor to bear all the costs associated with his or her actions. This company is external-izing—or "socializing"—the costs of disposing of its entropic industrial byproducts by forcing them to be borne by others. An externality, in this context at least, is only an economist's way of talking about property trespasses, a failure to respect the inviolability of another's boundaries. The government, largely through its court system, has historically allowed businesses to engage in such trespasses so as to avoid firms having to bear expenses that might be detrimental to them. Such decisions by the courts have helped to confuse our understanding of the orderly nature of a system of private property.

A similar problem arises from what is called "the tragedy of the commons."[3] When grazing lands are owned in common by various sheep farmers, each farmer will have an economic incentive to continue adding sheep to his herd to graze upon such lands. If any one shepherd were to refrain from adding sheep, each party reasons, the others would nevertheless add their sheep, which would work to his comparative disadvan-tage. As a consequence, each farmer will find it to his self-inter-est *not* to restrain his sheep's consumption of grass, leading to the ultimate destruction of the commons. These dynamics,

---

[3]William Forster Lloyd, *Two Lectures on the Checks to Population* (Oxford: Oxford University Press, 1833); Garrett Hardin, "The Tragedy of the Com-mons," *Science* 162 (1968): 1243–48.

which are also at work in such unowned areas as oceanic fish-
ing territories, underlie a number of environmental concerns.
While this dilemma is often presented as evidence of the
harmful nature of individual liberty, it in fact reflects the adverse
consequences of collective ownership: what is owned by *everyone* is owned by *no one*. There is no one decision-maker who
has both the unfettered control and the responsibility for the
property, no single owner upon whom all the consequences of
usage will devolve. If such lands were divided into privately
owned parcels, no owner would need to fear the over-consump-
tion of his grass by his neighbor's sheep. When property is privately owned and boundaries are respected, there is no division between those who will incur the costs and those who will
enjoy the *benefits*, a lesson that even small children learn from
a reading of *The Little Red Hen*. Indeed, the "enclosure acts" in
England privatized such collective lands for the purpose of
resolving this problem.

The owner knows that if he is to continue enjoying the benefits of his property, he must be responsible for the costs of its
maintenance, including a self-rationing of his use of it. The
property owner makes his own calculations, assesses his own
risks, and bears the consequences, be they good or ill. Each
farmer will have an incentive to forego immediate consumption and not overgraze because, to do otherwise, will result in
long-term costs to himself that outweigh the short-term benefits
he would derive. This is why the authority to control one's own
property fosters responsible behavior: the actor experiences the
consequences.

This analysis also helps to explain the troublesome nature of
political decision-making: those who benefit from political action
(e.g., "special interest" groups) do so disproportionately to the
costs they incur in promoting such ends. Ironically, this is what
politically-oriented conservation and environmental organizations have in common not only with most other lobbying groups,
but with private and governmental entities that socialize their
costs by imposing them, via pollution, on the general public. *All*
governmental action involves the creation of externalities, in that

some people (e.g., taxpayers, property owners) are forced to incur burdens not of their own doing or choice. Like the United Updike Company, conservationists and environmentalists who call upon the state to regulate the property interests of others, receive *benefits* whose costs they prefer others to bear. The state, like the polluter, is externalizing costs.

We should not be surprised that so many of us find it attractive to divide the enjoyment of benefits from the bearing of costs. Because we are self-interest motivated, we desire to keep our *gains* for ourselves, just as we are eager to share our *losses* with others, an attitude that keeps insurance companies in business. There is nothing remarkable in this, nor is there a property violation regarding private insurance, as insureds freely contract, for a fee, for the sharing of risks. But such motivations ought to be kept clearly in mind when assessing the relative merits of any governmental programs. This motivation, when combined with a refusal to adhere to the property principle as a way of limiting the scope of our pursuits, produces a disruptive dichotomy.

This Janus-faced tendency can be illustrated in an example. If X's neighbor constructs a hideously grotesque shack on his land and paints it chartreuse, X will bring a nuisance action and insist that the neighbor compensate him for any perceived diminution in the market value of his home, even though the neighbor had committed no trespass. If, on the other hand, that same neighbor had built a beautiful mansion that increased the value of X's property, X will not consider himself obliged to share his gain with the neighbor who made it all possible. X will, instead, content himself with the thought that his good fortune was simply one of the benefits of a free market system!

Likewise, real estate developers and the owners of professional sports franchises have figured out ways to get local governments to use their powers of eminent domain to take, by legal force and at taxpayers' expense, lands belonging to others, while, at the same time, forcing taxpayers to pay for the construction of facilities such as sports stadiums. When those who reap the benefits of such acts are privileged by the state to pass their costs onto unwilling parties, property trespasses are occurring in every bit the same way as when a manufacturer dumps its unwanted costs onto others in the form of pollution. Were we to learn to think in a principled manner and to become aware of the consequences that are implicit in our behavior, we might discover how government policies we so eagerly impose upon the lives and property of others, can produce troublesome externalities we had not intended.

There seems to be a deeper meaning to environmentalist thinking that requires exploration. Our willingness to identify ourselves with institutions and other abstractions, and our pre-occupation with "ego-boundaries," are not confined to separating ourselves from other people. One of the many victims of our divisive thinking has been nature itself. Western civilization—drawing upon the Old Testament's "Book of Genesis"—has long had a separatist attitude toward the rest of nature. "Man" was to have dominion over all living things on earth, a vertically-structured relationship founded upon the subservience of nature to human control which, like any political relationship, is bound to produce conflict. The biblical view of nature as being inferior to man is further evidenced in the "garden of Eden" story, wherein mankind was expelled from "paradise" and sentenced to what Westerners have since regarded as a second-rate neighborhood. Even our language reflects our sense of alienation from the earth, as we speak of being born *"into"* the world instead of *"emerging from"* it. If our daily thinking was better informed by what the biological sciences have to say about the origins of life, we might better understand how mankind has grown from the earth; that the earth is our *home*, not our *prison*; and that nature does not need to be subdued or dominated, but only understood and appreciated.

By regarding ourselves as dominant over nature, we made ourselves separate from it. In so doing, we also made ourselves both *superior* and *inferior* to it. Our superiority is expressed in our anthropocentric power over the world, while our sense of inferiority derives from our belief that, having been banished to earth for the "sin" of being human, that we became trespassers upon the property of others. This idea is so deeply embedded in our thinking that it emerges not only in the environmental and animal "rights" movements, but in the condemnation of Europeans for having discovered the "New World," as well as in the notion that humans ought not to behave in ways that "upset the balance of nature" (i.e., to exhibit any human influence). Such attitudes, while ostensibly respectful of nature, divide mankind from it and, consequently, generate the very conflicts that the environmentalists condemn. How does mankind—an expression of nature—upset the "balance" in the environment any more so than the wolf or crabgrass, each of which seeks to expand its presence in the world? If we are "apart from" nature, instead of "a part of" it, the rest of nature will continue to be just one more "other" to be subdued and controlled.

It should be clear that if we are only able to act in the pursuit of our respective self-interests, and if we continue to insist upon thinking of ourselves as differentiated from the rest of nature, including our neighbors, we will continue to pursue our interests in dominating, strife-ridden ways. If, in our concern to protect nature from the consequences of our thinking, we are unable to move beyond the simplemindedness that insists upon posing the "good guys" against the "bad guys;" of "socially responsible" activists against "greedy" businessmen, we shall only continue to play out the vicious, coercive games of "us against them" that have gotten us precisely to where we are now. In this regard, the industrial polluter and the politically-active environmentalist are both engaging in the same conflict-ridden war against nature: socializing the costs of pursuing their interests by disrespecting the boundaries of others.

Perhaps there is a direct correlation between our disrespect for *nature* and our disrespect for the concept of *private property*. After all, polluting the air, waterways, or lands of others, are just other ways of disrespecting property boundaries—of not confining our decision making to what is ours to control. Why should we be surprised that, in a society that has so little regard for private property, people would fail to make the distinction between what is and what is not within the proper range of their behavior? Furthermore, experience with collective ownership should inform us of the advantages of privately owned property. We know, for instance, that the owner of a parcel of land, or a business, has a greater incentive to care for and conserve the value of the property than does a non-owner. As we saw in the "tragedy of the commons," individuals have an incentive to take as much from collectively owned property as they can. Finally, when the state sets the social example of disrespecting the lives and property of others, why should we be surprised to discover men and women exhibiting the same disregard not only for their neighbors, but for the rest of nature?

Perhaps it is more appropriate to begin our inquiry not with the question of whether private ownership and voluntary practices can protect the rest of nature, but whether political systems—founded as they are on force and conflict—could ever conceivably do so. The range of our actions will be limited either by the property principle confining us to the boundaries of what we own, or will be defined by state regulations. The latter approach, which does not necessarily invoke property-based limitations, tends to socialize the costs of satisfying the preferences of those unwilling to incur the costs of negotiating with owners.

Lest we be seduced by the trappings of political power in the course of our desire to enhance and protect life, we ought to ask ourselves whether we are respecting life, human or otherwise, when we confront it with coercive practices. Our current social pathology is grounded in "command and control" systems that rob life of its self-directed, autonomous, and spontaneous character. Since nature is the expression of life on this planet, any system that denies life its self-controlling qualities, reflects hostility to nature itself. Any who doubt the dispirited and dehumanizing consequences of trying to control life processes, are invited to compare the quality of the lives of American Indians living freely within their traditional tribal cultures, and those living on government managed reservations.

I had a discussion with a number of my students one day on the question of whether the state, under the guise of protecting people's health, ought to have the authority to prohibit the sale of foods made with trans-fats, artificial sweeteners, chemical preservatives, or other ingredients deemed "harmful." Should the state be allowed to prohibit individuals from smoking, or from engaging in dangerous activities? A number of these students acknowledged such rightful powers by the state, arguing that if people didn't look after their own health, the government should do it for them. I asked them if the essence of liberty did not include people being free to calculate their own risks and to act on the basis of what their judgments informed them. They dismissed this suggestion as "idealistic." I reminded them of a previous political leader who was bent on using the power of the state to eradicate cancer, an end that included the prohibition of tobacco. I informed them that this man favored government-supported medical research, but not upon animals and that, in his obsession with making his country healthy, certain categories of human beings came to be looked upon as "diseases" to be eradicated. That leader's name, of course, was Adolf Hitler,[4] a revelation that seemed not to dissuade these students from *their* ambitions to save humanity from the consequences of "wrong" choices.

I asked these students why, since they had no respect for other people, they cared whether they lived or died as a result of their lifestyle habits? "The essence of life," I suggested to them, "is autonomous self-direction, and you are prepared to deny this to those who would make decisions in their lives that differed from the choices you would make in your own." I received plate-glass stares in response, and suggested to them that they be wary of those who seek to sterilize the world.

Many self-styled "environmentalists" express concern over what they perceive as the menace of commercial or residential development, a matter that does not preclude them from enjoying a home that was the product of earlier such developments. Their conditioned response has been to call upon the state to

---

[4]See Robert Proctor, *The Nazi War Against Cancer* (Princeton, N.J.: Princeton University Press, 1999).

limit, or even prohibit, development in areas they would like to see preserved. Such efforts generate conflict not only between themselves and other property owners, but also with the state and those affected by the restrictions. A more socially harmonious approach, one whose efficacy is a matter of record, is found in agreements with property owners. A number of privately owned, voluntarily supported organizations have been responsible for preserving literally millions of acres of forests, wetlands, watersheds, redwood trees, and other natural resources. Some environmental groups have made increased use of contracts, rather than state violence, to purchase wetlands, forests, water rights, or other property interests from owners, to accomplish their objectives. "Conservation easements," purchased from landowners rather than forcibly taken by regulation or eminent domain, have become an integral part of a system of voluntarily supported environmental practices.[5] I know of two communities whose residents were desirous of preventing a developer from purchasing adjoining land for the purpose of creating a housing development; individuals committed their own resources to purchase the targeted land from its owner, thus controlling by property ownership the nature of their town.

When we lived in the Midwest, our family had a membership in a very large, private forest preserve along the Missouri River. This organization accepted no government money, relying instead on the voluntary support of people who valued the preservation and expansion of the forest. When local residents found injured wild animals, as we did on one occasion, they often took them to this preserve, where a veterinary staff cared for the creatures until they could be returned to the wild. While recovering from their injuries, these animals were displayed in cages that created a transient zoo that people could visit. Similar organizations provide such facilities and services throughout the country.

---

[5]See, e.g., www.rffi.org/InTheNews.html. See also, www.nature.org/aboutus/howwework/conservationmethods/privatelands/conservationeasements/.

In contrast to those who believe that a respect for the environment necessitates a separation of humanity from "nature," this forest preserve encourages hiking along its trails, offers instruction in plant and animal life, and even sponsors programs such as Halloween trail walks for its members.

A major problem with a politically-based environmental movement is that it seeks to compel a kind of identity with and respect for nature where it does not freely exist. This is the underlying shortcoming of *all* political programs: by forcing people to act inconsistently with their own non-trespassing preferences, the state introduces conflict into society. Because there is a division between what individuals *want* to do with their own lives and property and what the state *compels* them to do, the result is to generate the increasing lack of integrity one witnesses in politically-structured societies. We are now suffering the political, economic, social, and environmental consequences of having learned to separate and distinguish ourselves from the world—including our neighbors—in which we live. In the words of Mark Twain, many of us tend to believe that "[n]othing so needs reforming as other people's habits."[6] Unless we can fundamentally alter our thinking, we may be destined to make human society even more intolerable. But most environmentalists, like social reformers generally, have little patience with mankind learning a new paradigm; like fanatics of every persuasion, they want results *now!* Thus, they try to force the *consequences* of an altered consciousness without such a transformation first taking place.

In spite of the limited understanding associated with all complex systems—the interrelated nature of the earth's geologic, atmospheric, and life processes in particular—many environmentalists presume to impose upon all mankind standards of conduct that will bring the rest of us into conformity with their inconstant speculations. Should any of us believe these warnings to be valid, we are capable of effecting a change of consciousness

---

[6]Mark Twain, *Pudd'nhead Wilson* (1894), *Pudd'nhead Wilson's Calendar*, chap. 15.

that would cause us to change our behavior. To that degree, we would be reducing, or even eliminating, our contributions to what we perceive to be a problem. But such individualized transformations are rarely satisfying to those in a hurry for change.

There is a self-righteousness in employing force to bring about the kinds of behavioral changes that would otherwise result from an alteration in thinking. Such arrogance underlies the modern tendency to treat preferences, values, tastes, and attitudes not as a range of options from which men and women can freely make choices, but as *political* issues to be resolved by compelling an undeviating conformity upon others. Since tastes and values are constantly changing to accommodate vacillating fashions, having the state enforce any set of preferences upon others tends to frustrate those whose own understanding is at a different stage of development. It may also arrest further change within those whose choices have been preempted. Those who insist upon employing such methods rarely bother to inquire into the costs—particularly the personal and social conflict—associated with such practices.[7] But then, patience, as well as a sense of humility and perspective, are rarely exhibited by the zealots of *any* social or political cause who, burdened by the illusion that their values represent "objective" truths, are much more inclined to see existing conditions as crises to be overcome at all costs.

Those desirous of reforming the behavior of others have an impatience with the marketplace because of its foundation in people freely committing their own resources to ends they value. A free market analysis only tells us *how* we humans make decisions, not *what* decisions we will make. The content of our decisions, in other words, depends entirely upon our personal, subjectively determined preferences—upon the content of our

---

[7]See my "Violence As A Product of Imposed Order," in *University of Miami Law Review*, 29 (1975): 732–63. Reprinted, Menlo Park, Calif.: Institute for Humane Studies, Studies in Law No. 4 (1976); republished in Ken Templeton, ed., *The Politicization of Society* (Indianapolis, Ind.: Liberty Press, 1979), pp. 447–99.

consciousness. If a person principally values monetarily quantifiable results, these values will predominate in the pursuit of his or her self-interest. On the other hand, to the extent one values such non-quantifiable factors as aesthetics, sensitivity to the suffering of others, the pursuit of abstract philosophic principles, or simply living in harmony with others, *these* values will be given great weight in the motivations of such a person. There is no better evidence of the economic ignorance of most people than the commonly held assumption, too often fostered by economists themselves, that *economic* motivations are always and exclusively defined in terms of increased monetary rewards. The history of the early private turnpike companies in America demonstrates a continuing commitment to the building of roads known, in advance, to be monetarily unprofitable. Broader social benefits were apparently the motive for persons to invest in such projects.[8] Those are few and far between who understand that a person who refuses a lucrative defense contract out of a revulsion against war is also making a profit-maximizing decision. All of us act in order to be better off afterward than we would have been had we not acted. How each of us defines "better off" is subject to as many translations as there are values that motivate us.

The free market, in other words, is a barometer of the strength of people's varied tastes and values, as reflected in their willingness to devote their own assets to a purpose. By contrast, the relatively cost-free expression of values in public opinion polls or voting booths tells us very little about the extent of people's commitments to such ends. It is not the marketplace that limits any of us to the pursuit of material values, but the limitations we have placed upon our own thinking. Furthermore, the marketplace maximizes the opportunities to advance our values by allowing us the unrestrained authority to invest our property interests on their behalf. One who is sensitive to the importance of protecting the environment is capable of developing a market,

---

[8] See, e.g., Daniel B. Klein, "The Voluntary Provision of Public Goods? The Turnpike Companies of Early America," *Economic Inquiry* 28 (1990): 788–812.

a demand for the satisfaction of these values, as surely as the more narrowly focused, monetarily defined profit maximizer will seek the satisfaction of his interests. Whether we choose to do so or not is but a reflection of the intensity of our demands in choosing to pursue our values.

Impatience with the values of others is commonplace in our politicized world. Indeed, the disregard most of us have for the inviolability of privately-owned property derives from the realization that, in a free society, outcomes we desire depend upon the choices others make regarding their own lives. It is far better, many of us reason, to compel others to comply with our interests. Such attitudes prevail not only in commercial or industrial pursuits, but in the fostering of social, ideological, or other philosophic values.

As individuals, we may experience some insight into a fundamentally different sense of our relationship with other people and the rest of the world. This new vision begins to inform our consciousness in a significant way. But instead of allowing this experience to play itself out within our mind, many of us become anxious to confirm its validity by projecting onto others the behavior that we believe are its consequences. We become driven to control the behavior of others so that *their* conduct will reflect our new vision. In such ways do we try to bolster our own newly-discovered resolve by imagining that the coerced obedience of others is a reflection of shared values. As with so many other aspects of our lives, we have learned to regard our inner experiences as unimportant. Rather than permitting such insights to develop themselves into a radically altered personal consciousness, we settle for the ersatz transformation of our outer world, which we deceive ourselves into believing can be produced through coercive, political means. Is it any wonder that we rarely become what we dream or feel?

If you and I are to experience a spiritual revolution, I suspect part of the change will consist in our learning to think of "life" not just as a material entity, but also as a *process*—less as a *noun* than a *verb*. As long as we regard life only as objects and things, we will—as McLuhan suggested—want to manage and "care" for it in some smothering, paternalistic fashion. Most of us have treated life as little more than a "resource," useful for the achievement of the ends of those wanting to control it. This is what has made conservationists and environmentalists such a depressing lot. Like missionaries of every faith, religious and secular, they are able to recite the gospel and exude all the proper shibboleths, but exhibit very little of the élan vital that is the very essence of life.

As suggested earlier, we need to remind ourselves that our interest in pursuing such nonmaterial values as spirituality, aesthetics, alternative lifestyles, physical and emotional well-being, environmentalism, and a host of other philosophic interests, has arisen as a consequence of our having figured out how to produce material prosperity. The same conditions of respect for liberty, the inviolability of property boundaries, and voluntarily-based relationships that allowed us to discover the superiority of the marketplace for our material well-being, will provide the same base from which to pursue other ends as well.

The arrogance that seduces men and women into a passion to control others should be tempered with an awareness of orderly systems that do not arise from the limited understanding of the conscious mind. As the study of chaos and complexity illustrate, the ability to foretell the outcome of a course of action is dependent upon the identification and analysis of so many interconnected and constantly fluctuating variables as to make the behavior of complex systems—including the environment—uncertain.

Much of the environmental movement is driven by an implicit faith in the ability of state-directed systems to identify and regulate to desired ends factors affecting global temperatures, the ozone layer, population growth, the extinction of species, the depletion of rainforests and agricultural lands, pollution, and other matters. Far too often, this article of faith is more an expression of fidelity to an antiquated, abstract dogma than a product of empirical inquiry. It is reinforced by the deeply engrained assumption that a complex world operates on the

basis of linear regularities rather than the inconstant dynamics
of nonlinearity. When predictions of mass human starvation,
species extinction, increased numbers of hurricanes, and environmental collapse have been measured against the resulting
data, the expected doomsday scenarios have failed to materialize.[9] This failure of expectations has not prevented the eigh-
teenth-century social prophet, Thomas Malthus, or such modern descendants of his views as Paul Ehrlich, Edward O. Wilson,
Lester Brown, and others, from continuing to be revered even
as their dire predictions have failed to materialize. Perhaps an
increasing familiarity with the dynamics of complexity will
make us more aware that the capacity to predict rests upon a
"sensitive dependence upon initial conditions," that such pre-
science can never be known to us, and that the power to coercively regulate human affairs in such matters would nowhere
be so dangerous as in the hands of people whose hubris will
not allow them to see the limitations of their understanding.
   One of the propositions uniting the environmentalists is that
we humans are depleting the ozone layer, and that this condition will be detrimental to all life on the planet. Because we
have only recently discovered this hole in the ozone, we have
no way of knowing what conditions existed there before our
presumed collective depletion of it, nor what state of the ozone
is or is not conducive to life. Furthermore, while "global warming" is an established fact, there is no consensus—the polit-
ically-inspired speculations of Al Gore and Bill Clinton notwithstanding—among scientists as to how much of this change
has come about as a result of human activity, and how much is
an expression of millions of years of temperature fluctuations
that preceded human presence on Earth.[10] The suggestion has

---

[9]See, e.g., Bjorn Lomborg, *The Skeptical Environmentalist* (Cambridge: Cambridge University Press, 2001).

[10]Contrary to the efforts of many environmentalists to create the impression
that their views on human caused climate changes reflect a consensus among
scientists, there are numerous works that either refute or raise serious doubts
about such conclusions. A very brief listing of such works include Lomborg,
ibid.; Ronald Bailey, ed., *The True State of the Planet* (New York: The Free Press,

even been made by some scientists, that global warming may *increase* speciation by expanding territories into which more life may flourish,[11] a conclusion that would seem to contradict earlier views that such warming would foster the extinction of some species.[12] Furthermore, before giving too much credence to the gloomy forecasters of the effects of "global warming," let us recall those equally authoritative voices (some of them the same persons!), who two and three decades ago were prophesying a "nuclear winter" and the return of an "ice age." What this suggests is that the dire warnings of the environmentalists are highly speculative at best, and remain subject to the admonitions of the students of "chaos" about the inability to make extended predictions regarding complex systems. If the environmentalists are in error, governmental policies extended across the entire planet are likely to be quite costly to all of life.

Nor should the rashness of those who presume to control the life processes on earth go unchallenged in the face of such scientists as James Lovelock who has offered the "Gaia" hypothesis[13] to

1995); Ronald Bailey, *Eco-Scam: The False Prophets of Ecological Apocalypse* (New York: St. Martin's Press, 1993); Stephen Moore and Julian L. Simon, *It's Getting Better All the Time* (Washington, D.C.: Cato Institute, 2000), pp. 183–205; S. Fred Singer, *Hot Talk, Cold Science: Global Warming's Unfinished Debate*, revised 2nd ed. (Oakland, Calif.: The Independent Institute, 1999); S. Fred Singer and Dennis T. Avery, *Unstoppable Global Warming: Every 1,500 Years* (New York: Rowman and Littlefield Publishers, Inc., 2007); Orrin H. Pilkey and Linda Pilkey-Jarvis, *Useless Arithmetic: Why Environmental Scientists Can't Predict the Future* (New York: Columbia University Press, 2007); Henrik Svensmark and Nigel Calder, *The Chilling Stars: A New Theory of Climate Change* (Thriplow, Cambridge: Icon Books, 2007). See, also, *17,200 Scientists Dispute Global Warming*, www.oism.org/pproject/s33p36htm; *Breaking: Less Than Half of all Published Scientists Endorse Global Warming Theory*, http://epw.senate.gov/public/index.cfm?FuseAction=MinorityBlogs+contentRecord_id=B35C36A3-802A-23AD-46EC-6880767E7966; *A Layman's Guide to Man-Made Global Warming*, www.climate-skeptic.com/2007/09/table-of-conten.html.

[11] See, e.g., Anthony D. Barnosky, *Climate Change and Speciation of Mammals*, www.actionbioscience.org/evolution/barnosky.html.

[12] See, e.g., Chris D. Thomas et. al., "Extinction risk from climate change," *Nature*, 427 (January 8, 2004): 145–48; Guy Gugliotta, "Extinction Tied to Global Warming," Washingtonpost.com, January 21, 2005, p. A03 (online only for pay).

[13] James Lovelock, *Gaia: A New Look at Life on Earth* (Oxford: Oxford University Press, 1982).

explain the spontaneous, fluctuating processes that have maintained a life-sustaining atmospheric balance since long before the emergence of humans. His original work suggested that life processes on earth, with the oceans and atmosphere functioning as the regulatory mechanism, maintain the conditions that are conducive to life. More holistically, Lovelock expanded his theory to include the entire earth—organisms and the physical environment—as an integrated, self-regulating system.[14] "Gaia," a concept he later referred to as "geophysiology," can be seen as a complex, self-regulating system, able to respond to changes in external conditions (e.g., an increase in the output of energy from the sun) so as to preserve environmental stability.[15] Lovelock's thesis finds support in the 18th century work of James Hutton, regarded by many as the father of the study of geology, who characterized the earth as a "superorganism," with geologic circulatory systems analogous to those found in biological systems.[16] A similar analogy was later voiced by T.H. Huxley,[17] as well as more recently, by Guy Murchie,[18] and Lewis Thomas.[19] If our planet can be thought of as a self-organizing, self-regulating system—a holographic system, if you will—might not a similar view of human society offer us a more effective way of addressing the uncertainties and complexities of life?

Let us not forget that, because of entropy, nature has always been a hard and uncertain place; that most of the species that have ever lived on this planet became extinct long before mankind's arrival; that life sustains itself only by feeding on other

---

[14]James Lovelock, *The Revenge of Gaia: Earth's Climate in Crisis and the Fate of Humanity* (New York: Basic Books, 2006).

[15]Ibid., p. ix.

[16]From James Lovelock, "The Evolving Gaia Theory," paper presented at the United Nations University, Tokyo, Japan, September 25, 1992. www.unu.edu/unupress/lecture1.html.

[17]Ibid.

[18]Guy Murchie, *The Seven Mysteries of Life* (Boston: Houghton Mifflin Company, 1978), pp. 388–95.

[19]Lewis Thomas, *The Lives of a Cell: Notes of a Biology Watcher* (New York: Bantam Books, 1974).

life, only by converting natural resources to the use of the actor; that the rest of nature produces forest fires, pollution, poisoned rivers, earthquakes and continental drift, deadly tornadoes and hurricanes, tsunamis, and soil erosion without the help of human beings; that the universe itself probably came into being as the result of a fiery explosion and may very well end in a cosmic gridlock that physicists call the "big crunch"; and, finally, that life as we know it today was able to emerge *only* because of the most catastrophic act of pollution in earth's history, namely, the appearance some two billion years ago of oxygen in the atmosphere, which poisoned all anaerobic life forms and made way for the rest of "us."[20] And in our quest to save "endangered species," let us also remember that it was the extinction of the dinosaurs, perhaps brought about by a comet- or asteroid-caused atmospheric pollution that made way for the proliferation of "us" mammals.[21] Nature is quite orderly, although its patterns of regularity proceed from no apparent agenda, and are not always beneficial to existing interests.

Those who wish to employ their own energies and resources to do something to preserve natural resources, rather than just holding press conferences to condemn developers, lumber companies, or petroleum companies, or to call upon the state to create yet another intrusive bureaucracy, have every opportunity to do so. In fact, many have discovered the increased effectiveness of themselves employing, rather than violating, property principles to accomplish their purposes. Environmental groups have spent many millions of dollars in courts, legislative halls, government agencies, and the media, fighting lumber companies over the fate of the redwoods. How many acres of such timberland might have been purchased and preserved, through private ownership, with this same amount of money? How much greater feelings of closeness to nature, rather than just a coziness with politicians, lobbyists, lawyers, and bureaucrats,

---

[20]Lovelock, *Gaia: A New Look at Life on Earth*, pp. 31–32.

[21]See, e.g., Stephen Jay Gould, *Hen's Teeth and Horse's Toes: Further Reflections in Natural History* (New York: W.W. Norton & Company, 1983), pp. 320–31.

might have been fostered by people devoting their resources directly to the private purchase of forests, marshlands, and coastlines, rather than political influence? What genuine sense of empowerment might have been experienced by those who could have exercised control over such lands as *owners*, rather than interlopers? How much social conflict, including depriving farmers of opportunities to profitably till their own soils, or causing severe injuries to lumbermen by the tactics of some violent environmental groups, could have been avoided by treating their fellow humans—who are also a part of nature—with the same respect that other animals accord the ownership claims of members of their species? As indicated earlier, that a number of organizations have recently been using private money to fund agreements with property owners shows how a change in perspective can achieve mutually desired ends without resorting to violence.

Bearing in mind that the production of entropy is an inevitable part of the life process, might adherence to the property principle provide insight into how to reduce the dumping of entropic wastes into the atmosphere, waterways, and the lands of others? To what extent have industries and governments contributed to these conditions by failing to internalize the costs of disposing of the unwanted byproducts of their activities? Are the environmental problems we experience anything more than an unintended consequence of our refusal to respect the inviolability of one another's property boundaries; of our failure to live responsibly by incurring all of the costs of our actions? Can we transcend the divisive mindset that allows us to see others, and their property, as resources to be plundered in the least-costly manner possible?

If we were to view life from a holographic perspective, we might understand that we are more than just "mankind": we are "life" itself. We might then experience our interconnectedness with all of nature. Becoming aware of how the survival of a particular species depends upon the resiliency that comes from the capacity for change and variation, we can then understand how these same conditions are essential to the survival of the life system on earth. Life itself—not just human life—thrives best in an environment in which variation and mutability provide it an extended range of options with which to respond to changed circumstances. Just as nature did not settle upon the dinosaur as some ultimate expression of life processes, despite it having enjoyed many millions more years of planet-dominating success than we humans have thus far managed, mankind may not prove itself capable of sustaining its need for resiliency and change. Should this be the case, the life system may have to turn to alternative expressions of its expansive needs. Perhaps the dolphins will replace us as the repository for nature's experiment with advanced intelligence. *Mankind* may not need a proliferation of other mammals, birds, or plants in order to survive, but *life*, itself, may require a wide range of species in order to maximize its opportunities for flexibility in its continuing experiment on this planet. At the same time, however, while the life system has advanced to highly complex forms of expression, it has kept its options open: nature has not given up on single celled forms. Should the more specialized species prove unable to respond to changed conditions, they may—like the dinosaurs and civilizations—find themselves swept aside, with life continuing its experimentation in either simpler or more complex forms.

There is a trait shared by many environmentalists and animal-rights advocates that I find troublesome. In the name of respecting and protecting "nature," many tend to keep human beings—a significant part of nature—out of the equation of interests to be considered worthy of attention. A popular motion picture theme has involved humans endeavoring to liberate animals from various confinements or life-threatening situations. Such films as *Born Free*, *Turtle Diary*, *Free Willy*, and *Fly Away Home*, have permitted us to experience, albeit vicariously, a strong emotional sense of closeness to other living things as they struggle to pursue their unrestrained nature. But as I listen to the uplifting music and lyrics from *Born Free*, I cannot help but wonder why these same sentiments and insights rarely find expression in films about the repression of human beings. If a story about people liberating turtles from a zoo is so emotionally compelling, what about a film involving the liberation of children from those zoos we call government schools? To those concerned with the fate of dolphins trapped in tuna nets I would ask: what about the condition of human beings whose lives are caught up in the restraints of government regulations? If it is important for *other* species to enjoy the liberty and spontaneity that represents the very essence of "life," why are *human beings* not accorded the same considerations? Are we so fearful of confronting the anti-life implications of our institutionalized thinking and attachments that we can do little more than transfer to other animals our needs for autonomy, spirituality, spontaneity, and respect? Science fiction writers, Montesquieu, and such utopian and dystopian novelists as George Orwell, Aldous Huxley, Samuel Butler, and Jonathan Swift, have created fictionalized societies for their writings as a way of deflecting attention from their own societies, thus masking a criticism they chose not to make directly. Are we so unwilling to openly examine what we are doing to ourselves? And, if so, why?

It seems clear that a change in our perspective could and perhaps will contribute to peaceful social change. In order to illustrate the "butterfly effect" of such a change, I would like to relate an experience I had, a number of years ago, with one of my students. This young woman is a fervent champion of the "rights" of animals, and she once told me that her principal reason in attending law school was to become a competent lawyer who could represent the interests of animals. She even seemed to have some clear idea of what their interests were! In one of our many discussions, I asked her about the wisdom of using political methods to accomplish the changes that she desired. "If individuals effected a change of consciousness so as to become more sensitive to the suffering of animals," I inquired, "would legislation serve any valid purpose?"

"Of course not," she responded.

"And if people did not experience such attitude changes," I went on, "would legislation cause them to do so?"

"Probably not," she admitted.

"And so, if people who do not share your sentiments become legally obliged to stop doing what they want to do, and to act as you want them to act, are they not likely to feel resentment and conflict?" I asked.

"Probably," she acknowledged, "but what else can we do?"

"Have you considered peaceful alternatives that do not rely on political enforcement that only creates more conflict?" I replied.

"But that might take a long time," she went on.

"Do you know how long it takes to get one single case through the courts, or to get a piece of legislation enacted? And this says nothing about the monetary costs of doing so," I answered.

"But the approach you're suggesting assumes that other people will change," she said.

"Were *you* always a vegetarian and animal rights advocate?" I asked. This young woman acknowledged that she had not been, and went on to relate how her conversion came about when, in high school, she had had a conversation with a friend on the subject of eating meat.

"Did this friend try to force or intimidate you to become a vegetarian?" I inquired. She answered in the negative, adding that her friend was not even a vegetarian himself, but had only been challenging her thinking with questions.

"And so, what caused you to change?" I asked.

"I simply became aware of how we were making animals suffer, and I couldn't be a part of that anymore," she responded.

"Do you think that *other* people might also be capable of experiencing such an awareness?" I queried. "Furthermore," I continued, "do you think that you—as an animal rights proponent—might be at least as effective in helping others to understand this, as your high school friend, who was not a vegetarian, was in helping you to become aware?"

My student had no immediate response to this. During the remainder of our conversation that day I asked her whether she thought it might be possible for her to devise methods of protecting animals that would not put her in a position of conflict with those who did not share her sentiments. She said she would think about it. In fact, as she later told me, for the next few weeks she went through a good deal of self-questioning about whether it even made sense for her to remain in law school. I didn't see much of her during this time period, but then, one day, she stopped by my office with the brightest smile in her eyes. "Did you read the article about the seal hunters who gave up hunting, and now use their ships to take people on Arctic tours to observe seals, whales, and the like?" she asked.

What a lovely example of how a change in perspective, a rephrasing of the question, can make us more sensitive to the consideration of alternative solutions to what we perceive as problems. This is the only way in which any meaningful social change can ever take place; it will either arise within each individual, or it will not occur at all. It will either manifest itself through the commitments men and women make with their own lives and property, or it will only amount to political posturing, empty rhetoric, and the proliferation of conflict with others. Those who insist upon change coming from above, as something to be imposed upon mankind by institutional authorities, have given up on people. They have lost their confidence in the life processes that exhibit themselves only within individuals. We have tried gods, institutions, laws, rulers, and ideologies, in a futile attempt to establish order in society by the assumption of power over the lives and property of other persons. It is now time to give people a chance to bring order to the world by bringing *themselves* to order. Let us begin with ourselves. If it is truly our purpose to help lead others toward a greater respect for nature, then let us lead by our example of learning to respect nature as it manifests in the lives of our neighbors.

Chapter Nine
Individualism vs. Collectivism

It seems obvious to me now—though I was slow coming to the conclusion—that the institution of private property, the dispersion of power and importance that goes with it, has been a main factor in producing that limited amount of free-and-equalness which Marx hoped to render infinite by abolishing this institution.

— Max Eastman

The most materially and spiritually depressing systems of social organization are those that embrace the mechanistic and degrading premise of collectivism. Mankind has, for thousands of years, suffered under these most oppressive and dreary social systems. In its political manifestation, it provides society with a herd-oriented image. Perhaps it is genetic memory—certainly not pragmatism—that is recapitulated in the appetites of so many moderns for collective systems.

The twentieth century demonstrated to thoughtful men and women the totally inhumane nature of any system premised on political collectivism. A sign on a church in the former East Berlin that read "nothing grows from the top down," succinctly identified the anti-life nature of all forms of institutionally-directed, collective control over people. Collectivism is the ultimate expression of the pyramidal model of the universe. It is the epitome of power-based thinking (i.e., that it is appropriate for some people to exercise coercive authority over the lives and property of others). Judged by its own materialistic premises, collectivism is unable to withstand any rigorous economic analysis. If the twentieth century resolved anything, it is the superiority of free market economic systems over command-and-control state systems in the production of goods and services. And when measured against such spiritual needs as the sense of personal dignity and self-worth that come from having complete authority over one's life, collectivism is even less attractive. It was so thoroughly discredited in the Iron Curtain countries as to help bring about the collapse of those regimes, and remains held together in China only through vicious military repression. It has proven itself both an economically and spiritually bankrupt system.

As suggested at the outset of this book, in discussing collectivist thought and systems, one must clearly distinguish collective and cooperative behavior. As social beings, cooperation is both natural and essential to our well-being. None of us would have survived birth for more than a few hours without a family—or someone filling the family role—caring for us. We might otherwise have been dropped beside a trail or, currently, placed in a dumpster shortly after having been born, a practice which, if generalized, would have led to the extinction of our species. Cooperative undertakings arise when individuals freely choose to associate and "work with others in a common effort."[1] The focal point for cooperative efforts is individuals coming together, voluntarily, to further mutual purposes.

A number of our allegedly "primitive" fellow humans have developed some sophisticated tribal forms of group cooperation which, at the same time, inhibit the development of political power. Tribal chiefs, far from being coercive authorities over others, are often the means by which centralized power is discouraged. Tribal chiefs—a role that does not even exist in some tribes—have been burdened with so many ceremonial functions as to deprive them of opportunities to pursue power over their fellows. His failure to perform the prescribed rituals

---

[1] *Webster's Third New International Dictionary,* p. 501.

would cause him to lose face within the tribe.[2] As Pierre Clastres has observed: "Humble in scope, the chief's functions are controlled nonetheless by public opinion. A planner of the group's economic and social activities, the leader possesses no decision-making power; he is never certain that his 'orders' will be carried out."[3] Such cooperative, non-coercive forms of social organization contrast with the systematized violence of the modern nation-state, whose very existence depends upon the inculcation of an enforced collective mindset.

Collectivism is "a social theory or doctrine that emphasizes the importance of the collective (as the society or state) *in contrast to the individual*."[4] By definition, the collective entity is the focus, both as to purpose and direction. With the exception of voluntarily organized communal societies such as the religious or philosophical communities that sprang up across America in the nineteenth century,[5] or twentieth-century cooperatives, collectivism has generally been coercively constituted. In comparison with the mutually-supportive, face-to-face relationships in smaller, cooperative groups, modern institutionalized collectives such as the state have had to rely on artificial, abstract identities through which total strangers can be compressed into contrived multitudes. As we saw in the discussion of "ego boundaries," collective entities are comprised of persons who subordinate themselves to a group identity. Organizations,

---

[2]See, e.g., Pierre Clastres, *Society Against the State* (New York: Zone Books, 1989).

[3]Ibid., p. 37.

[4]*Webster's Third New International Dictionary*, p. 445; emphasis added.

[5]See, e.g., John A. Hostetler, *Amish Society*, 3rd ed. (Baltimore: The Johns Hopkins University Press, 1980); Steven M. Nolt, *A History of the Amish* (Intercourse, Penn.: Good Books, 1992); Donald B. Kraybill, ed., *The Amish and the State* (Baltimore: The Johns Hopkins University Press, 1993); James J. Martin, *Men Against the State* (Colorado Springs, Colo.: Ralph Myles Publisher, 1970); Robert V. Hine, *California's Utopian Colonies* (Berkeley: University of California Press, 1983); Charles Nordhoff, *The Communistic Societies of the United States* (New York: Dover Publications, Inc., 1966); Jay O'Connell, *Co-Operative Dreams: A History of the Kaweah Colony* (Van Nuys, Calif.: Raven River Press, 1999); Charles Gide, *Consumers' Co-Operative Societies* (New York: Alfred A. Knopf, Inc., 1922).

particularly the state, encourage and exploit such behavior in order to channel the energies of individuals into group-serving purposes. It would be impossible to organize massive forms of social destructiveness such as wars and genocides unless sufficient numbers of people first had their sense of identity mobilized into the collectivist mindset. When we so organize ourselves, we become alienated not only from all who do not share our abstract identities, but from any inner sense of self that cannot be harmonized with group purposes.

We can also experience a sense of alienation from the material world in which we live as a result of allowing coercive collectives to usurp control over our lives. The defining characteristic of political collectives is the centralized authority over property within the group. This, in turn, produces within people a fragmented, depersonalized relationship to property. We learn to think of property as something *apart from*, rather than *a part of*, our lives. We babble political catechisms that "human rights are more important than property rights," not being aware that such thinking strips away any real world meaning to the exercise of liberty, leaving us clinging to empty abstractions for an understanding of what it means to be free. In embracing such hollow bromides, we participate in the Orwellian delusion that we can enjoy liberty even as the state directs, regulates, and confiscates what we like to pretend is "our" property. The debate over private, individual ownership versus collective, political control of property, has nothing to do with "social responsibility," or "greed," or "economies of scale," or "fairness," or "public goods" analyses, or "equality," or protecting the environment, or ending racism, or helping the poor. Such purported ends are simply the sales pitches used to rationalize the transfer of authority from individuals to the state. The real debate, which institutionalists do not want to see staged, has to do with where the locus of control over our lives and property is to reside. *All* "human rights" are property rights, the issue always turning into the inquiry: *who* has the "right" to *do* what, and *with* what?

We become collectivized not through force of arms, but by our willingness, brought about through years of careful conditioning begun in our childhood, to identify ourselves by reference to one or more abstractions. We are, by nature, social beings with need for companionship, cooperation for the achievement of mutual benefits, and a sense of community. Such needs, however, have been exploited by institutional interests desirous of having us organize ourselves around abstractions that serve organizational purposes. Through words, ideas, symbols, and other images, we develop the "ego boundary" identities discussed in chapter four. By reference to nationality, race, gender, religion, language, or any of a number of other abstractions, we come to think of ourselves not as *individuals*, but as members of some *collective*. Although we still act within and upon our world in order to further our survival— activities that necessitate decision making over property—the purpose of our action shifts from enhancing the well-being of specific *persons* (e.g., our selves, spouses, children, parents, etc.) to that of various abstract entities (e.g., the state, church, corporation, etc.). This depersonalizing, collectivizing process is nowhere more evident than in the methods used by the military (e.g., shaving one's head, wearing uniform clothing, and formal training to get the soldier to repress his individually-directed behavior in favor of obedience to constituted authorities) to mold troops into an institutionally-cloned mold of fungible robots.

As we move from personal, individualized priorities in our lives—David Riesman's "inner-directed" person[6]—to abstract, collectively-defined persons, our relationships to property also change. In becoming "other-directed," we make ourselves subservient to institutional interests, transferring decision-making power over our lives and other ownership interests to such entities. By creating "individual" versus "collective" divisions within ourselves, we experience both *internal* conflict, and conflict with the "others" who are behaving as we are toward the objects of their ego-boundaries. This is how our world got into

---

[6]David Riesman, with Nathan Glazer and Reuel Denney, *The Lonely Crowd* (New Haven, Conn.: Yale University Press, 1950).

its present mess, and only a reversal of our thinking will get us out of it. But just as we cannot end conflict without privatizing our sense of self, i.e., by withdrawing our energies from institutionally-managed ego-boundaries; we cannot move to a system of privately owned property without dismantling the divisive, conflict-ridden thinking that has collectivized our sense of who we are. Our sense of humanity is not to be found in either an isolated hermitage, or as undifferentiated members of a herd.

It would be gratuitously generous to the state of intellectual discourse in this culture to imagine that there has been a significant debate over the competing values of "individualism" and "collectivism." To undertake such an inquiry would force a close examination of the nature and importance of property, including the central question of self-ownership. Ideologues and members of the institutional establishment would find such a focused discussion destructive of their principal purpose: to promote their respective interests through the control of human beings. This, in turn, would necessitate asking the most spiritually relevant of all social questions: does *life belong to the living, or to institutional collectives?* It is the Dred Scott question again: is each of us our own property, or the property of *others?*

Institutions provide the most poignant examples of behavior that is highly *energized* yet lacking in the *spiritual* dimension of life. Their energies are supplied by men and women who, in order to advance their individual interests, largely have to repress those values that do not serve the institution. While a kind of ersatz spirituality is provided to people as an added inducement for their participation in organizational purposes (e.g., "patriotism," "comradeship," "holiness"), such values are always secondary to the paramount interests of the institution. They arise from outside rather than from within the individual. Any display of spiritual dimensions that arise from within the individual as an expression of his or her independent sense of being may be tolerated by established authorities, but *not* if they are taken seriously so as to interfere with preeminent systemic purposes (e.g., "conscientious objection" to participation in wars). The temptation to experience or express such inner energies is discouraged by admonitions such as "don't get emotional."

While people often express their spirituality in association with others, such sentiments have transcendent meaning only if they resonate within the individual independently of any purposes external to the person. Just as emotions such as love, happiness, or excitement can occur only within individuals, spiritual expression arises from inner voices speaking from both the collective unconscious of mankind and the personal experiences of the individual. We may share our endeavors with one another, our transcendent experiences are peculiar to each of us. There is no more of a "collective spirit" to mankind than there is a collective DNA, an endless cloning of some idealized person. Furthermore, experiencing our spiritual nature necessitates that each of us have a realm of authority in the world that is inviolate from the intrusions of others. Only as we insist upon the liberty to actualize our "inner" being in the "outer" world, can we end the conflict-ridden division in our lives and discover a genuine connectedness with others and the rest of nature.

The spiritual and emotional bankruptcy that affects so many of us is reflected in our inability to integrate psychic and materialistic needs so as to live without contradiction and be able to express a sense of wholeness in our daily lives. We cannot discharge our bankruptcy and learn to live with a sense of integrity until we assert the will to be the owners and controllers of our own lives. It is in this sense that the personal ownership of property becomes inextricably intertwined with an emerging spiritual renaissance: if we regard ourselves as a sufficient reason for being, we will enjoy a realm of unfettered authority—as defined by our property interests—with which to express our personal sense of being.

Because such inquiries threaten the reduction, if not total withdrawal, of our energies from institutional purposes, there has been an understandable resistance to this spiritual reawakening. Institutionalists bleat their contempt for what they label the "irresponsibility" of the "me generation," hoping, thereby, to shame us back into our assigned organizational stalls. The statists condemn us for our preoccupation with acquiring material wealth, all the while scheming to despoil that which we have accumulated. We are urged to limit our sense of wonder to institutionally crafted technologies, and to confine our inquiries to those amenable to the scientific method. Admittedly, science does a wonderful job answering the kinds of questions science is willing to ask. But more and more of us understand that the kinds of questions we are in greater need of asking are those that offer little in the way of material, quantifiable answers.

Whether we approach our understanding of economics from a socialistic or free-market perspective, very little inquiry is directed to anything but materialistic considerations. Marx's "dialectical materialism" seems to have set the tone for most modern comparative analyses of "command-and-control" versus market-driven systems. There appears to be an implicit agreement, even among most free-market advocates, that quantitative "bottom-line" outcomes are sufficient to measure the superiority of one system over another. But mankind's material prosperity, important as it is, is not the only factor in the equation. The collapse of state socialism did more than alter the means by which material values are best provided for in our world. It also raised the question about how we regard both ourselves and our neighbors; do we see ourselves as autonomous but cooperative individuals, or as interchangeable "units" in one or another collective?

From the perspective of institutions, individuality becomes a form of entropy (i.e., energy otherwise unavailable for their productive purposes) that they insist on repressing. Liberty is a very volatile condition, conducive to all kinds of uncertainties and unpredictabilities. Institutions prefer uniformity, standardization, and the sense of security that comes from knowing that their interests will not be upset by diverse and spontaneous influences that cannot be exploited for organizational ends. A society of free-spirited, self-interest motivated individuals cooperating with one another for their own productive purposes will be quite vibrant, but unsettling to established entities that regard their interests as ends in themselves. For such reasons, since institutions regard the fate of both civilizations and human beings as secondary to their own purposes, individuality must be quashed in favor of a more standardized and controllable humanity.

Collectivist systems have depended upon the mechanistic, reductionist paradigm represented in Newtonian thinking. A belief that nature is structured in relatively simple patterns capable of being reduced to identifiable and measurable calculations, is essential to hierarchically planned and controlled societies. To a collectivist, the world consists largely of "matter"—human beings included—whose qualities and differentiations are largely confined to chemical or mechanical description, and whose essence is to be servo-mechanisms in some giant, institutional purpose. Thus does the soldier become little more than expendable cannon fodder,[7] whose appearance and behavior is uniform in every respect; while other individuals are vulgarly dismissed as "the masses."

As we saw in chapter five, most collectivists find comfort in such self-contradictory sentiments as Pierre Proudhon's "property is theft,"[8] and George Bernard Shaw's "property is organized robbery."[9] Were their thinking more focused, they would have become aware that for "theft" and "robbery" to occur, there must be an owner to be despoiled. From whom do they imagine such property to have been taken, and upon what basis did these phantom prior owners base *their* claims? If the answer is some amorphous "mankind," how is control exercised by an entire species, and what are the boundaries by which such

---

[7]The late White House Press Secretary Tony Snow inadvertently let slip the state's depersonalized characterization of soldiers when, in response to an inquiry about 2,500 dead soldiers in Iraq, calmly replied "it's a number" (*Chicago Tribune*, June 15, 2006; *USA Today*, June 15, 2006). See www.usatoday.com/news/world/iraq/2006-06-15-iraq-deaths_x.htm.

[8]Pierre Joseph Proudhon, *Qu'est-ce que la Propriete* (1840).

[9]From George Bernard Shaw, *Major Barbara, in Bernard Shaw and George Bernard Shaw, The Wisdom of Bernard Shaw Being Passages from the Works of Bernard Shaw* (Whitefish, Montana: Kessinger Publishing, 2004), p. 325.

interests are defined? Is it not clear that these very statements negate the legitimacy of the alleged earlier claimants? If it is an act of "theft" for a specific individual to assert a claim of ownership over a precise item of property against an undefined "owner," how does a "claim"—and made by whom?—advanced on behalf of a nonexistent collective over undefined property, rise to a level worthy of respect? Such is the confused and wholly abstract base upon which collectivist thought rests.

Because collectivism presupposes a uniform and undifferentiated treatment of people, it has long embraced the doctrine of "egalitarianism," a concept wholly inconsistent with the inconstancies and variations implicit in individual liberty. The notions of equality and stability are closely related, each implying a resistance to practices that generate differences among people. Many acknowledge the importance of diversity and pluralism in fostering the life-sustaining adaptability of a species or a culture, and then turn around and embrace a doctrine that erodes the foundations of such negentropic values.

The study of chaos informs us that liberty, which is essential to a diverse culture, is a necessary condition for both producing and responding to the fluctuations upon which far-from-equilibrium systems work to generate the more complex patterns that help resist entropy. Adaptability to turbulence is essential to any vibrant system. Those who insist upon conditions of uniformity tend, much like brain-injured people, to be challenged by complexity and the processes of growth and change that are necessary for creativity and life itself. Creativity necessitates change, and change is a most uneven process. By contrast, the doctrine of equality is premised on a commitment to inflexibility and nonvariation (and with it, the suppression of individual liberty), requiring the maintenance of equilibrium conditions that further the entropic decline of a society.

This is why, contrary to our accustomed thinking, political systems based on egalitarian sentiments (e.g., state socialism, welfarism, social leveling) are inherently conservative in nature. The turbulence that accompanies change is most threatening to those with established interests, many of whom now have an incentive to promote political policies that discourage change. Such programs are focused upon the redistribution of some existing body of privately owned property, and the enactment of governmental policies (e.g., graduated income tax, antitrust or licensing laws, or other regulatory measures) that impede the processes of creativity and change that produce greater diversity. It is yet another example of the paradoxical nature of our world that such political programs, while appealing to the sense of envy and resentment upon which egalitarianism is based and purporting to dismantle the benefits of concentrated wealth, have had the opposite effect. It is no idle coincidence that the most firmly established institutions (e.g., the state, major corporations, churches, and universities), whose well-being depends upon preserving the status quo in order to protect their wealth, have been some of the most vocal advocates of egalitarian policies.

Contrary to such doctrines, *liberty*, as a catalyst for change, provides the best opportunity for wealth to be both created and subject to a continuing process of redistribution. A condition of liberty is no friend to those allied to the status quo, who see it more as a form of entropy to be eliminated. In the engineering concept of "equipartition of energy," we get a partial explanation of how energy tends to get evenly distributed throughout systems.[10] The way in which heat gets evenly distributed within a pan of boiling water illustrates this principle. It provides a metaphorical example for why, in an unrestrained marketplace, wealth that is produced tends to get redistributed throughout the economy without anyone having intended to bring about such a result. Wealth provides a means for enhancing one's well-being by securing the cooperation of others—be they employees, suppliers, or customers—which will occur only if others expect to better their own conditions in the exchange process.

Such are the consequences of the dynamic produced by the interplay of individual self-interests in a setting in which parties are free to respond to the specific conditions before them.

---

[10]Briggs and Peat, *Turbulent Mirror*, pp. 125–27.

Furthermore, unrestricted entry and free competition would be the most effective means of redistributing wealth out of the hands of those who lack the resiliency to respond to energized rivalry. But by impeding the processes of change, government taxation and regulatory policies have helped entrench the positions of the more established economic interests. *Standardization* becomes a tool for narrowing the range within which others, who might otherwise emerge as competitive threats—may operate. This is why established institutions have been consistent supporters of the political structuring of the marketplace.[11]

Even more compelling is the fact that egalitarianism is premised on the illusion that wealth consists of some fixed body of property, and that the rich have taken from the rest of mankind more than their "fair share" of such wealth. Proudhon's and Shaw's descriptions of the nature of property are grounded in such fanciful thinking. Furthermore, unlike most other species, humans not only *consume* wealth, but *create* it, an attribute that has been our greatest source of resiliency. We have not simply taken from nature, but have transformed resources to produce what did not previously exist! There is, of course, one expression of equality that collectivists are most anxious not to permit. As long as each of us has an unrestricted decision-making control over our own lives and property, there is an *equality of authority* that prevails among us. This is what institutionalists fear the most, and why there is such widespread hostility to

---

[11]See, e.g., Gabriel Kolko, *The Triumph of Conservatism* (New York: The Free Press, 1963); Gabriel Kolko, *Railroads and Regulation, 1877–1916* (Princeton, N.J.: Princeton University Press, 1963); James Weinstein, *The Corporate Ideal in the Liberal State, 1900–1918* (Boston: Beacon Press, 1968); Robert Cuff, *The War Industries Board: Business-Government Relations During World War I* (Baltimore: The Johns Hopkins University Press, 1973); Murray Rothbard, *America's Great Depression* (Princeton, N.J.: D. Van Nostrand, 1963); James Gilbert, *Designing the Industrial State: The Intellectual Pursuit of Collectivism in America, 1880–1940* (Chicago: Quadrangle Books, 1972); Ron Radosh and Murray Rothbard, *A New History of Leviathan* (New York: E.P. Dutton & Co., 1972); Ellis Hawley, *The New Deal and the Problem of Monopoly* (Princeton, N.J.: Princeton University Press, 1966); Robert Himmelberg, *The Origins of the National Recovery Administration* (New York: Fordham University Press, 1976); and my *In Restraint of Trade*.

the private ownership of property. It is in the practice of evenly distributed authority throughout mankind that "liberty" and "equality" are quite harmonious. But when egalitarianism was seized upon by the politically ambitious as a tool for gaining power over their fellow humans, the divisive nature of all political systems ended up destroying this harmonious and mutually respectful relationship. Rather quickly, "equality" came to be regarded not as a claim to *immunity* from state coercion, but as a condition to be conferred upon people by political force! But the exercise of the power to redesign and alter the lives of others—an authority enjoyed by a select few—can hardly be reconciled with notions of equality. If one scratches any egalitarian deeply enough, one finds a very deep-seated animosity to expressions of individual liberty as well as a commitment to totalitarian thinking and behavior.

All political power is premised on the *unequal* distribution of authority in society, for some people (e.g., politicians, judges, bureaucrats, and the special interests who enjoy the use of such power) are permitted to exercise control over not only *themselves*, but others. The allegedly "classless" Iron Curtain countries, with government officials living in comparative luxury and enjoying special privileges *vis-à-vis* their so-called "comrades," were a clear example of this phenomenon. But the practice prevails in *every* political system, by virtue of the coercive nature of politics itself. Thus, an egalitarian principle, in which each of us exercises 100 percent authority over our own lives and property, becomes corrupted into an elitist undertaking, in which our personal autonomy is reduced to, let us say, 70 percent, while the effective decision making of state officials, along with those who advance their special interests through political means, is increased far beyond the range of their own self-ownership. This is why a politically based equality is both self-contradictory and totally incompatible with a condition of individual liberty.

Egalitarian thinking squeezes such nonlinear factors as individual uniqueness, spontaneity, and autonomy out of the meaning of life. Inquiries into the *quality* of life become subjected to a *quantitative* analysis, with linear calculations and comparisons dominating and standardizing the mind.

As long as we conceive of the world in reductionist, mechanistic, fragmented ways; as long as we accept Cartesian mind/ body dualism as part of our understanding of "reality," we are inclined to look upon life in behavioristic ways. We are then disposed to the operant conditioning of systems intent upon exploiting us for their purposes. From there, it is easy to consider ourselves as little more than a given organic mass that goes through life acting, and reacting, on the basis of causal factors lying outside us. At the same time, we see one another as human billiard balls, responding to forces that we neither influence nor direct, and delude ourselves that our movements around the table are the products of "free will." It is just such a dreary, Skinnerian view of life that has sustained the institutionalized slaughter and human degradation that defined the twentieth-century and works to stamp its imprimatur upon the twenty-first. Whether political regimes parade under the banner of "communism," "socialism," "God," "fascism," "Keynesianism," "corporate statism," "Allah," "democracy," "welfare statism," or the "New World Order"—systems whose superficial differences mask their fundamentally synonymous nature— they all share in the collectivist premise that existing lives and property are subject to a superior claim of rightful authority by the state.

Our institutionalized training has conditioned us to fear individualism, to assume that it equates with isolation from and antagonism toward others. The "individualist" is often portrayed as the "loner," the misanthropic recluse who exhibits no regard for the interests or well-being of others. We are told that, only through collective agencies—the state, the church, the corporation, the labor union, etc.—can we find a sense of cooperation and wholeness. The debate between individualism and collectivism has arisen out of our willingness to allow institutions to insinuate themselves into our thinking and our lives.

We ought to have learned from basic biology that the individual is not only the carrier of DNA (hence, life itself) from one generation to the next, but also the carrier of the values upon which a civilization depends if it is to retain its vigor. Individuals have produced the art, music, literature, philosophies, scientific discoveries, inventions, and engineering and technological innovation that underlie great civilizations. The statue of David was conceived and sculpted by Michelangelo, not by an artists' guild. The Mona Lisa derived from the genius of Leonardo da Vinci, not from some corporate "paint-by-the-numbers" kit. Philosophic and religious thinkers—from Plato and Aristotle to Locke and Marx, and from Zoroaster to Moses, Jesus, Muhammad, and Martin Luther—continue to have their personal influence upon the minds of subsequent generations. Beethoven, Bach, Mozart, Verdi, Wagner, and numerous other composers, discovered deep within themselves musical compositions that have greatly enriched the human spirit. The writings of Shakespeare, Milton, and Dante were the products of individual minds, not a writers' workshop. It was Thomas Edison, not a local labor union, who worked in his simple workshop for long hours, often at subsistence levels, to invent many of the technological underpinnings of modern civilization. Entrepreneurs such as Andrew Carnegie, John D. Rockefeller, James J. Hill, Henry Ford, Cornelius Vanderbilt, and countless other creative individuals produced the commercial and industrial "instruments of expansion" upon which the American civilization has depended for its material well-being. In turn, merchants and other tradesmen exchanged such wares with the rest of the world, extending their benefits to others and receiving the goods of other peoples in return. None of these works were mandated by state coercion; they arose out of the liberty of individuals to pursue what their minds and spirits drove them to accomplish.

Even the most well-intentioned collectivists have never been able to divorce their genuine desires to benefit others from their need to exercise coercive power over the lives and property of their fellow humans. To such minds, "good" motivations excuse harmful behavior. Nor are their egalitarian sentiments able to transcend their collective leanings to embrace the individualistic sentiments in e.e. cummings' observation that "equality is what does not exist among equals."[12]

The holographic model provides a fitting metaphor for ending the institution-serving division between our *individual* and *social* natures, allowing us to see that they are complementary aspects of the same dynamic of self-interested behavior. The boundary lines in our dualistic thinking that help to separate us from one another, begin to dissolve once we see them as fabrications of our minds. In their place, perhaps, may arise the vision of ourselves and our neighbors as interconnected individuals. Each of us is a biologically and experientially unique person who, at the same time, needs the companionship, support, and cooperation of others in order to survive. We are neither isolated hermits nor fungible cells in some monstrous, six-billion headed leviathan that moves about the earth in response to an imagined collective will. The *individual* and the *numerous* are manifestations of the *wholeness* that lies hidden beneath our dualistic divisions of reality. A jar of beans, for instance, can appear to us as an individual bean-filled vessel, or as a combination of individual beans, whose absence leaves only an empty jar. Recall how the examples of Seurat paintings or newspaper photographs remind us of the interconnected nature of the singular and the general.

There is a popular notion, so long unquestioned as to rise almost to the level of a settled truth, that individuals are motivated, in large part, to preserve and promote the well-being of the species. In his book *The Selfish Gene*,[13] Richard Dawkins proposes a more realistic explanation of behavior: we are motivated at an unconscious level by a desire to perpetuate our individual genes. Just as the member of any other species acts to advance its own interests, our genes seek to perpetuate themselves

---

[12] e.e. cummings, "Jottings," originally published in *The Harvard Wake* (1951), reprinted in e.e. cummings, Six Nonlectures (Cambridge, Mass.: Harvard University Press, 1962), p. 70.

[13] Richard Dawkins, *The Selfish Gene* (New York: Oxford University Press, 1976).

from one generation to the next. To accomplish this, of course, requires the cooperation of another individual equally driven by this need. Such individual self-interests combine, through sexual reproduction, to produce the uniqueness of each child. This, in turn, fosters genetic diversity, an unintended consequence of which is to enhance the resiliency of the species itself. Just as we see in the dynamics of the marketplace, self-interest driven behavior can, without anyone intending to do so, bring about the well-being of an entire species or society.

The collective model upon which pyramidal systems are grounded prefers the institutional entity (e.g., the corporation or the state) as the fundamental reality, the "person" for whom human beings function as little more than subservient, fungible units. Those who would discourage the separation of the individual from the numerous do so solely as a means for gaining collective control over human beings. Through the divisions generated by thought, we come to distrust others, save those who, in exchange for the authority they demand over our lives, promise us protection from these contrived fears.

A holographic system of social organization, on the other hand, is one in which both the purpose and the authority for decision making is distributed throughout the social system through the principle of private ownership. Only as decision making is horizontally distributed can a peaceful and creative social order emerge from the boundless diversity and imaginations of free individuals and autonomous groups each seeking the full expression of their sense of being.

The fanciful nature of collectivist thinking has kept us confused in such matters. The holographic model presumes all of us to be composed of a seemingly endless variety of traits, dispositions, preferences, values, beliefs, ambitions, and other qualities. It presumes that in the pursuit of individually defined interests we are likely to bump into one another on occasion, or to desire the same resource, and that, in order to accomplish our purposes, it is desirable for each of us to minimize the conflicts and injuries we might have with one another in these pursuits. This holographic paradigm is premised not on some collectively defined undertaking, but on a recognition of the limitless diversity that inheres in the individualized nature of our being and, as a corollary, the common interest we share in a social environment that allows for the full expression of such diversity. It is the spontaneous, autonomous, and diverse nature of our individuality that is spread across the holographic film, not the homogenized image of some make-believe "common man."

Because institutions have set their purposes apart from and superior to those of people, their existence depends on an *e pluribus unum*, "melting pot" mentality that turns otherwise decent and responsible *individuals* into *masses* to be manipulated and directed toward dehumanizing, collective purposes. In the words of Doctor Murnau in the motion picture *Kafka*: "A crowd is easier to control than an individual. A crowd has a common purpose. The purpose of the individual is always in question."[14]

It is the uniqueness and energy of life, as reflected both in the singular nature of our respective DNA's and our autonomous and spontaneous character, against which collectivism wars. What is both remarkable and ennobling about life is its personal and insistent struggle against the inevitability of the second law of thermodynamics. It is another example of the interconnectedness of what, to our dualistic thinking, appears to us as contradiction: we live in a terminal state and yet are open systems who can take in energy from outside ourselves as we valiantly act to overcome, or at least delay, our fate. Though our lives may have no greater purpose beyond what we give to them, we search for some transcendent meaning to our existence that we hope will have eternal significance. But our pursuit of such ends requires us to be open to and supportive of this creative process, including having an awareness of the conditions that make possible such responses to our entropic destiny.

By eliminating distinctions among individuals, egalitarianism fosters the centralizing thinking and practice of dividing

---

[14]*Kafka* (produced by Baltimore Pictures, distributed by Miramax Films, 1991).

people into exclusive groups, within which people are expected to find meaning and direction for their lives. The increased centralization of authority in institutions has come about as a consequence of the enlarging of our "ego-boundaries" to embrace various abstract collectives. Because most of us have not found a capacity for generating transcendent experiences within ourselves, we enlarge our ego identities in the hope of realizing a fuller life experience in the greatness we imagine to lie in certain institutions or other abstractions. As we have seen, however, in attaching ourselves to a collective identity, we increase the likelihood of bringing ourselves into conflict with others (i.e., those who identify themselves with other abstractions). Because we now have an expanded boundary definition of ourselves, usually in forms that assume national or worldwide dimensions, "our" interests are bound to confront a much wider range of persons. When our boundaries become enlarged, we experience an increase in trespasses by others. As wars and genocides amply demonstrate, millions of men, women, and children, with whom we have never had a personal dispute, can suddenly become our sworn enemy, not because of anything they have personally done, but because of our respective ego attachments. Wars and other conflicts are most likely to occur along the boundaries that separate us, whether geographical, religious, ideological, or economic in nature. This makes the ego-boundary game a much more confrontational practice than relating to others from an individually-centered perspective.

Furthermore, in identifying ourselves with such large-scale collectives, we greatly restrict our felt sense of purpose in, and control over, our lives. Collectivism deadens the spirit and, in so doing, helps to produce a passive humanity. People succumb to the mass of power that confronts them in the form of an external, collective body and, feeling overwhelmed, may simply give up trying to discover a deep meaning and purpose in their lives. A more inner-directed man or woman, on the other hand, might find the designing of a building, or the raising of a child, or the creation of works of art, or the competent performance of one's work, or the development of a centered base of awareness, sufficient to satisfy their needs for transcendent, spiritually-grounded experiences. Because such ends, and the means of accomplishing them, are more narrowly focused, the achievement of their purpose is more within the capacities of the individual. Such man or woman has the power to develop a personal sense of order by acting upon the resources within his or her immediate control. The woman who seeks fulfillment in sculpting need only improve her skills, discover more interesting materials with which to work, or continue her own insightful explorations as to what is meaningful for her to express in her work. She need not concern herself with satisfying legislative committees, or getting the right candidate elected to office, or hoping that others will experience a change in consciousness.

But once we identify ourselves with an abstraction, the focus of our activity shifts from our individual selves to collectives. The externally-directed feminist who can find satisfaction only in changing what she perceives as male-dominated cultural patterns; or the "God-fearing American" who will not be content until his religious and political visions are enforced upon all; or the animal rights advocate who will not rest until the lives of all animals are respected by all humans, will eventually discover that the conditions necessary for their sense of accomplishment are not within their power to control. Having projected their sense of self onto abstract collectives over which they have no genuine control, they are left without the resources upon which to act in furtherance of their desired order. The "butterfly effect" illustrates how effective we can be when the focal point of our actions is more individualized. But most of us still cling to our collective image of "self," basking in the reflected light of some institution, a practice that generates personal frustration and infuriation. Such anger, partially explained by the "frustration-aggression" hypothesis,[15] has been a major contributor to the modern environment of confrontation and violence that

---

[15]"Violence As a Product of Imposed Order," pp. 742ff.

accounts for so much of our social—and all of our political—lives.

By its very nature, collective ownership generates confusion and conflict due to the bifurcation of the elements of *claim* and *control*. Who is entitled to make decisions over property, and who is responsible for the consequences of such decisions? When property is privately owned, these elements are integrated in the hands of the owner, and we know to whom to look for answers to both questions. In a system of collective ownership, by contrast, there is uncertainty as to who the "owner" actually is and, as a consequence, confusion in answering both these questions. Who does own Yellowstone Park? Is it the President of the United States, or the Secretary of the Interior? Is it the head of the United States Park Service, or perhaps the camp rangers who are actually in control of the park? Presumably not, since none of these people could sell the park and pocket the proceeds. If the answer is the abstraction, "the United States of America," what human decision-maker exercises his or her ultimate will on behalf of this entity?

If you were to telephone the Park Service and ask them this question, you would probably get one of those high school civics class answers that "the American people" own the park. And if you go on to ask: "does that mean that *I* am an owner?," you will probably receive an affirmative reply. But, if you then ask the Park Service to identify *your* portion of Yellowstone so that you can exert your control over it, you will quickly discover that your alleged interest does not, in fact, exist. Should you insist on entering "your" park at times contrary to the posted admissions signs, you will probably be arrested for the crime of "criminal trespass." If you were to engage in an activity prohibited by park officials, you would likely be arrested for this offense as well. The absurdity of the arrangement regarding collective property ownership was reflected in a sign in a city park somewhere in Kansas that declared: "No loitering! No bicycle riding! No picnicking! No ball-playing! REMEMBER: This is Your Park!"

The idea of collective ownership explains why there is so much conflict and confusion over the policies and curricula of government schools. First of all, by being taxed to support these schools, taxpayers erroneously believe that they have some property based interest that entitles them to control what "their" schools are doing and teaching. Once again we are reminded of the conflicts over government school curricula and methodologies that have become a regular topic in news reports and on radio talk shows.

Like two children fighting over a CD player given to them jointly, the parents of government-school children angrily insist that *their* schools teach *their* values to *their* children. Privately-owned schools experience fewer conflicts, not because they have more intelligent administrators or better curricula, but because there is no illusion as to who owns the school. The owners announce school policies, curricula, and other matters of interest to parents who then make decisions as to whether to enter into a contract with the school for the education of their children. If the school later decides to change its policies, the parents can freely enter into a contract with another school that is more to their liking or, if no such alternative meets their standards, they may decide to home-school their children.

The individual liberty that is implicit in decentralized systems not only fosters more options for both the suppliers and consumers of goods and services, but in so doing, generates individual responsibility. In selecting from numerous alternatives available to them, parents must engage in a more critical assessment of the curricula and teaching methods of schools, become more aware of the developmental stages of their children, formulate expectations they have of schools, and create a sense of mutuality of purpose and respect for their children. In the case of alternative health practices, individuals become more active in identifying and communicating symptoms to doctors or other practitioners, and seeking out alternative explanations and/or treatments for their ailments, instead of being passive recipients of standardized evaluations and treatments. In matters of a spiritual nature, individuals seek alternative forms of expression that appeal to their inner, spiritual sense, rather than wrenching and conditioning themselves in an effort to conform to externally derived dogmas and rituals. With an environment of liberty allowing individuals to control their lives and property in furtherance of their chosen options, each becomes an unrestrained free agent, rather than a fungible subject of a captive audience.

The sharp contrast in responsibility between *privately-* and *state*-owned property is nowhere better illustrated than in comparing the care and maintenance of a private amusement park, such as Disneyland, and almost any city-owned park. Disneyland is immaculate in its cleanliness; no youth gangs run loose to annoy people; and crime is virtually nonexistent, thus permitting families to wander freely without fear of being molested or attacked. By contrast, many city parks are overrun with trash, graffiti, unsavory characters, and muggers. No responsible parent would dream of taking his or her family to such a park for an evening of enjoyment. Or, compare the upkeep of a private school with that of all too many government school buildings with their broken windows, graffiti-covered walls, and prison-like steel fences. Nor can we forget the lessons learned from the erstwhile Iron Curtain countries: privately owned farms were much more productive than collective farms, just one of the many liberalizing influences that helped to dismantle the system of state ownership in such countries.

There are a number of motivational factors that cause privately-owned facilities to be better managed and more productive than those that are owned collectively. Where property is owned privately, there is a direct correlation, to the owner, between the costs and the benefits associated with the use of such property. Because I will reap the benefits of doing so, I have a greater incentive to incur the expenses of repairing a building that I own than I have to contribute to the repair of the city hall. We can recall Robert Ardrey's observation that among animals, personal territory carries with it a sense of energy sufficient to provide an owner with the capacity to repel trespasses even by stronger attackers.

Collective ownership, by contrast, fosters both the "tragedy of the commons" and "free rider" problems, wherein individuals are neither motivated to ration the use of a collective good or service, nor to incur the cost of providing such a good or service that they are able to enjoy without doing so. Still, politicized minds would rather use coercion to compel participation in state-owned activities than to rethink their assumptions by privatizing collective activities. As a result, we witness the inevitable increase in state coercion that accompanies rejections of private ownership and control of property. It is no coincidence that the bloodiest police-states in recent history (i.e., the Soviet Union, Nazi Germany, China) practiced collective ownership and/or control of property.

Such examples should remind us, once again, that whatever is said to be owned by *everyone* is owned by *no one*. It should also remind us of the earlier point that blurring the boundaries of our information systems—be it language, knowledge, or property—helps to generate the social disorder that is essential to the interests of the state. Wartime slaughter, genocides, and other forms of state tyranny have, like the atrocities committed by other organized mobs, been produced by the illusion that we can collectively pursue ends for which none of us need be personally responsible. Few of us would have the stomach to personally confront a neighbor, or even a total stranger, and do to him what we thoughtlessly approve of government officials routinely doing to millions of others through their collective authority.

By identifying both ourselves and others with any abstraction, we externalize our sense of reality. Inquiries into "the good, the true, and the beautiful" produce standardized responses that conform to the interests of those entities with which we associate ourselves. We think of ourselves as being in a world that is "out there," beyond us, a world that operates on the basis of "objective" principles that we learn to substitute for our inner, intuitive sense.

The collectivist mindset has depended upon a belief in *objective* values, particularly in economic matters. The presumption is that the *price* for which a product sells in the marketplace, which price *is* objective, correlates with the *value* of such product to market participants. In fact, the exchange value of a product will never equate with its price. Because we are motivated to act only out of an intention to be better off afterward than we would be had we not acted, any transaction between a buyer and seller is premised upon each anticipating a net gain. This means that the seller will subjectively value the item *less* than the money the buyer is willing to pay for it, while the buyer will value the product more than he will the money he is prepared to exchange for it. But subjectivity necessarily implies individualized decision-making and a multiplicity of preferences and actions, a condition that would be fatal to all collective systems. This process by which *subjective* values get translated into *objective* prices is what makes the study of economics—particularly *micro*economics—such a fascinating window into human behavior.

Believing that economic values have an objective quality to them, has led to the popular belief that any price received by a seller in excess of this "value" constitutes "exploitation." One sees this attitude expressed following a natural disaster, when retailers are able to sell scarce commodities at higher prices than usual. The mindset also surfaces in eminent domain cases, when the state pays a supposed "fair market value" for property taken from an unwilling owner. A "market price" for anything can be determined only when an owner's claim is voluntarily transferred.

Were this idea simply confined to the economic analysis within a system of thought that has proven itself unviable in human affairs, it might make for only a footnote here. But the underlying sentiment persists beyond the realm of economics and permeates much of our social thinking. We hear it commonly expressed in the idea that there must be a "winner" and a "loser" in every transaction.

I confront this notion quite frequently in my classes. My response has been to ask the student uttering such beliefs if he or she has ever purchased an automobile from a dealer. I usually get a "yes" answer to my inquiry. The student will then go on to recite another article of faith in this view, namely, that the businessman, by virtue of his more abundant resources, enjoys an "unequal bargaining power" over the buyer, enabling him to "exploit" the buyer. One such discussion continued as follows:

"Are you aware of this 'unfair advantage' before entering into the transaction?," I ask.

"Yes," the student proclaims.

"So that, before agreeing to purchase the car, you know that you are going to be taken advantage of by the seller and, further, that you will 'lose' (i.e., be worse off afterward) in this transaction?"

"Yes," the student responds.

"Then why would you enter into such an agreement in the first place?," I ask. "If you have voluntarily entered into an economic transaction, knowing that you were going to be exploited, what would have motivated you to do so?"

"Because I have no choice," he or she answers.[16]

This is the kind of muddled thinking produced by collectivist thought, a confusion that feeds the interconnected strands of personal irresponsibility and popular demands for political remedies for imagined "wrongs." Such thinking conflates the exploitation that does exist in the world—such as acquiring the property of another through acts of theft, fraud, eminent domain, taxation, embezzlement, etc.—with one's failure to anticipate the consequences of his or her voluntary acts.

---

[16]After reading cases that speak of the "inequality of bargaining power"— an article of faith upon which many judges, bureaucrats, politicians, and academicians base their authority to superintend our transactions—I invite my students to go to retail establishments and bargain for lower prices for goods that are listed. In almost unanimous fashion, the students reject the suggestion. After informing them of numerous examples of former students who successfully pursued such a course, most still treated it as an unrealistic proposition. On one occasion—after my suggesting that they discover just how much bargaining power they *do* have in the world—one of my students raised his hand and announced that, prior to coming to law school, he had been an assistant manager at a major Los Angeles department store, then said: "we did this all the time."

For the collectivists to denounce, as "exploitation," transactions in which individual property owners freely make decisions with one another, is not only to condemn life processes, but to fail to distinguish peaceful from violent behavior. The exploitation that derives from violence (e.g., an act of theft) constitutes a violation of the property principle. A voluntary act of exchange by an owner, on the other hand, represents not only the very essence of ownership, but is a real world expression of what it means to be a free, independent individual. If a worker's property interest in his or her work is "exploited" by the worker choosing to be employed by the businessman, under what circumstances will the collectivist acknowledge said worker to be free to make such a choice? When, in other words, does the worker acquire an existential authority over his or her own labor? Such is a moot question, of course, for such independence is precisely what no collectivist can abide.

The socialist, of course, will argue that the worker is not paid adequate compensation for his or her work—as though economic values have an objectively defined quality to them. It is also contended that the employee has no real "choice" in working for "exploitative" wages. From the perspective of the worker, however, such employment is the best of the available options. When collectivists endeavor to prevent the importation of goods manufactured in Third World countries by workers who are paid lower wages than are paid in America, for example, such efforts—when successful—deprive the foreign workers of employment options, thus worsening their lot.

Socialistic thinking, grounded in notions of "alienation" of workers from their work has, ironically, contributed to the disconnectedness many people have as a result of not being able to influence, through negotiation, their relationships with others. Collectivism requires the mindset that the individual is helplessly caught up in a presumed mass of humanity, the powerful forces of which he can neither comprehend nor deal. A.E. Housman's lament, "I, a stranger and afraid, in a world I never made,"[17] provides a lyric to the sense of personal inadequacy and vulnerability upon which all political systems depend. Only within a powerful group, it is believed, can one's interests be effectively pursued. We see, herein, yet another example of the problems that can arise from divisive, dualistic thinking that fails to respect the inviolability of individual decision making. In teaching us to think of voluntarily transacted and compensated work as a form of "exploitation," employees have increasingly allowed the state to preempt their authority to contract for themselves. Even worse, such dogmas—to the degree they are believed—weaken the listener and generate a sense of helplessness, the very mindset necessary for collective rule.

The same thinking has metastasized into other sectors of human activity. Landlord and tenant agreements, product standards, sales and employment practices, and the relationships of family members to one another, are further examples of the collectivist premise that the state should superintend our dealings with one another. Even the most personal of matters—including what food and drugs people may consume, their weight levels, and how they treat their pets—are now considered appropriate subjects for political/legal decision-making. As we saw earlier, personal behavior that was once confined to the domain of "manners" to be addressed by *social* pressures, has provided an ever-expanding list of public offenses to which the state is expected, by many, to respond. It is difficult to imagine any facet of human activity that, in today's politicized climate, could be said to be safely reserved to individuals and beyond the reach of state power. We have become so passive in the management of our own affairs that we regard it as an accusation to want to "take the law into our own hands," something we do whenever we freely negotiate with one another for the rules, i.e., a contract, that will govern our mutual relationships. In a free society, one supposedly grounded in a "social contract", in whose hands *should* "the law" reside? What sense of personal

---

[17]A.E. Housman, *Last Poems*, no. 12 (1922).

alienation is engendered by the state presuming, contrary to our will, to act for our alleged benefit?

Because collectivist thinking, with its insistence upon objectively-defined values, has come to dominate the material dimensions of our lives, even non-material values (e.g., aesthetics, morality, religious and political principles) have been co-opted by "objective" thinking. That notions of "good" and "evil," "beautiful" and "ugly," and the like, are steeped in subjective preferences, has not discouraged many people from self-righteously imposing their standards upon others.

Having already been taught the importance of security and the dangers of uncertainty, and believing that the state is capable of planning for and managing society for beneficial ends, we eagerly embrace the political structuring and regulation of our lives and property interests. Like dogs who carry their own leashes in their mouths, we readily subject ourselves to the rigid discipline of institutional authorities and channel our energies in ways that serve their ends.

Long before humanity embarked upon the Industrial Revolution, the life process had discovered the evolutionary and survival benefits of a system of exchange for mutual advantage. Might such arrangements in nature suggest to us that the roots of marketplace economics go much deeper than abstract, ideological preferences? Might a system of *laissez faire* be an expression of the need for life to be spontaneous and autonomous if it is to remain creative and thrive?

As we learn to think of our world more holographically, the divisive exploitation theories upon which all collectivist systems depend, begin to evaporate. At the same time, such a shift in consciousness may likely cause us to see how our well-being, as humans, is dependent upon the well-being of other life forms. It is not just the loss of individual species that should concern us, but the loss of the interactions among various species that could have produced a multiplicity of strategies for survival. It is out of this symbiotic dance, whose complexities, as the study of chaos tells us, are far too numerous to be prescribed or predicted, that biological diversity is strengthened.

To think of the world holographically, we must see through the dualistic processes by which our minds have created divisions in our lives. Nowhere is this more necessary than in our social relationships. We separate our individual and collective well-being, not recognizing that our mutual interests lie in preserving our individual liberty and property interests. The dichotomy into which we have been conditioned works to the benefit of institutions—most particularly the state—that promise to regulate our conduct so as to "balance" our allegedly "competing" interests. But this separation is wholly an artifact of our thinking. Were we to understand that what we have in common is a need to respect and protect the inviolability of one another's lives and property, this false division would end. As long as we think of our individual interests as opposed to one another and seek wholeness within collectives, we end up institutionalizing the collective, turning it into an end in itself, the result of which is to produce the kind of rigidly ossified, coercive structures that destroy civilizations.

Because of the divisiveness generated by traditional thinking, we find it plausible to believe that our interests are fundamentally incompatible with one another. The twentieth century, alone, should have disabused us of the destructive and demeaning illusion that social order requires the subordination of the individual to some fanciful collective good. A holographic model of society does not imply collectivism dressed up in new costumes: quite the contrary. The holographic premise *ends* the divisive thinking that sees individual and social interests as being inherently in conflict.

Our acceptance of collectivist thinking has been the major contributor to the debasement of our lives. Being premised upon the subservience of individuals to institutional purposes, collectivism is unavoidably a system, in varying degrees, of human sacrifice. The degradation of the individual implicit in such thinking finds clear expression in the motion picture, *Casablanca*, when Rick declares: "I'm no good at being noble, but it doesn't take much to see that the problems of three little people don't amount to a hill of beans in this crazy world."[18] In a society whose members respected the inviolate, self-serving purpose of each person, such a statement would be met with contempt. It would be generally recognized that there is nothing "noble" in the sacrifice of even one person in furtherance of political adventures.

Through playing out the conflicts and contradictions inherent in the collectivist doctrine, we have turned human society into the dystopia that Hobbes[19] envisioned arising from the *absence* of systems brought about through such thinking. Nazism, Stalinism, Maoism, and other fascistic and socialistic nightmare societies with their slave labor, death camps, wars, genocides, and other calculated cruelties, uniformly attest to the monstrous consequences of forcibly herding human beings. The fate of the Soviet Union, alone, a system in which so many well-intended persons had invested their intellectual energies, ought to be a warning as to how the exaltation of collectives ends up destroying the opportunities for individuals to realize their mutual interests through genuine cooperation and, in so doing, diminishes civilization, itself, as a viable, creative system.

From the works of a number of historians, we may induce an inverse relationship between a condition of liberty and the collapse of civilizations. If liberty is thought of as life pursuing what it chooses to pursue in order to produce the values upon which its viability depends; and if the structuring of life processes frustrates those ends, we may wish to consider that life has a dynamic of such a compelling nature that it will eventually bring about the collapse of structures that impede its expression.

We need to put aside the political and ideological myths that we continue to recycle as received wisdom and become aware of the dynamics that either produce or destroy a healthy society. The creative richness of a civilization derives from the behavior

---

[18]*Casablanca* (produced by Warner Brothers, 1942).

[19]Thomas Hobbes, *Leviathan* (1651).

of individuals, not from some imagined collective genius. The creative process depends upon men and women being free to experiment; to generate and pursue any of a variety of options; to be mistaken; and to offend the habits, tastes, sensibilities, prejudices, or established interests of others. As we experience in "brainstorming" sessions, it is the interplay of individual insights and responses that gives birth to the new; a process that presumes the liberty of people to act upon the world.

The vibrancy of any system depends upon its capacity and willingness to both generate and respond to change. Neither individuals nor civilizations can remain creative unless people are free to direct their own energies and to convert some portion of the material world to their self-interested purposes. The death of civilizations, on the other hand, is facilitated by a movement from individualized to collective patterns of thinking and conduct. Fear mobilizes mass-mindedness which, in turn, produces the state's deadliest expressions: wars and genocides. Nuclear and neutron bombs, with their capacities for killing hundreds of thousands of people in one strike, are the logical technological consequence of herding individuals into collectives. The indiscriminate slaughter of people and the massive destruction of cities, factories, transportation systems, and other forms of material wealth, are inconsistent with the creative processes of civilization. History reminds us that civilizations are created and sustained by individuals; they are destroyed by collectives.

Whether this civilization collapses from its accumulated entropy, or is able to transform itself into a more resilient system, will depend upon whether we are able to reform our organizational thinking and systems so as to enhance life-sustaining practices. Such fundamental alterations, however, must occur within each of us rejecting the collectivist premise that the interests of organizational entities have priority over those of individuals. If we are to transform our civilization, there must be a profound shift in both the thinking and practices that now threaten it, including our insistence upon identifying ourselves through collective "ego-boundary" attachments. We must begin by acknowledging that "life" belongs to the living, not to venerated abstractions or institutions; that human society exists for the mutual benefit of individuals pursuing their own purposes and meanings in life, rather than for the aggrandizement of institutional collectives. We need to discover new principles and systems within which we can freely cooperate with one another to achieve personal and mutual ends. We need to learn from the experience of the tens of millions who have suffered under various forms of collectivism that becoming attached to a collective is both a material and a spiritual dead end, for one has no capacity to direct its course to their purposes. Systems premised upon a decentralized, holographic model of organization may provide the best means of generating social behavior capable of protecting both individual liberty and cooperative undertakings; thus ending the divisiveness that inheres in institutionalism. We must liberate ourselves from the albatross of collectivism.

Chapter Ten
Property and the State

For what property have I in that which another may by right
take when he pleases to himself?

— John Locke

Different people invariably have different interests, perspectives, and tastes in mind when it comes to the uses to be made of particular forms of property. A real estate developer, a naturalist, a farmer, and an artist, may each have a different opinion as to the use that could best be made of a given parcel of land. Furthermore, what one person regards as her sense of artistic expression in the design of a house on her land may be considered a nuisance by her neighbor. Given the diverse range of preferences we humans exhibit, it is the height of arrogance for any of us to believe that our peculiar tastes and states of awareness are so intrinsically valid as to be entitled to coercive enforcement upon the rest of mankind. The idea of state formulated, uniformly enforced "master plans" to coercively direct the development of entire communities, is a collectivist concept that should be relegated to the past.

Because the essence of ownership lies in control, whoever exercises the ultimate decisional authority over any subject matter of property, even if a thief, must, in the most realistic, functional sense of the word, be acknowledged as its "owner." Perhaps the fragmented and dualistic nature of our thinking has made it easier for us to accept a division between formalized "title" to some entity, and our "control" over it. It is easy to see how our confusion over the meaning of property ownership has paralleled the increased loss of authority and control over our lives.

The focal point of all political systems is found in the conflict generated over how property is to be controlled. This is why *all* political systems, in varying degrees measured by the extent of their claims over property, are divisive and violence-prone. The principal disagreement between the advocates of *private* capitalism and *state* capitalism has to do with whether the ownership of productive property shall remain in private hands or be confiscated by the state. It is wrong to characterize the Marxists as being *opposed* to property. Marx, himself, was preoccupied with the interconnected relationship between private property and power, an alliance intensified by the rise of capitalism. One searches Marxist literature in vain for the expression of any values that are not tied to a condemnation of private ownership and its replacement by collective ownership. The Marxists only oppose *privately* owned property, and desire to get their hands on as much of it as possible. The first thing any Marxist regime has done when it seized power was to begin confiscating, on behalf of the state, hitherto privately owned property. Their passions to expand control over property have been no less than those men of industry whose motives and actions they sternly condemned. Unlike *private* capitalists who, as long as they operate within a marketplace, rely upon voluntary, contractual exchanges of property claims with others, the Marxists have resorted to naked violence to achieve their ends.

Nor are intrusions upon privately owned property confined to avowedly socialist regimes. It is no exaggeration to suggest that the overwhelming recourse to governmental regulation and confiscation of private property has come from within the business community, from persons who are the first to scream

"socialism" when such practices emanate from "leftist" ideologues. "Mercantilist" or "corporate-state" political systems are
no less grounded in a disrespect for private property simply
because they have come from men of commerce and industry.

No form of tyranny accomplishes its horrors in purely abstract
ways. Rather, all political systems direct and compel people in
how their lives, their bodies, their incomes, their accumulated
wealth, their lands, their tools and personal belongings, their
homes, their businesses, their crops and livestock, their savings
and investments, their books and newspapers, their methods of
communication, and their vehicles and systems of transportation, are to be used, disposed of, or transferred to others.

Because property has been one of the most misunderstood
of our social practices, and because of the central importance it
plays in fostering liberty and order in our world, attention must
be devoted to clarifying the nature of this concept and practice. The importance of doing so becomes all the more crucial as
we move toward unstructured, decentralized systems of social
organization.

As we saw earlier, whether we are considering abstract
"ego-boundaries" or concrete property interests, conflicts occur
along boundary lines, out of a failure to respect the inviolability of another's interests. Such conflicts arise out of state-gener-
ated fears and uncertainties regarding those whose ego identities confront our own. Believing that the state can resolve such
anxieties, most of us are eager to confer upon it expanded powers over our lives. As Randolph Bourne informed us, it is our
reaction to such concocted fears that is essential to the exercise
of state power. Because of our willingness to huddle at the feet
of political officials whenever we feel ourselves threatened, the
state will feed us an endless supply of fear-objects with which
to assure our continuing submission. This is why the well-
being of the state is dependent upon the war system.

To presume that uncertainty provides a justification for state
intervention in our lives is to retreat into childhood. As we
become more familiar with the dynamics of complexity, we will

likely increase our awareness of the uncertain and unpredictable nature of our world. Because our understanding of complex systems is unavoidably limited, when we allow the state to make decisions for an entire population, we run the risk of utter disaster should the basis of such actions prove wrong. Such is one of the many lessons deriving from the studies of chaos and complexity. In an inconstant world, we need all the options our minds are capable of mustering, from which each of us can choose our most appropriate path of survival. We need to heed the warnings provided by history regarding the dangers of collective actions taken on the basis of limited information. We need, as well, to pay attention to the lessons that biology offers concerning the anti-life implications of trying to stabilize and standardize life processes. Life expresses itself in the explosion of energy—perhaps a reverberation of the "big bang"—that occurs only within the autonomous and spontaneous nature of individuals, not collectives. Mankind needs nothing so much as for each of us to shift our thinking away from the arrogance of having power over others, to a more humble contentment in living harmoniously with our neighbors as mutually-respecting, self-controlling individuals. We need, in other words, to learn to respect one another's boundaries.

The very existence of the state helps blur the boundaries that separate our respective realms of decision making. Politics is born out of the belief that neither the lives nor property interests of individuals are inviolate, but remain subject to the claims and control of others, a proposition that renders the boundaries of one's authority uncertain. When the state is permitted to share control over property with private owners (e.g., zoning laws, housing codes, etc.), or when it engages in more blatant disrespect for boundaries (e.g., eminent domain, conscription, asset forfeiture, etc.), there is a confusion of the lines that separate our respective areas of decision making. This helps to produce the boundary disputes identified by Perls as the causes of conflict.

Because political systems are dependent upon conflict, it is no surprise that the interests of the state have always necessitated confusion as to the meaning of words, including the concept of property. One sure way of generating conflict is to blur the boundary lines that separate one word (or other abstraction) from another. Most of us have learned from George Orwell how easy it is to distort the meaning of words, and how such corruption of language produces the conflict and confusion that is essential to all forms of tyranny. Since our willingness to sanction political power is entangled in words and the images they connote, the state has been able, with the aid of both intellectual obfuscators and our own sloth, to expand its powers by corrupting the meaning of words beyond their inherent haziness to embrace meanings we would reject if done forthrightly. Such phrases as "war is peace," "freedom is slavery," and "all animals are equal, but some are more equal than others," have their modern counterparts in the Strategic Air Command's "peace is our profession," police departments' "to serve and to protect," and the Defense Department's Vietnam War policy of "destroying villages" in order to "save them."

The inherent ambiguity in language has helped delude us into thinking it possible to limit the powers of governments by writing words on paper. The United States government is the most powerful political system known in human history, and yet it functions under a constitution theoretically designed to limit its powers. A most sincere effort was made by the drafters of this document to limit the boundaries of the federal government by dividing political authority into three discrete branches, each with its jurisdictional boundaries and insulating, through a "bill of rights," the boundaries of individual liberties that the government was not to violate.

But even a cursory reading of this document reveals that it is replete with the vaguest of words—"justice," "domestic tranquility," "common defense," "general welfare," "unreasonable," "due process of law," "necessary and proper," "probable cause"—whose haziness creates a vacuum of understanding that the state, through its courts, is all too willing to interpret to suit its interests. Indeed, the government, through the judiciary, has presumed such powers of interpretation without any language in the document establishing such authority. The accepted definition of every government is that it is an institution with a monopoly on the use of force within a given geographic area. When such an entity is further acknowledged as having the power to define the boundaries of its authority, nothing but mischief should have been expected to ensue.

We pay too little attention to history, and fail to understand that the power to exercise absolute control over our lives is implicit in the state's assertion of authority to control our lives and property for even the most limited of purposes. Just as "the power to tax involves the power to destroy,"[1] the sanctioning of state authority to regulate even one percent of our conduct is to admit its authority as to the rest. The reason for this is that—as Korzybski warned us—any words delineating governmental authority will, by the inherent nature of language, have enough vagueness to them to require interpretation. If the state enjoys the ultimate power to interpret such language, it requires little imagination to see that the construction will proceed from the self-interested motivations of the state itself, as well as from the institutional interests that profit from having access to such power.

Unlike relationships grounded in *contract*, which involves a voluntary negotiation for the transfer of property claims between or among owners, political authority is grounded in *force*, which is not a respecter of claims to immunity from trespass. A lawful monopoly on the use of coercion negates, by definition, the principle of the inviolability of private property. A monopolist must have tangible assets upon which to exercise its exclusive power. Because the state generates no wealth of its own, but only confiscates that produced by others, the property interests over which such coercive authority will be exercised will always be that of private persons. Thus, a conflict of decision-making authority will necessarily ensue. If the owner resorts to force in order to resist the use of state power, the latter will, as the acknowledged lawful monopolist, be entitled

---

[1] *McCulloch v. Maryland*, 17 U.S. (4 Wheat.) 316 (1819), p. 431.

to prevail. By warring with the property interests of individuals, the state always engenders conflict within society.

Because your voluntary consent is irrelevant in political behavior, once you sanction the state's power to impose its will upon you, is it not evident that it can *extend* such authority at its will, at least up to the point where you are able to successfully resist it? Once you admit to the principle that permits the state to decide, without your agreement, how you are to spend as little as five minutes of your time each week, is it not clear that it can increase the scope of its authority—by being able to interpret such powers—to ten minutes, or to twenty-four hours, or for the entire seven days? Is it not evident to you that this, in fact, is precisely the way in which the power of the state has expanded in America, and that no change in the language of the Constitution was needed to bring this about? It is our willingness to give up authority over our own lives and property, *not* the increments in which it is given up, that has been the threat to our liberty.

A late friend of mine, Sy Leon, once provided a vivid example of the futility of limiting state power through the use of words. He proposed a hypothetical constitution in which a government was restricted to the power to regulate *time*. He then proceeded to demonstrate how Congress could enact laws prohibiting people from spending their "time" consuming drugs, or working for less than a prescribed minimum wage, or driving their cars faster than 55 miles-per-hour, or discriminating against others on the basis of any named criteria. This same power to regulate time could also be used to require people to spend two years of their "time" in military service, or four months of their "time" earning income to pay to the state. Step-by-step he showed how the current breadth of government authority over our lives could be rationalized through interpretations of what innocent minds might consider a "limited" function. His exercise confirmed the observation of Anthony de Jasay when, in discussing the concept of "limited government," he observed that "collective choice is never independent of what significant numbers of individuals wish it to be."[2]

As suggested earlier, a thorough exploration of the self-ownership question has very radical personal and social consequences. If you claim self-ownership, why do you tolerate the state controlling any aspect of your life? And if you are not prepared to assert such a claim, what possible objection can you mount to anything another person wants to do to you? Because every political system is grounded upon some degree of governmental taking of private property, those who identify themselves with any political party or doctrine tend to be quite uncomfortable playing out the implications of this question. What does it mean to even speak of self-ownership within a political context? After all, if you and I do not own ourselves, then who does?

Whether we conclude that our lives belong to *ourselves* or to the state, reflects our attitudes about where we think life has its principal expression and meaning: within the *individuals* who embody life, or within abstract *collectives*. Is the power to control your behavior governed by *your* will, or by that of institutional *authorities*? Will it be *centralized* in the hands of the state, or, as suggested by a holographic model of social systems, *decentralized* among us in the only expression of "equality" that nature seems to have bestowed upon all living things: the capacity for self-governance? These are just some of the questions that are almost never asked, the options that never appear in our institutionally administered multiple choice examinations or public opinion polls regarding alternative sources of authority for our lives.

What aspects of our lives can be said to be immune from state control and direction? The state regulates what substances we may ingest and what products we may purchase; what health care practices we may employ; the terms and conditions of our employment; how we are allowed to spend and invest

---

[2]Anthony de Jasay, *Against Politics: On Government, Anarchy, and Order* (London: Routledge, 1997), pp. 59–60.

our money; how we are to raise, educate, and care for the next generation of its conscripts; what occupations we are allowed to pursue, and what businesses we may operate; the risks we are permitted to take; what decisions we may make concerning our home and other property; whether, and to where, we are permitted to travel; what we are permitted to read and communicate to others; and whether we are at liberty to end our lives. Such regulation is in addition to the 40–45 percent of our wealth that is taken through various forms of taxation, as well as the enormous taxation of our estates upon our deaths, and to the conscription of our lives into military service on behalf of the state. We like to imagine that the Thirteenth Amendment to the Constitution *abolished* slavery, whereas it only *nationalized* the practice.

Since control is the essence of property ownership, any exercise of governmental control over people amounts to an assertion, by the state, of its claim of ownership over those it commands. When the state controls our property, it is controlling our lives, for it is limiting the choices we are permitted to make. It constrains us to act within boundaries established by the limited understanding or the special interests of those who enjoy the power to command by force. Every political system reflects a mix of peaceful private ownership and coercive state control of people and their property. Our answer to the question of whether we have ownership of ourselves will determine the future of political institutions. If we answer in the affirmative, the *state's* future will be a bleak one. If we answer in the negative, *our* future will become increasingly bleak!

On the other hand, reclaiming authority over our lives will necessitate our confronting what, for many of us, will be a very troublesome question: is it really possible for others, particularly the state, to control our actions? Can other people make us do things we do not want to do? It is comforting to most of us to believe so, to imagine that we have been the "victims" of someone else's wrongdoing and, therefore, bear no responsibility for doing what others "made" us do. But isn't such a response a denial of the existential freedom each of us always enjoys, no matter what the circumstances, to control how we will use our energies? If I do control my energies, how can my response to threatened punishments or desired inducements be anything other than my chosen action? If others can "make" us do what we do not want to do, why do they bother trying to *persuade* us, whether with carrots or sticks, to obey them? The state does not control us with its threats: rather, it threatens us with the loss of something we value, or the imposition of something we do not want in order to overcome our resistance to its demands. Translated into the language of economics, the policeman, like a mugger, puts a gun to our head in order to raise the costs to us of failing to obey his commands. It may be discomforting to our egos to admit it, but each of us always has a choice under such circumstances, even though we do not like the options available to us. The threat of force, such as a gun, may be a sufficient inducement to secure our compliance, but we have to make a conscious choice to do so: the *gun* does not make that decision for us. If the state could truly control us, it would not need to have every piece of legislation backed up with threats of fines or imprisonment: it would simply *direct us*, much as we direct our automobiles or computers, to accomplish its desired ends. That the state must resort to threats in order to secure our compliance, is an admission of its inability to control our behavior.

Our compliance with the demands of those who threaten us may, at the time, be a most prudent act. But for the sake of clear thinking, we must acknowledge the volitional nature of our response. Otherwise, we become habituated to a lifetime of thinking of ourselves *not* as self-controlling actors, but as passive, non-responsible beings who are acted upon by others. Such an awareness might also cause us to begin questioning the legitimacy of social systems that are unable to secure the participation of people other than through the threatened use of violence.

Since "freedom" and "self-control" are synonymous terms, and because self-control necessitates the exercise of one's will to be a decision-maker over one's life, it is possible for us to choose to abdicate such self-control. Again, if you do not want to claim

self-ownership, you can be assured that there are others prepared to claim what you do not want. This is what occurs when
men and women become "other-directed" people, allowing
their thinking and their actions to be directed by others. This is
not to deny the inherently self-controlling nature of all human
action (other-directed people are always free, in fact, to reas-
sert their self-directed control), but only to point out that people
who are not self-directed can appear, particularly to themselves,
to be controlled by others. This is why, when external restraints
on other-directed people are removed, they often react with violence or other antisocial behavior. Such are the dangers inherent
in consensus definitions of reality.

That each one of us controls our own energies, including our
free will, and that no other person can ever make us do something, is evident from the contrary responses of young men to
military conscription during different wars. Most of us who
grew up in the 1940s and 1950s believed, without much thought
to the contrary, that the state had a rightful claim upon our lives
and could rightfully send us off to war to risk being killed for
some vaguely defined or understood "national interest." If we
had been asked whether we had any choice in the matter, most
of us would likely have said "no, we are compelled, by the government, to serve in the military."

If the state was able to literally force earlier generations of
young men to go to war, what can be said of the responses of
many young men of a later generation who, in the 1960s and
1970s, refused to go along with conscription? These men were
faced with the same options those of twenty years earlier had
faced: when the state tells us that we must put on a uniform and
go off to Lower Ruritania to fight the Slobovian invaders, each
of us must decide whether or not to do so. In the 1960s, many
men made the conscious choice to not cooperate with the government's demands during the Vietnam War, decisions whose
cumulative effect helped to bring that war to an end.

Government officials are also responsible for the consequences of their behavior, including conditioning us to become
dependent upon their judgments. The fact that they, unlike the

rest of us, enjoy the exercise of legal force, adds to the moral accountability for their acts. But as they are burdened by the same fear of self-responsibility as the rest of us, they try to shift the responsibility for their failures to a virtual cornucopia of scapegoats. Parents, television, rock music, and motion pictures, are accused of fostering children's lack of respect for constituted authority, while teachers blame the collapse of learning upon lazy students, unsupportive parents, or the unwillingness of taxpayers to provide more financial support. The "war on terror" is another example of this phenomenon, with the American political system shifting the consequences of decades of its brutal, interventionist foreign policies onto its unwilling recipients.

The division between control and responsibility has become virtually synonymous with all forms of governmental behavior. From the days of the feudal maxim "the king can do no wrong" to its modern equivalent of "sovereign immunity" or "implied powers," the state insists upon the absolute reach of its authority while, at the same time, greatly limiting, or even denying, responsibility for harms visited upon others as a result of the exercise of that authority. By refusing to be answerable for the injuries it inflicts, the state manifests an ethic no higher than that of a riotous mob. In teaching that responsibility can be separated from the exercise of power, it has helped to foster the all-too-prevalent attitude among the rest of us that we, too, need not be accountable for the consequences of our actions.

Herein lies the difficulty many of us have with the prospects of a life of freedom: taking the responsibility for our own thinking and actions. Like the teenager who pleads that his friends "made" him do something he now regrets, most of us are uncomfortable calling ourselves to account for our behavior. Neither the IRS, nor the Selective Service System, nor a judge, nor a police officer, nor any other government official, makes us obedient. From at least the time of the Stoics, history has afforded us examples of many men and women who chose suffering or death rather than submit to established authority.

This point can be illustrated with the example of a late friend of mine, Howard Moore. During World War I, he was ordered to report for military service. Howard refused to do so, declaring that he was conscientiously opposed to war. He was prosecuted, convicted, and given a twenty-five year prison sentence for his refusal. At each step in the proceedings, he was given the opportunity to change his mind, to finally admit, in other words, that the state owned his life. Howard refused all such offers. When he arrived at the federal prison in Utah, he was ordered to participate in such prisoner activities as cleaning up the grounds. Again, Howard refused such commands, for which he was tortured, beaten, and made to sleep on a concrete floor. After the war, the sentences of conscientious objectors were commuted, and Howard was one of the very last to be released, because of his continuing refusal to acknowledge the authority of the state over his life. Even though Howard had been born two months prematurely, with a defective heart, he lived to the age of 104. He was too kind a gentleman and too respectful of life to have taken any delight in having outlived all those who had subjected him to such treatment. It would also be incorrect to suggest that he had lived as long and as well as he had "in spite" of his painful insistence upon maintaining his own sense of integrity: I like to think that he lived this long because of such resolve![3]

Whether we remain as free individuals or not depends upon how strongly we insist upon respect for our claim of self-ownership. For men like Howard, it is the determination to insist upon our own inviolability that is a predicate to any meaningful experience of freedom and self-dignity. The implications of such attitudes for our survival are reflected not only in Howard's life, but in the experiences of Viktor Frankl, a survivor of Nazi concentration camps. Frankl observed that "under the influence of a world which no longer recognized the value of human life and human dignity," people "lost the feeling of being an individual, a being with a mind, with inner freedom and personal value." Those who managed to survive the concentration camps, said

---

[3]Howard Moore, *Plowing My Own Furrow* (New York: W.W. Norton & Co., Inc., 1985).

Frankl, were those whose lives were more centered, and who understood that what "makes life meaningful and purposeful" is a sense of "spiritual freedom," which he went on to describe as "the last of the human freedoms—to choose one's attitude in any given set of circumstances, to choose one's own way."[4] If we choose to accept whatever definition of "rights" our masters bestow upon us, how does our condition differ, in any meaningful way, from the status of slaves?

When we assert a "right" to be free, we are making a claim, which we hope others will respect, to be the exclusive decision-maker over whatever is subject to being controlled, by us, toward some end that we have chosen. In making such a claim, we desire others to acknowledge the propriety of our claim and, in the process, respect our claim to immunity from being trespassed by others.

The necessary interconnectedness of individual liberty and decision-making concerning property should be apparent upon examination. Whether freedom of religion, or of the press, or of speech, or of assembly, exists in any society, centers on the question of whether individuals will be permitted to own and use church properties, printing presses, speaking facilities, or assembly halls. The freedom to travel, or enjoy privacy, or operate a business, or to raise one's children, or to select one's system of health care, all presume the unhindered exercise of control over some claimed property interest (e.g., one's body, or home, or relationship with one's children, or productive assets). This is why no serious objection has been raised concerning the freedom of people to *believe* what they want to believe. Because the state has thus far been unable to directly control individual thinking processes, judges and other government officials are willing to make this concession as evidence of their liberality. But if such thought processes could be controlled, you can be assured that the state would be working to implement control mechanisms to do so, using the same rationale it now uses to

---

[4]Viktor Frankl, *Man's Search for Meaning* (New York: Washington Square Press, 1963), pp. 78–79, 104, 106.

constrict our other liberties: "rights are not absolute." Only its own power does the state consider to be "absolute," knowing no limitations other than what it chooses to acknowledge.

Minds that have been trained to believe that the competing interests of individual liberty and state power can be reconciled through a process of "balancing," overlook the fact that the "balancing" is done by the state with its legal monopoly on the use of force. The "balancing" concept is one that has been employed by the courts to reconcile individual and political interests, a trick that begs the question as to whether—and by what means—the state has ever acquired a legitimate claim over the lives of people. What is unavoidable in this relationship is that the struggle for liberty ultimately reduces itself to the question of whether *property* principles or the coercive mandates of *state power* will be regarded as absolute. One or the other must prevail. The existence of the state depends upon conflicts that it promises to resolve by restraining people's lives and other property interests. Lenin understood this quite well when he observed that "it is nonsense to make any pretence of reconciling the State and liberty,"[5] a position essential to the collectivist system he was helping to create. To believe that liberty can be compromised and "balanced" with the demands of monopolistic force is to further the kind of illusory thinking that the history of constitutional government has shattered. Like a wolf entrusted with balancing its interests with those of a sheep, the outcome of the arrangement ought not surprise intelligent minds.

In a holographic system in which private property principles prevail, individuals and other minorities need not fear being at the mercy of more numerous groups enjoying the exercise of coercive power to advance their interests. With each of us assured of the inviolability of our own lives, social behavior would move from "majority rule" divisiveness toward consensus-based associational activity, wherein mutually beneficial

---

[5]Quoted in Albert Jay Nock, *The Memoirs of a Superfluous Man* (Chicago: Henry Regnery Company, 1964), p. 211.

decisions can be arrived at through general agreement, and without the use of force. "Consensus" derives from "consent," and implies a "unanimity" or "group solidarity in sentiment and belief,"[6] all of which negates any sense of being coerced into submission. Those who favor a particular program would be free to pursue it, and to attempt to persuade others to join their efforts, while those who did not, would not be obliged to participate in it. Respect for property boundaries keeps one from acting beyond the limits of what he or she owns which, by definition, also sets limits for the actions of others. Respect for a principle of inviolability would free us from a need for defensiveness and allow us to become more willing to consider cooperating with others.

One of the numerous rationales used by the state to justify the extension of its control over property has been the idea that resources are "scarce," and state regulation is required to avoid their depletion. The conservation movement, though largely fostered by business interests as a way of restricting competition,[7] continues to feed itself on this notion. Such thinking is commonplace among socialists, who operate from the premise that wealth of all kinds is in a fixed supply, and has been "unfairly" distributed into the hands of a few people through marketplace mechanisms that they do not begin to comprehend. The idea that new wealth can be created, and that what we call "natural resources" is a flexible concept, forever changing as our inventiveness and technology change, rarely enters the minds of such persons.

Government-mandated conservation programs are grounded not only in the dogma of scarcity, but implicitly (and often explicitly) in the collectivist premise that natural resources belong to

---

[6]See, e.g., *Webster's Third New International Dictionary*, p. 482.

[7]See, e.g., my *In Restraint of Trade: The Business Campaign Against Competition, 1918–1938* (Lewisburg, Penn.: Bucknell University Press, 1997), pp. 145–81.

the nation. Long-standing common law principles have recognized oil, gas, and minerals to be part of the boundary of a parcel of land and, therefore, to be the property of the surface owner. For resources discovered in unowned territories (e.g., ocean floors), the first person to take control of them under a claim of ownership would be the recognized owner. What underlies such common law thinking is the idea that individuals are entitled, as self-owning beings, to lay claim to previously unowned resources; that their purposes and strategies for overcoming entropy and pursuing what each regards as a meaningful life, provide a sufficient basis upon which to claim some portion of the world.

When one examines the legislative history of government conservation policies, however, they discover the hand of many business corporations using this fair-sounding theme—coupled with state power—as a means of curtailing production by their competitors and, thus, stabilizing prices. Such efforts have often paraded under the banner of preventing "waste." That the owner of any valuable resource has an incentive not to *waste* but to *protect* it, is a point often lost in legislative chambers. But upon closer examination, it becomes evident that the "waste" industry members often sought to prevent was not *physical* in nature, but *economic*. Resources were being put into the marketplace by some firms at prices lower than what their competitors found comfortable. Thus did the president of Standard Oil (Indiana) testify before a congressional committee in 1934:

> **Mr. Cole**: You say there is an excessive supply of crude oil today. Where does it go?
>
> **Mr. Seubert**: Well, speaking for my company, it is going into storage, both crude oil and refined products.
>
> **Mr. Cole**: Then, speaking of the man who does not have storage facilities, where does it go?
>
> **Mr. Seubert**: Well, it finds its way to the market.
>
> **Mr. Cole**: None of it is wasted?

Mr. Seubert: Well, it is wasted in the fact it is put in
the market at demoralizing prices and is wasting to the
extent of demoralizing the general industry.[8]

The economist Fritz Machlup has observed that "[t]he chief
purpose of production restriction is price maintenance, which
is . . . made possible by large-scale collusive activity between oil
companies and governmental authorities."[9] In such self-serving
ways have members of the business community been a dominant force in the expansion of state power over the ownership
of property.

Since at least the time of the ancient Greeks, humans have
feared that a rising population would soon threaten mankind
with mass starvation, a fear that failed to account for improved
methods of agriculture that have made possible increased levels
of production from increasingly fewer acres of farmland. When
radio and television broadcasting first began, government regulation of such media was rationalized on the grounds that the
airwaves were "scarce", and, of course, in yet another manifestation of collectivist thinking, belonged to "the people." But
with changing technologies (e.g., fiber optics, cable systems, satellites, etc.), such explanations for government regulation have
disappeared—but the regulation has *not*. The ghost of Thomas
Malthus still whispers his outmoded economics to modern conservationists who, at the same time, ignore current voices who
speak of the destructive consequences of planning and regulating complex systems.

Such thinking reflects an ignorance of the fact that all resources
are, by definition, "scarce." This is what creates a market demand
for their use and consumption. Is oxygen scarce for most people
in a city? Clearly not, but for a heart patient, or someone atop
Pikes Peak, it might be, thus creating opportunities for suppliers

---

[8]From "Petroleum Investigation," *Hearings on H. Res. 441* (Washington,
D.C.: Government Printing Office, 1934), pt. 1, 485, reported in William Kem-
nitzer, *Rebirth of Monopoly* (New York: Harper & Bros., 1938), p. 119.

[9]Fritz Machlup, *The Political Economy of Monopoly* (Baltimore.: The Johns
Hopkins University Press, 1952), pp. 302–03.

to sell this resource. Furthermore, "scarcity" is largely a function of our minds; a deprivation of some desire produced by our thoughts. Things become scarce because we want them, and we often want them because we have psychological attachments to things outside ourselves. Was there a scarcity of electricity in ancient Babylon? Did Henry VIII experience a scarcity of computers or CD players? Did the emigrants on the Oregon trail experience a scarcity of automobiles or television sets? Is there a current shortage of witch-doctors or stagecoaches in London? Does the depletion of wild game that led the Man-a-hat-a Indians to sell to the Dutch, in 1626, the island that bears their tribal name, continue to impoverish modern New Yorkers?

Given the apparently insatiable appetite for material things in our culture, it may be said that there is a greater scarcity of goods in modern America than there is in more undeveloped cultures in which people seem content with the fruits of their hunting and gathering efforts. This failure to satisfy our seemingly unlimited expectations of material rewards accounts for a good deal of the anger and frustration of people in our modern, industrialized world. Even though each of us enjoys goods and services that even the most despotic of ancient monarchs could not command (e.g., air conditioning, telephones, electricity, television, the Internet, automobiles), as long as our fantasies remain unfulfilled we will be attracted to the dogmas of "scarcity." Such an attitude helps to keep us subservient to the institutions that promise us a steady flow of such externally derived benefits in exchange for our continued submission to their authority.

Of course, the statists would never entertain the countervailing argument that "authority" is a scarce resource that has become "unfairly" and increasingly concentrated in the hands of political officials and ought, therefore, to be "redistributed" to the many. It takes little imagination to see that the case against private wealth is grounded in hostility to private ownership, a system that forever stands as a barrier to those with ambitions for power over others.

As our world has become increasingly politicized, another form of "scarcity" has materialized: the reduced opportunities for people to evade the reach of state control. As we saw in chapter four, the frontier once served as a territorial refuge into which independently minded men and women could move in order to live relatively free of formal restraints. The image of the pioneer, or the mountain men, or traveling peddlers, or the cowboy, or the "traveling people" of Ireland, remind us of ways of living vastly different from the constantly regulated, policed, fingerprinted, searched, surveilled, licensed, identification-numbered, and documented modern society. The song, *Don't Fence Me In*, reflected a frame of mind that valued spatial and personal independence.

An ancient tradition known as "sanctuary," was grounded in the recognition of the inviolability of certain property boundaries. It once served as a check upon the authority of the state. There were recognized places, usually churches, wherein individuals could find refuge, free from the powers of arrest or legal process. A parallel practice has long prevailed in the world of nation-states in the form of "neutral" countries, which could provide sanctuary for persons caught in the middle of wars, or allow warring nations to indirectly deal with one another. The same practice has been used by some parents in recognizing a "safe place" (e.g., beneath a table, or in the child's bedroom) to which the child could repair for refuge from parental authority.

Each of us has a need for space that is recognized as immune from the trespasses of others, a role served by the practice of privately owned property. The maxim "a man's home is his castle" is a reflection of this need for sanctuary. But such claims to inviolability are increasingly disrespected by autocratic states that insist upon their powers to engage in the surveillance of homes, wiretap telephones, break down doors, engage in "sneak-and-peek" entries without the knowledge or consent of the owner, and otherwise regulate the behavior of individuals within their own homes. The contrast between the respect our ancestors showed for sanctuary within churches, and the modern American government's willingness to burn to death Branch Davidians who resisted violent attacks within what was both their home and church, illustrates how far removed we are in our thinking from any understanding of the important role property principles play in the maintenance of free, peaceful, and humane social systems.

If social conflict erupts because of the failure of individuals to respect the inviolability of one another's boundaries, and if we believe that political systems are necessary to deal with such transgressions, why should we assume that government officials—who are as self-interest motivated as other people, and whose methods consist of coercion, threats, and other trespasses—have any greater awareness of the importance of respecting one another's impregnability than the rest of us? Are we imbuing political authorities with a greater disposition for such respect than we have ourselves? Do centuries of politically organized strife and butcheries warrant such confidence? Carrying such an inquiry into the international arena, would a world government end such conflict and violence or only *redefine* it? Why should we expect such a super-state to function any differently than local or national political systems? Do we believe that while nation-states are incapable of planning and directing the behavior of tens of millions of persons to achieve predictable ends, government functioning on an ever-more-complex world level, involving *billions* of people of even more diverse cultures and interests, could do so? And are our judgments so unburdened by history as to lead us to imagine that the corporate interests that have manipulated the machinery of *national* governments to suit their ends, would be disinclined or unable to employ the powers of *international* governments for the same purposes? If conflict and violence can end only within the consciousness of each of us, why would we expect any authority to be able to compel an end to our disorder?

When we understand that liberty and order imply one another, we will end the division and conflict our thinking has created. Self-control, reinforced by respect for property boundaries, defines the conditions for social harmony, and helps to explain why political systems, which substitute coercive state regulation for individual self-control, destroy the symmetry between peace and liberty, producing the social destructiveness that now characterizes our institutionalized world. Defenders of the established order may argue that concerns for individual liberty are exaggerated, that the state rarely exercises such a degree of control over us as to substantially diminish the quality of our lives. But the hundreds of millions who have been made victims of wars, genocides, police brutalities, and government regulation of economic behavior (whose hidden costs are not shown on the eleven o'clock news shows) would contend otherwise.

Furthermore, such a defense by institutionalists misconstrues the nature of life, treating it in purely materialistic and mechanistic terms. Contrary to the commercial and industrial footings upon which our modern culture has been built, life also has its spiritual and emotional dimensions. As Viktor Frankl reminds us, the sense of degradation that accompanies the violation of our personhood by the forcible preemption of our free will, diminishes life every bit as much as a physical trespass, if not more. The feelings of humiliation suffered by rape victims, beyond the physical pain and injury, express this psychic dimension to life. But such inner qualities reflect the idiosyncrasies and temperaments of individuals that do not translate into resources available for institutional purposes. Consequently, their costs tend to be disregarded in favor of collective, mechanistic calculations of organizational policies and practices. How, after all, can such nonquantifiable costs be taken seriously in a "bottom line" society that regards the nonmaterial as immaterial?

As we are discovering from the study of chaos and complexity, the universe is inherently orderly, regardless of the particular courses of action we pursue in our self-interests. Most of our politically-engendered social problems are occasioned by two factors. The first is reflected in the fact that the diversity of our interests fosters a variety of competing definitions of orderliness. What the buyer of a low-priced widget regards as an expression of an orderly marketplace, the manufacturer might treat as an example of "predatory price-cutting" to be punished by the state. The second factor arises from the tendency to regard our ignorance of the complex interconnections of our world as manifestations of "disorder" to be rectified by governmental intervention.

We have, unfortunately, failed to circumscribe the limits, if we admit to them at all, as to what is appropriate for each of us to control in our efforts to create order in our lives. Unless we simply give in to the arrogance of power, and allow some to define their sense of order at the expense of others who are not allowed to do the same, we must discover principles of conduct that are fundamentally different from those that plagued our public life in the twentieth-century. But to undertake such an inquiry requires that we explore the deeper philosophical and spiritual question of whether we regard each person as his or her own reason for being, worthy of pursuing their respective self-interested ends. In this regard, we might wish to revisit the civilizing attitude of "tolerance" for others, a concept that has long been shouted down by strident voices who angrily and self-righteously contend with one another at the boundaries of their respective "ego identities."

Is there a principle by which social order can emerge as the unintended consequence of people pursuing their own interests and freely negotiating with one another for those patterns of regularity that serve their mutual purposes, but without presuming to forcibly impose those patterns upon others? Can our thinking transcend its own conditioning, and imagine order arising without anyone's intention to create it?

If the *political* means of endeavoring to impose orderliness upon society via property trespasses has produced the conflicts, wars, economic recessions and dislocations, and other disorder in our world, is it not time to rediscover the *social* means? We must begin to consider that a system of individually owned property, wherein each of us enjoys an unhindered authority over what is his or hers, an authority that necessarily ends at each person's boundaries and thus respects the inviolability of one another's interests, may be the only means of experiencing the kind of orderliness that serves us all, rather than just the arrogant few who control state systems of power.

What impact will the continuing transformation of our social systems likely have upon the state? In an age of computerized information and transactions, as well as other technological creations that allow us more rapid and individualized dealings with one another, life will take on too great a speed and range of expression for government planning and direction to have much functional relevance. The state will become increasingly seen as but an agency of destructive violence, while the changeful forces of complexity will intensify the unintended and uncontrollable consequences of political decision making.

Now that the decision to start a world war is no longer the prerogative of presidents, prime ministers, and chairmen, but can be made by a handful of angry men representing no formal political system; now that the obliteration of a city can be accomplished by one man with a nuclear suitcase, or a vial containing a biological agent that can be dumped into a water supply; and now that it is beyond the capacity of governments to either predict or control such acts, it is time for us to acknowledge that the state has reached a terminal condition. The decentralization of destructive power, occasioned by the contradictions and inefficacies of vertically-structured forms of organization, is producing a decentralization of political power, . . . and all the king's horses and all the king's men will be unable to put the system back together again!

Chapter Eleven
Conclusion

I am striving . . . to discover whether man still has a place in this tangle; whether he still has any authority among these colossal masses in movement; whether he still can exert any force whatever on the statistics which are slipping from his hands into the abstract and the unreal. Can he have a place, authority, and the possibility of action on a better basis than ill-founded declarations of hope or blind acts of unreasonable faith?

— Jacques Ellul

We are living in "interesting times." The question is how do we respond to the tumult in which we find ourselves? Most of us, caught up in the important but narrowly detailed matters of our lives, fail to stand back and observe the broader canvas upon which larger events are playing themselves out. As our present social systems continue to collapse around us, our very existence demands that we examine and discover alternative models for social organization.

Our world is undergoing major processes of decentralization, changes that can provide peaceful, liberating, and creative opportunities if we approach them intelligently and without fear. There will, of course, be those with intense and unquestioning attachments to the old order who, like their Luddite ancestors, will strike out with fear and anger at whatever portends a deviation from the familiar. The state—the incarnation of the status quo—will continue to insist upon its destructive divide-and-conquer games in a desperate attempt to continue its power over us. It will provide various groups with differing benefits, e.g., subsidies for one, special privileges for another, tax breaks for yet another, and lucrative government contracts for still another, in an effort to preclude us from developing a sense of common interest.

It is for each of us, however, to see through such contrived divisive practices, and to rediscover our mutual interests. We can find a genuine sense of community in our need to respect and defend the inviolability of each other's lives, property, and autonomy. And that experience of community would be fatal to the political classes. An etymological dictionary informs us of the interconnected history of the words "peace," "freedom," "love," and "friend."[1] What might our ancestors have known about the nature of relationships—an understanding that has long since been lost by allowing the state to repress our sense of *community*? Might people who treat one another as "friends" generate the "love" that produces a "free" and "peaceful" society? If so, how would we expect those who exhibit such traits to regard their neighbors' interests? Is it possible that the ongoing decentralization of social behavior will allow us to reclaim our humanity with one another?

In a period of significant change, we must be prepared to engage in significant learning, rather than just reaffirming what we already know. We need to constantly remind ourselves of the tentative and limited nature of our understanding; of how our thinking is necessarily restricted by our experiences. Such an awareness becomes all the more compelling as the processes of change escalate.

Each of us has a sense of "reality" that can be represented as a circle (see figure 3). At any point in time, what we profess to know about ourselves and our world is contained within the boundaries of our particular circle. Because your experiences

---

[1]Eric Partridge, *Origins: A Short Etymological Dictionary of Modern English* (New York: Greenwich House, 1983), p. 235.

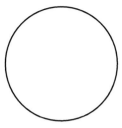

Figure 3.

differ from mine, the contents of our respective circles will also differ, a fact that not only underlies many of our social problems but, at the same time, creates the diversity that makes cooperation possible. Learning and other forms of creativity involve a continuing synthesis of the known and the unknown. We can expand the range of our understanding only by expanding the circumference of our circle of reality. Throughout our lives, we are confronted by various teachers, who may include parents, school teachers, mentors, writers, friends and relatives, whose own circles of reality can be represented by the dotted line in figure 4.

Figure 4.

Such teachers seek to persuade (or cajole) us to expand our definitions of reality by moving from our present boundaries of understanding outward toward theirs. The kind of learning most of them induce, however, is largely *linear* in nature, consisting of new information or modifications in our methods of analyzing information already known to us. Examples of such learning may be found in taking a survey course in history that is followed by an advanced course in French history, or learning a foreign language after having mastered your own, or progressing from an understanding of simple mathematics to calculus. A metaphor for this kind of accretive learning can be found in the nautilus or the snake, which expands its shell or sheds its skin to accommodate its continuing growth.

Because these linear methods of learning tend to be gradual and evolutionary in nature, they pose no "clear and present danger" to our established patterns of thinking. Through negative feedback, we reinforce—and thus stabilize—our prior learning. To the extent our thinking has been institutionally-directed, these conservative influences help restrict change to within limits that can be accommodated to the interests of such formal systems. But to the degree processes of change are restricted, the negentropic vitalities of both the individual and the broader social system are threatened, producing ossifying tendencies which can eventually bring about the societal collapses previously identified. For an individual or a civilization to maintain its sense of vibrancy, a more fundamental kind of learning must be employed: *paradigm breaking*. While this kind of learning emerges from what has been previously known, its implications tend to be more *revolutionary* than *evolutionary* in nature. Not surprisingly, given the conservative nature of institutions, paradigm breaking has always been resisted by institutional hierarchies, creating the conflicts between individual and societal needs to resist entropy, and institutional interests in preserving their established positions.

All learning—even that which is linear—generates uneasiness, as we move from comfortable confines into the uncertainties of the unknown. As I tell my first year law students, the most important factor in learning is to become comfortable with uncertainty; to welcome the unknown; and to be willing to look foolish in the eyes of others. Drawing upon the study of chaos, learning consists of having your thinking put into turbulence, then looking for patterns that bring order out of the resulting tumult. The alternative, of course, is to simply give up and allow the turbulence to collapse into entropy. Having sufficient experiences with linear learning, we are disposed to tolerate the distress it produces—not unlike learning to tolerate the discomforts of dental work.

But with paradigm breaking, the learning is *nonlinear* in nature. Again, as the study of chaos illustrates, any system, including our learning, can reach a bifurcation point, at which it moves from its regular, linear state into turbulence and irregularity. Operating from a particular model of reality (e.g., Newton's mechanistic description of the universe), we continue our gradual accumulation of information. But over time, exceptions to such mechanistic interpretations begin to appear. For a while, such deviations are dismissed as "measurement errors" and conveniently ignored. But with the passage of time, such exceptions become more numerous and more difficult to explain away under the prevailing model. Then, as Kuhn reminds us, a paradigm breaker emerges and suggests *not* simply a linear accretion to a body of accepted knowledge, but a more fundamental transformation of the previous model. Settled and regularized patterns of thinking are then thrown into a turbulent state. A *new* paradigm is presented for consideration (e.g., quantum mechanics, or chaos theory).

Whereas the role of the linear teacher is represented by the dotted line (figure 5), the paradigm breaker can be represented as being at point "x," far outside—but still related to—the older circle of reality. At such a point have stood the likes of Copernicus, Newton, Pasteur, Darwin, Freud, Einstein, and

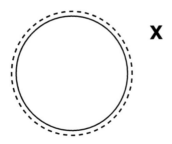

Figure 5.

now, apparently, those working in the studies of chaos and complexity. By being so far removed from the accepted range of understanding, however, the paradigm breaker is more easily seen, by those within their respective circles of reality, as outrageous, dangerous, or even insane. Thus have avant garde poets and artists been called "madmen;" inventors and pioneering scientists labeled "crackpots" and even "criminals;" and philosophers and religious teachers stigmatized as "heretics" or "deluded paranoids." From the persecution of Socrates to Lenny Bruce, from Galileo to Wilhelm Reich, from Jesus to Ezra Pound, defenders of the institutional order have exhibited little tolerance for those who dared to expand the existing circles of human understanding.

We tend to forget that many major discoveries and creations produced by mankind, whether in the arts, the sciences, agriculture, business, medicine, technology, philosophy, religion, or social practices, have come about only as a consequence of a few men and women being willing to stand far outside the accepted circles of understanding and appear to be outrageous to their contemporaries. These people did not create what they did by remaining faithful to the prevailing thinking of their times. Such outrageous people moved outside their circle of understanding, which, like the forces of gravity, pressure us to return to the status quo of the center, and teased or coaxed the rest of us to step outside our existing circles in order to gain a different perspective on reality. As we amass the courage to do so, we also learn something about the transient nature of *all* paradigms.

We are presently moving into a fundamentally new social environment, one as dissimilar to that into which we were born as today's world would be to that of my grandparents. How we choose to respond to such changes will tell us much about the future of our civilization. Perhaps we can take a lesson from the astronauts who first landed on the moon. They had crossed the boundary into a frontier known to no other human. While their safe return home was dependent upon the linearly-structured spaceship that had brought them to their destination, their behavior on the moon was—like that of the earthbound pioneers on the overland trails—governed by the thinking and values they had taken with them. There were no familiar freeways upon which to drive their vehicles, no speed limits to obey, nor any "safety-net" to protect them from unanticipated problems. They had to adapt themselves to new experiences with the lunar gravity which, unlike the earth's, was not as constraining. What an apt metaphor in our efforts to discover a world lacking in what has become familiar to us.

Learning, as with other processes of change, can be likened to the "cutting-and-filling" functions of a river. As the river pursues its meandering course, the centrifugal forces on its outer side are stronger, and cause the river to eat into the surrounding banks, bringing dirt, gravel, and silt into the flow. On the inner side—where the force is weaker—silt accumulates to form new land masses. Through this process, the river continues to redefine its boundaries and move into new territory.

We live in a culture in which people like to imagine themselves on the "cutting" edge of change, a function that would include "paradigm breaking." But like the ongoing life of the river, attention must also be given to the role of the "filling" side of change. After all, it is on the filling side of the river that the silt gathers to provide a bed for the growth of new plant life.

The cutting and filling interplay finds expression in the roles played by *linear* and *nonlinear* forms of learning and thinking. The architectural genius Frank Lloyd Wright engaged in nonlinear, outside-the-circle behavior in designing his buildings. At the same time, he relied upon more linear, mechanistic thinking in addressing such matters as structural supports, the most efficient distribution of building forces, and other physical ways in which form and function became integrated into pragmatic forms of artistic expression. Painters and sculptors have to become disciplined in specific skills in order to give an outward embodiment to their inner sense. All creative acts depend upon such interaction.

An example of the creative interplay between the forces of *change* and *stability* implicit in the "cutting-and-filling" metaphor, was the emergence, in the 1960s, of a number of independent social movements that challenged the established mindset. Fundamental changes in thinking began to arise among people interested in civil rights, peace, libertarian systems, the environment, the role of women, and a variety of alternative social practices and lifestyles. I vividly recall the dynamics occurring during these years. There was a highly-energized, spontaneous flow of ideas emanating from a mixture of intuitive insights, emotions, unbridled speculation, and the observations of earlier philosophic thinkers. It was initially an exciting period of self-discovery, in which inquiries from within became the focus of our questions to the outside world. "Why have we allowed ourselves to live in ways that served systemic interests rather than our own?" was asked in each of these social arenas, as we continued cutting into the banks that surrounded us.

Rather quickly, however, attentions shifted to the filling side. Abstract conclusions were drawn from what often turned out to be superficial insights, and new belief systems emerged. Free and open speculation became structured into ideologies, moralistic dogmas, political movements, and, ultimately, statutory mandates. New "isms" were thus born, as men and women surrendered the joys of imagination and exploration for the security of attachments to new sets of fashionable doctrines. In the words of Frank Chodorov, expressed during this time period, far too many limited themselves to "wanting to clean up the whorehouse, but keeping the business intact."[2]

The question mankind has always faced is how to maintain the dynamics of this "cutting-and-filling" interplay. Previous successes have a seductive quality that attracts us to make permanent the forms that produced past benefits, a temptation that gives birth to institutions and endangers opportunities for continuing creativity. It is the interconnected processes of change that sustain an individual, a business firm, a society, or even a civilization. If surrounding conditions are not receptive to such

---

[2]From a talk Chodorov gave at The Freedom School in Colorado, circa 1961.

changes, they may fail to take root and become instruments for growth. The Greek engineer Hero of Alexandria who died in 70 A.D., invented a steam engine that was seen as little more than an object of amusement. It was not until the seventeenth century that the practical implications of this tool began to develop. So, too, the Industrial Revolution flowered in England and America, rather than such countries as France and Russia, for reasons that included opportunities for creative undertakings.

While Western civilization appears to be in a state of rapid decline, the societies that have housed this culture are not destined to collapse. Historians are fond of addressing "the decline and fall" of earlier civilizations, as though their deaths ended their influences upon humankind. But in much the same way that our biological descendants continue our genes long past our lives, so-called "dead" cultures retain their influence in the present. Ancient Greek philosophers still provide a starting point for most modern philosophic studies, just as Greek thought and language influenced Rome's culture in the years following its decline in the west. Roman law and engineering inform current practitioners in these fields; and the Saracens introduced Europeans to the concept of "zero," which, itself, had been borrowed from India, making possible not only more sophisticated forms of mathematical analysis, but modern computers. The Saracens also brought paper and papermaking from China to the West, and replaced Roman with Arabic numerals. Along with the Greeks and Romans, the Saracens were significant contributors to one of Western civilization's most creative periods, the Renaissance, a word meaning a "renewal" or "revival" of classical influences. Human language, regardless of its specific form, continues, like a meandering river, its ongoing processes of change and adaptation, deriving its contents from centuries of interconnections. In varying degrees of influence, the history of mankind will continue to perform its filling functions as we go on with life's game of challenging the *familiar* with the *novel*.

Western civilization is in a state of turbulence, and seems to have reached a bifurcation point at which the thinking that underlies it, and the forms such thinking expresses, will either generate systems that are more supportive of life, or collapse into an entropic death. Technological changes continue to astound us, and may provide a base from which a social metamorphosis might occur. We humans are a pragmatic lot, and have ways of borrowing from other cultures and civilizations methods that are useful to our efforts to sustain ourselves. As individuals, we will find Roman engineering more suited to our purposes than Roman military techniques. Our creative efforts will, of course, be resisted by weak and destructive people who continue to dream of empires and conquest, and work to dam up the river lest it cut into new territory. But, as with any dam, the river will eventually prevail, providing the rest of us with opportunities for filling in and adapting creative changes to our daily lives.

The life force, in whatever form it finds expression, has always been adept at circumventing barriers placed in its way. Plants and trees maneuver themselves around rocks or fence posts in order to get more direct sunlight. In human affairs, the marketplace has long found ways of satisfying the demands that the state chooses to make unlawful. Why we tolerate the erecting of restraints—which increase the costs to life sustaining itself—is a question deserving of inquiry, particularly in assessing the conditions necessary for maintaining a vibrant civilization.

We are intelligent and resilient beings who can, and do, find new ways of achieving our productive ends. At the same time, we are social beings who require organization and cooperation with one another not only to survive, but to maintain our sanity. Our present institutionalized practices, however, do not serve such needs well. Our traditional model of a centrally-directed society, in which order is presumed to be the product of rules imposed upon mankind by coercive means, may be all but defunct. Because of the sharp contrast between institutional interests in stability and uniformity, and individual interests in autonomously-directed variation; and because most of us have accepted the conflation of *institutions* and *society* into a single entity, with the former being the expression of the latter, we have managed to make social conflict a nearly universal feature in our lives. Those who can only confront the resulting violence, economic dislocation, institutional bureaucracy and ineffectiveness, anger, depression, despoliation, alienation, despair, and other symptoms of social discord, with an intensified outpouring of proposals grounded in the same interventionist premises that have produced these problems, fail to grasp the fact that our institutionally structured world is in a state of utter disrepair.

Naiveté alone sustains a faith in the capacity of traditional thinking and institutional systems to overcome the disordered and destructive world they have produced. Our world is in crisis, and only a fundamental shift in our thinking can reverse our entropic course. Thomas Kuhn's analysis—in chapters one and three—of the history of scientific inquiry may provide a beginning point for understanding the social transformations currently taking place in our world.

Beginning at least in the late nineteenth century, and continuing throughout the twentieth, the anti-life implications of the established model became apparent. The most virulent manifestation of these symptoms, the state, became increasingly expansive in its systems and mechanisms of power, as well as more destructive of human life, not only through wars and genocides, but through the regulation of economic activity which it was presumed state authorities had the capacity to direct for the sake of human well-being.

Many social and political philosophers who antedated the twentieth century had, through their insights and reasoning, warned us of the dangers inherent in depending upon state systems. But, like the alcoholic who does not see the long-term implications of short-term conduct, most of us failed to allow such warnings to affect our illusionary expectations. Now, in recent decades, our idealized hopes have collided with the harsh reality that the playing out of such systemic premises has proven destructive of the conditions necessary for the survival of mankind.

In hindsight, one can see that Plato's pyramidal archetype was ill-founded. The state has long depended for its existence upon the popular illusion that it is capable of planning for and controlling events in order to accomplish desired ends. But as we become more aware of the uncertainties inhering in complex systems, the futility of trying to regularize our lives in conformity with this belief becomes increasingly apparent. Political history, whether in the realms of foreign or domestic policies, economic regulation, or other aspects of life subject to governmental authority, is a testimony to the failure of this traditional model to achieve expected ends. Inability to account for outcomes inconsistent with such expectations produces a crisis—"turbulence"—to which a response must be made. Either of two options then seems available: (1) to bring about no change at all, and allow the system to collapse into total entropy, or (2) to generate a basic "paradigm shift" that will produce a more sophisticated, orderly system. On the assumption that an intelligent response to the present organizational crisis will obviate the first alternative, the next question becomes whether there is a sufficient basis in our thinking for bringing about the necessary transmutation. As Kuhn has made clear, such a paradigm shift will occur only if a better model is available to overcome the failures and shortcomings of the prevailing one.

Like passengers shipwrecked on a previously undiscovered island, or our ancestral pioneers entering a new frontier, we must explore uncharted territory. As in survivalist stories and training programs, we bring with us a variety of tools that may prove to be either useful, or a hindrance, in our efforts to sustain ourselves in a new society. We will also bring with us, of course, our prior thinking, derived from the formal learning and other experiences that have produced our fragmented and limited understanding. Should we try to concoct an alternative model out of a reshuffling of abstract ideas, our efforts would suffer from the same shortcomings found in all utopian thinking. Unless we are consciously aware of the influence of Heisenberg's "uncertainty principle" at work upon our minds, our efforts may accomplish little more than to confirm the prior thinking that got us to the troublesome place where we find ourselves. A belief system can never rise to a higher level of authenticity than the thinking of its creators. The unintended consequences resulting from our acting upon belief systems—which, by their nature, are inherently limited by our prior experiences—may lead us to produce the kinds of paradigm shifts discussed by Kuhn. An awareness of both the limited nature of our understanding, as well as how our acts of observation influence what we see, may help transform our *hubris* into *humility*.

If our explorations are to be a catalyst for change, rather than a hindrance, we must be prepared to think outside the circle of prior learning and find comfort in the uncertainties that accompany our endeavors. As with the advance of scientific understanding, regularities that can be more readily explained by a new paradigm will likely bring about a shift in our thinking. We may discover patterns by which living systems organize themselves without conscious, external direction. Will the order upon which our lives depend be found within the regularities that arise, spontaneously and without design, from the interplay of human behavior; or shall we continue to seek such patterns within consciously formulated rules crafted in furtherance of the interests of those with access to the systems of power that generate such mandates? Will orderliness, in other words, express the central importance of autonomy and differentiation in human affairs, or the premises of a systematically directed uniformity? Will its emphasis be a reflection of the importance of social *processes*, or of institutional *forms*?

How we answer such questions will tell us how our lives and other property interests are to be controlled. We may discover that a self-organizing society can function only on the basis of decision-making authority being diffused into the hands of individual actors, each of whom will pursue their unique purposes in the concrete circumstances before them, a condition that necessarily implies the private control of property.

We must begin by casting aside the illusory thinking that sustains the collective systems that are destroying us. The pursuit of self-interest, which expresses itself in individualized spontaneity and autonomy, goes to the essence of all living things; such dynamics drive life in its varied manifestations. Coercion is anti-life, for it forces life to go in directions it doesn't want to go.

As long as we regard the lives and property of one another as interests to be forcibly exploited in furtherance of our respective ends, we ought not wonder why our world is fraught with wars, genocides, suicide bombings, rapes, street-gang violence, riots, murders, terrorist attacks on skyscrapers, robberies, and all the other atrocities we so unthinkingly accept as "human nature." Such behavior is the product of our assumptions about how human society is to be organized, which, in turn, are brought about by our thinking.

As command-and-control systems continue to erode, it is time to consider whether a holographic social model might be better suited to our purposes. Drawing upon the metaphor of Indra's Net, can we think of our relationships with others in terms of horizontal interconnectedness rather than the divisive categories to which we have been conditioned? Can we learn that most civilizing of all traits: to respect the inviolability of one another's person? Will we be able to understand that a system grounded in mutual respect for our claims to immunity from coercion can only be based on the private ownership of property, a concept that goes to the essence of the question of how authority will be exercised among people? Knowing how, and by whom, decisions over people's lives and property are made tells us whether a given society is organized through individual liberty or political violence.

As we synthesize our understanding of the incalculable nature of complexity with our expectations of social systems, we may develop a deeper understanding of the biological, social, and spiritual necessity for autonomy and variability. Instead of having such values as liberty and diversity tolerated as little more than atavistic expressions of ancient liberal sentiments, we may discover why our very survival depends upon them. Our institutionalized practices have been built upon a distrust of ungoverned life processes, but such formalized systems are destroying human life, society and, apparently, Western civilization itself. We need to reaffirm not just the *idea*, but the functional *reality* of spontaneity and dissimilarity within society.

In many respects, as our world has become more industrialized and institutionalized, it has fallen into patterns of uniform, standardized behavior and, what is far more dangerous, standardized thinking. The idea that human conduct should be restrained within templates of institutionally defined regularities is a long-standing article of faith within modern society. Nowhere is this premise more firmly entrenched than in the belief that a monolithic, state-controlled legal system must superintend human affairs.

As I have demonstrated, such institutionalizing practices are being challenged—and without centralized direction—across the tapestry of human society. Perhaps as a social expression of Newton's third law of motion, there has been a countervailing emergence of numerous subcultures within different nations. Such tendencies should remind us of the need for the proliferation of pluralistic values and practices within society if we are to remain vibrant and creative and, in the process, continue to resist our entropic fate. *Harmony* can arise only out of *diversity*. Where there is no diversity, no differentiation, there is only *monotony*. One of the most important lessons that chaos theory can provide is that our culture must become one in which the commitment to autonomy and diversity *is* the culture.

If the rest of nature has discovered the harmonious implications of the inviolability of property boundaries within a species, what prevents us allegedly intelligent and rational humans from having such an understanding? If property boundaries do not serve as the basis for social order, what will? We need not speculate as to the alternative, nor of its consequences. We need only look at our present world, where constantly changing whims and power alliances of some are forcibly imposed upon others; where differing groups compete with one another for control of the machinery of the state to plunder, coerce, and even destroy one another; and where "intelligence" is considered an integral part of the process by which people ritualistically slaughter one another. The twentieth century's two hundred million victims of wars, genocides, and "sanctions," should remind us of the deadly consequences of behavior that knows no boundaries—i.e., of practices not constrained by principled limitations that can reasonably assure each of us an immunity from being violated.

Our institutionally-directed society has taught us to think of "right" and "wrong" social behavior largely in terms of standards that the state promulgates. It is sufficient, for such thinking, that a legislative body or the executive branch of government has formulated rules that the courts are willing to enforce. In this way, liberty and the inviolability of the individual has given way to legalistic notions of "procedural due process" as a principle for restraining state power. Such a politically-based standard allows for any form of conduct, even that which causes no physical injury to another, to be labeled criminal or tortuous if a sizeable number of people object to it. The history of "victimless crimes" (e.g., drug use, prostitution, gambling, etc.) proves the point.

With the invasion of property boundaries as the standard for what is appropriately called "improper" behavior, the opportunities for state-enforced fashions or whims to limit the liberties of individuals is minimized. There is no "wrong" that does not reduce itself to a measurable trespass to private property interests. Indeed, any politically-defined and enforced "wrong" that does not rise to the level of a trespass would, itself, be a trespass upon the interests of those regulated.

This is why a book on property and liberty requires so much attention to the nature and forms of our social systems: these interests are unavoidably intertwined. If we are to live as free, self-controlling people, the underlying premises through which we cooperate with one another must reflect such purposes. *Cooperation*, the organizing principle of the marketplace, is grounded in a respect for the inviolate nature of each other's property boundaries. *Coercion,* the essence of all political systems, is premised on a rejection of the property principle.

It is critical for us to re-examine the basic assumptions upon which our social systems are to be based. What are the values and the practices we are to embrace? We might begin with the inquiry offered by Franz Oppenheimer, who distinguished the two basic methods for acquiring wealth. The first was the "economic means," which arose from the free exchange of property claims in the marketplace; the second was the "political means," which consisted of the use of violence to despoil property owners of their property interests.[3] As the state has increased both its powers and appetites, the political means has become ascendant in our world. But growing public opposition to wars, eminent domain, regulation of economic life, and taxation, has both encouraged and accompanied the processes of decentralization that are working to dismantle governmental structures.

The political establishment no longer enjoys the confidence that earlier generations placed in its hands. Its response has been to increase police powers and surveillance; expand penitentiaries and prison sentences; build more weapons of mass destruction; and create new lists of enemies against whom to conduct endless wars. The state has become destructive of the foundations of life, particularly of the social systems and practices that sustain life. Were its attributes found within an individual, it would be aptly described as a psychopathic serial killer! But its destructiveness can no longer be tolerated by a life system intent on survival. Unconscious voices are informing conscious minds that it is time to walk away from these instrumentalities that war against life. The state is like a chicken that has just had its head chopped off: it flaps and flails around in a noisy and messy outburst of disordered energy, spreading blood in its trail. But it is all reflexive action with no creative purpose

---

[3]Franz Oppenheimer, *The State: Its History and Development Viewed Sociologically,* trans. by John M. Gitterman. (New York: B.W. Huebsch, 1922); reprinted (New York: Free Life Editions, 1975).

beneficial to the life of the chicken, whose fate has already been determined.

Is it possible that the intellectual transformations that have driven scientific revolutions could teach us anything that might help bring about fundamental changes in our social thinking in order to extricate humanity from self-destructive practices? The study of chaos reminds us that our world is, indeed, quite complicated. At the same time, we are beginning to understand that, if we are to live well, our *thinking*—including the practices and systems that our thinking generates—had better *not* be complicated. To presume that a complex world can be rendered orderly through the imposition of elaborately structured systems and rigidly enforced rules, is to fail to comprehend nature's inherent orderliness, as well as the dangers associated with the disruption of such undirected regularities. As we learn more about chaos, including how our inherently limited knowledge and understanding can never keep up with the interconnected complexities of our world, we may discover that the quality of our lives depends on learning how to live with greater flexibility, diversity, spontaneity, and uncertainty than our institutionally-structured systems allow—qualities demanded by the unpredictable and uncontrollable nature of a complex universe.

It may be said that quantum physics, chaos theory, or holographic systems have, at best, metaphorical applications to human affairs. But such an objection begs the question, for our understanding of the world has always advanced through the use of metaphors. What our minds embrace as "truth" largely consists of a sophisticated labyrinth of interconnected abstractions, put together by our minds with such detailed consistency as to cause us to believe they represent objective truth. Abstractions piled upon abstractions have produced a base of conscious understanding grounded in metaphor.

It has been our practice to apply metaphysical models as broadly as possible. Hegel's "dialectic" was used by Karl Marx to explain his social and scientific models. Religious cultures have provided metaphorical explanations for regularities in nature as expressions of a divine will, just as Newton found it useful to interpret such orderliness in the mechanistic form of a giant clockwork. Our organizational practices have also been grounded in analogical thinking. Thus, the pyramidal model of social systems has its origins in beliefs about the nature of order in the universe. If we think of order as a quality *imposed* upon the world—whether by divine forces or so-called "laws of nature"—we will be inclined to embrace social systems that reflect such a model. As our understanding of orderliness is transformed, we should expect our social systems and practices to reflect such changed awareness. Thus, if the study of chaos, complexity, and quantum mechanics, informs us that order is a quality that *arises from*—rather than being *mandated upon*—human behavior, we may find ourselves attracted to a holographic metaphor for society.

The underlying premise of a holographic model is that orderliness is distributed throughout the system as the product of the interconnectedness of its subsystems. The regularities of the marketplace arise not through the designs of planners, nor even the intentions of market participants, but as the unintended consequences of people pursuing their disparate and often contrary interests. The interplay of such varied purposes, with each participant committing his or her resources on behalf of a desired end, generates widespread patterns for which all participants, but none in particular, are responsible. It is the diffusion of authority into the hands of resource owners that gives the marketplace its resiliency and viability. It is this same dispersion of energy that gives meaning to a holographic system.

A spontaneous order arising through adaptability, rather than design, is found throughout non-human nature in animal and plant life not known for being centrally-directed or supervised by outside forces. The concept of evolution is grounded in life forms responding to changed conditions by altering their behavior and/or biological structures, a practice echoed by mankind in the history of industrialization. In the continuing evolution of technologies, we see the same interplay of *stability* and *change* producing life-enhancing modifications beyond the capacities of centralized authorities to create.

Perhaps the metaphor provided by the dynamics of a river system can help us transcend our present mindset that so insistently wars against life. The words of Will Durant, with which I began this book, make a fitting contrast between the violence and destruction wrought by the force of the river, whose course has long entertained our dark side as the study of history, and the peaceful activities taking place on the banks where people live and produce the values necessary for the sustaining of life. It has been my purpose to explore the conditions that must prevail on the banks if a free, productive, and humane civilization is to exist.

The question that has always confronted mankind is whether society will be conducted by peaceful or violent means. Our conditioned thinking, however, has kept us from examining the implications of these alternative forms of behavior. The distinction between such practices rests on whether trespasses will or will not be allowed to occur. It is not that property trespasses can *produce* violence; they *are* violence, whatever the degree of force that is used. The property principle—in restricting the range of one's actions to the boundaries of what one owns—precludes the use of violence. As long as we choose to deny the necessity of this principle, we should cease getting upset over the political and private acts of violence that are the unavoidable consequences of failing to respect the inviolability of the lives of our neighbors.

The extent of the social harmony we generate can be measured by the degree of respect we accord this principle. The concept has been tortured, twisted, and misunderstood by people in virtually every segment of society, including political ideologues of both the "Left" and "Right," as well as by judges and lawyers. The reason for this confusion is rather clear: for men and women to understand the nature and importance of private property would call into question the entire political order, which is premised upon the formal usurpation of authority over people's lives and property. In our politically institutionalized relationships, divisive thinking manifests itself as coercively structured systems for transgressing one another's property interests.

Although we continue to recite bromides about our culture's commitment to the private ownership of property, most of us have little understanding of the nature of ownership, or how the state regularly transgresses such interests. The depth of confusion on the part of most Americans about private property was brought home to me a number of years ago when I was visiting London. While waiting for my wife and daughters in an indoor mall, I decided to check on the amount of film remaining in my camera. As soon as I took the camera from its case, a security guard came up to me and said, quite politely, "I'm sorry sir, but you cannot take pictures in here." After assuring him that I was not intending to take pictures, I asked why there was such a prohibition. "Because it's private property," he informed me. As I reflected on his response, I pondered how a security guard in a shopping mall back home in California might have responded to such an inquiry under similar circumstances. I imagined replies ranging from "because those are the rules," or "because I said so," to "I don't know: that's just what we've been told." I wondered how many American shopping centers I would have had to visit before finding a security guard or building manager who would regard it an adequate answer to respond "because it's private property." How ironic—although it may provide but another instance of the unity in apparent opposites—that, in a socialistic nation such as Great Britain, it should be considered a sufficient explanation that a property owner does not allow photographs to be taken.

The most compelling case for the private ownership of property lies in its implicit affirmation of the primacy of individual interests as the focus of any social arrangement. The measure of any society's respect for the innate worthiness of individuals is found not in abstract platitudes, but in the degree of commitment people have to the maintenance of exclusive realms of decision-making within which each of us is free to direct our own lives and pursue our dreams and ambitions. No society can reasonably claim to be humane and decent as long as the purposes and desires of individuals are regarded as secondary to any collective undertaking. Until we are able to grasp this fundamental point, and learn to move beyond our attachments and subservience to institutional identities, human society will never amount to much more than a form of bondage—of forced servitude and plunder carried out through "due process of law."

What I have endeavored to express herein is not just a new set of ideas, and certainly not an ideology. The property principle is a reflection of *how the world actually works*. That other living things follow such practices—with no known belief systems or dogmas to direct their behavior—should suggest to us some underlying principle common to life itself.[4] But mankind, whose collective arrogance presumes a special dispensation from nature, has ignored such a principle to its detriment. Only a very intelligent species has been able to construct systems, practices, and beliefs that have placed us and kept us in a state of perpetual war and misery with one another! Perhaps the awareness of what we are doing to ourselves will energize our intelligence and generate new patterns of living.

The study of both physics and economics informs us that there are costs associated with every activity. The fundamental conflict between a system of privately owned property and a political system is this: where private property interests are respected, the costs of human action are borne by those who desire a given activity and are prepared to pay the full costs thereof by committing their resources to its achievement. The nature of politics, on the other hand, is to forcibly transfer such costs to others. When we compel others to commit their lives and other property interests to programs they do not wish to support, we foster social conflict, which reveals itself in the form of trespasses against individuals. There is an integrity to a system of private property in that the *costs* borne, and the *benefits* received, by a given course of action are experienced by the

---

[4]In this empirical—rather than normative—sense, one might speak of such universal behavior as a "natural law."

owner. There is no integrity in political action, however, as the relationship of costs to benefits is fragmented.

Contrary to the polemics of Hobbes and other statists, every political system is an institutionalized means of forcibly transferring control of property from owners to non-owners. Of course, this is too candid and unvarnished a statement for most conventional, formally educated men and women to comfortably consider. The price of admission into the antechambers of the philosopher kings has been one's tacit agreement to never call a thing for what it is, for truthfulness and clarity would allow others to apprehend the nature of the game being played at their expense. Because we prefer our illusion that politics is a noble, socially responsible undertaking, we resist these more pedestrian explanations, or dismiss them as "simplistic thinking."

But what practices are more "simplistic" than those grounded in the belief that social order can be generated by an institutionalized elite using formal tools of violence to compel individuals to act as the elitists choose them to act? What arrogant assumptions underlie both the propriety of employing such methods and the belief that sufficient knowledge of means and outcomes lies in the hands of those enjoying the use of such coercive power? As we are discovering, life is far too complex and subject to far too many perturbations to any longer permit the illusion that human society can be organized and run from the top-down. It is time we gave Plato a decent burial.

Epilogue

If there is any period one would desire to be born in, is it not the age of revolution; when the old and the new stand side by side, and admit of being compared; when the energies of all men are searched by fear and by hope; when the historic glories of the old can be compensated by the rich possibilities of the new era? This time, like all times, is a very good one, if we but know what to do with it.

— Ralph Waldo Emerson

Index